KINTYRE
COUNTRY LIFE

KINTYRE COUNTRY LIFE

ANGUS MARTIN

Angus Martin
Campbeltown, 1993

JOHN DONALD PUBLISHERS LTD
EDINBURGH

To my wife Judy

ISBN 0 85976 195 9

The publisher acknowledges subsidy from the Scottish
Arts Council towards the publication of this volume.

Phototypesetting by Quorn Selective Repro, Loughborough.
Printed in Great Britain by Bell & Bain Ltd., Glasgow.

Preface

This is my third book about Kintyre, and my last, because there is not the making of another in the material remaining to me; and, in any case, thirteen years have passed since, in 1974, I began *The Ring Net Fishermen*, and enough is enough.

These books have been both my attempt to understand my native Kintyre — its culture and its history — and my celebration of the places and people that have filled my life.

Place-names taken from documentary sources are spelled exactly as they appear in these sources. For the rest, I have used 'standard' spellings wherever these existed. But the great majority of place-names in Kintyre are Gaelic, and there are no 'correct' anglicised forms of Gaelic names — the only correct forms are the Gaelic forms, if these are known, or can be deduced with certainty.

All *Mac-* names are spelled just so, except in the case of authors and others who have chosen to use 'Mc-'. There are those who would make a great issue out of the 'distinction' between the two forms, but really there is no distinction — except that *Mac-* is the full and correct Gaelic form, and 'Mc-' is an abbreviation. The whole subject is taken too seriously.

There is a marked north-south imbalance in the illustrations. Personal bias has no part in that — the reason is simply that no one in the Largieside, or in any other district of north Kintyre, responded to my appeals for material, published in the local newspaper.

A chapter was devoted to goats, and a couple of pages to pigs, in my previous book, *Kintyre: The Hidden Past*, so these animals are mentioned only in passing in this work.

I wish to apologise to Mrs Sheena Carmichael for remarks about her late husband, Alasdair Carmichael, in chapter one of *Kintyre: The Hidden Past*. These remarks caused her distress, which in turn distressed me. I trust that this sincere apology will heal both of us.

In writing this book I have been conscious always of the sturdy foundations of scholarship already laid down. The late Eric R. Cregeen remarked to me once that Kintyre was fortunate in having had so many industrious and perceptive local historians. He was right. I am particularly indebted to the work, both published and unpublished, of the late Duncan Colville and Andrew McKerral. The late Archibald McEachran, Father

James Webb, and Colonel Charles Mactaggart also deserve acknowledgement. I thank them all across the gulf of death.

There can never be perfection in the treatment of history. Writers are not infallible, and critics — many of whom have never suffered the agonies of assembling a big work — would do well to remember that. This book is flawed in many ways. It would have been even more flawed without the criticism, advice and general assistance of the following to whom I extend the full measure of my appreciation (while relieving them of any responsibility for the errors and other imperfections which may lurk in this work).

The maps are selectively compiled — within the limitations of the scale available — concentrating on places mentioned in the text, and particularly those places which are no longer inhabited. Current Ordnance Survey maps show those farms which continue to be occupied and the others not included in my maps.

Acknowledgements

Mr Murdo MacDonald, archivist, Argyll and Bute District Council, Lochgilphead, once again supplied a mass of diverse and indispensable material, and to him I am most of all indebted.

Mr Robert Smith, Blackness, West Lothian, and formerly curator of Auchindrain Country Life Museum, Argyll, painstakingly read and invaluably criticised all chapters except the last.

Dr Alexander Fenton, Research Director, Royal Museum of Scotland, read chapters 1-4, 6, 9 and 10, and was instrumental in arranging the copying of the photographs I collected locally.

For reading and criticising chapters of this book, with great benefit to me, I thank: Dr Alan Bruford, School of Scottish Studies, University of Edinburgh (11); Mr Michael Moss, archivist, University of Glasgow (7); Mr Geoffrey Stell, the Royal Commission on the Ancient and Historical Monuments of Scotland (8); and Mr Robert McInnes, Stewarton, Campbeltown (5 and 6).

I thank:

Mr Edward P. Lafferty, Campbeltown, who printed all but one of the photographs of my own which appear in this work, and who would accept no payment;

Ms. Janette Gillies, Killeonan, Kintyre, for her invaluable efforts in the collection of old photographs for me;

Mr Archibald Hogarth, Courier Office, Campbeltown, for allowing me unrestricted access to the back issues of the *Campbeltown Courier*;

Mr Kenneth D. MacDonald, Department of Celtic, University of Glasgow, for advice on Gaelic terms;

Mr John Tuckwell and Mr Gordon Angus, with the rest of the staff of John Donald Publishers Ltd., for their consideration over the years;

Ms. Alison Todd, head librarian, and the staff of Campbeltown Public Library for their generous and tolerant assistance at all stages of the work;

the staffs of the Scottish Ethnological Archive, National Museums of Scotland; the Scottish Record Office; New Register House (in particular Dr John Shaw); the Mitchell Library, and the Registration Office of Births, Deaths and Marriages, Lochgilphead (in particular Mrs Isabella Souden).

For various small services I thank (in Kintyre): Mr John Armour, High Tirfergus Farm; Mr Norman Campbell, Campbeltown; Mr J.D.F. Colville, Kilchenzie; Mr Rory Colville, Langa Farm; Mr Hugh Ferguson, Campbeltown; Mr Donald Irwin, Drumlemble; Mr Duncan McGeachy (my colleague in the Post Office, Campbeltown); Mr Allan McLay, Carradale; Mr Andrew Reid, Ballywilline Cottage; Mr Richard Semple, Campbeltown; Mr A.I.B. Stewart, Campbeltown; Mr Alister and Mrs Agnes Stewart, Campbeltown; Mr Donald

Woodrow, Campbeltown, and Mrs Effric Wotherspoon, Campbeltown (Kintyre Antiquarian Society). Also, Mr Alistair Lorne Campbell, Inveraray Castle; Dr J.A. Gibson, Kilbarchan, Renfrewshire; Mr Malcolm Docherty Jr., Glasgow; and Mr Eoghann Henderson, Gigha.

Finally, I thank all who loaned me photographs — many of which could not be included in this work — and all who opened their doors to my tape-recorder and me.

Principal oral sources used in this work

Angus Allan*, b. 1896, Gigha
Mary (McNair) Armour*, b. 1888, New Peninver
Calum Bannatyne*, b. 1900, Rosehill Cottage
Alistair Beattie*, b. 1906, Kerranbeg
Archibald D. Cameron*, b. 1894, South Carrine
John Campbell, b. 1904, Dalintober
Finlay Clark*, b. 1906, Uigle
Alexander Helm*, b. 1902, Ifferdale
Margaret (Black) Littleson*, b. 1881, Dalkeith
Donald MacCallum*, b. 1908, High Glenadale
Donald MacDonald*, b. 1891, Port na Cudainnean, Gigha
William MacGougan*, b. 1896, Upper Barr
Robert McInnes, b. 1917, High Glenadale
John MacKay, b. 1898, Darlochan
Duncan MacKeith*, b. 1887, Sunadale
John MacKeith*, b. 1889, Sunadale
Graham McKinlay*, b. 1895, Ayrshire (brought up at Whitestone)
Adam MacPhail*, b. 1907, Glasgow (brought up at Skernish)
Robert Russell*, b. 1901, Knocknaha
Neil Thomson, b. 1904, Muasdale
Donald Watson*, b. 1901, North Muasdale
William Watson, b. 1911, North Muasdale

N.B. An asterisk denotes an informant who, at the completion of this work, was dead.

Principal published sources used in this work

Cuthbert Bede (Rev. Edward Bradley), *Glencreggan, or a Highland Home in Cantyre*, London (1861), two vols.

Cuthbert Bede, *Argyll's Highlands*, Glasgow (1902).

Alan Bruford, 'Seasonal Festivities and Customs', in *A Companion to Scottish Culture*, ed. D. Daiches, London (1981).

Alexander Fenton, *Scottish Country Life*, Edinburgh (1976).

Nils M. Holmer, *The Gaelic of Kintyre*, Dublin (1962).

Peter MacIntosh, *History of Kintyre* (1857, and subsequent reprints).

Frank Forbes MacKay, *MacNeill of Carskey, his Estate Journal*: 1703–1743, Edinburgh (1955).

Andrew McKerral, *Kintyre in the Seventeenth Century*, Edinburgh (1948).

Thomas Pennant, *A Tour in Scotland and Voyage to the Hebrides*, Chester (1772).

John Smith, *General View of the Agriculture of the County of Argyll*, London (1805, but written c. 1795, to judge by internal evidence).

Argyll, An Inventory of the Ancient Monuments, Vol. I, *Kintyre*, HMSO (1971).

Statistical Accounts for Kintyre: Old (1790–95); New (1843).

N.B. Since this work is not provided with detailed notes and references, I have tried as far as possible to indicate sources within the text itself.

Contents

	page
Preface	v
Acknowledgements	vii
Principal oral sources	viii
Principal published sources	viii
1. Agriculture: A Changing Scene	1
2. Tilling and Fertilising the Soil	17
3. Crops	30
4. Cattle and Horses	53
5. Sheep	65
6. Peat-Cutting	83
7. Illicit Whisky	98
8. Crafts and Industries	1'8
9. Building the Houses	137
10. Hearth, Home, and Diet	156
11. Festivities, Customs, and Sports	172
Appendix 1. Tenants of the Argyll Estate Convicted of Malting or Distilling Illegally	193
Appendix 2. Illicit Whisky Distillers	194
Index	196

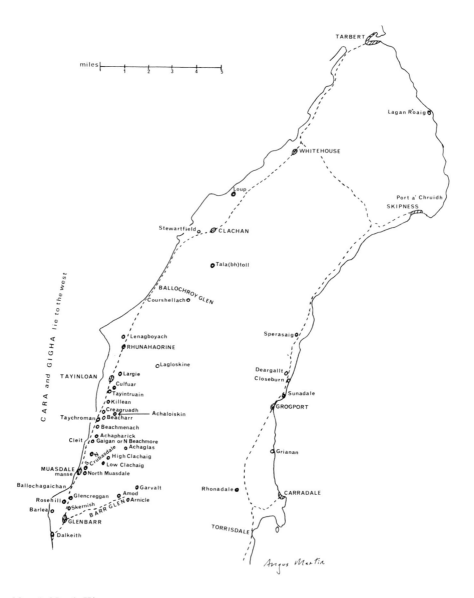

miles |—————————————————|
      1   2   3   4   5

TARBERT

Lagan R'oaig o

WHITEHOUSE

Loup o

Port a' Chruidh
SKIPNESS

Stewartfield o   CLACHAN

Tala(bh)toll o

BALLOCHROY GLEN
Courshellach o

CARA and GIGHA lie to the west

Lenagboyach o
RHUNAHAORINE

Sperasaig o

Lagloskine o

Largie o
Culfuar o
Tayintruain o
Killean o
Creagruadh o
Achaloiskin
Beacharr o
Taychroman

Deargallt o
Closeburn o

Sunadale o
GROGPORT

TAYINLOAN

Beachmenach o
Cleit   Achapharick o
         Gaigan or N Beachmore o
         Achaglas o
         High Clachaig o
Crubasdale o Low Clachaig o
MUASDALE o
manse   North Muasdale o

Grianan o

Ballochagaichan o
Rosehill o Glencreggan o Amod o Garvalt o
Barlea o   Skernish o   Arnicle o
         BARR GLEN
GLENBARR
Dalkeith o

Rhonadale o

CARRADALE

TORRISDALE

Angus Martin

Map 1: North Kintyre

Map 2: South Kintyre

CHAPTER 1

Agriculture: A Changing Scene

If it were possible to reconstruct accurately an aerial photograph of a cluster of Kintyre farms — any farms — so that they appeared as they had been in, say, the late seventeenth century, it is unlikely that many would be recognisable. The buildings would bear no resemblance to present-day farm buildings, and there might be so many of them that one would imagine a village had been there; the land would be almost entirely open, with scarcely a fence of any description to be seen; much of it might lie under water or be noticeably boggy. Even the ploughed fields and the tiny grazing forms of sheep and cattle would have an odd appearance. The system of farming then was *runrig*.

All that began to change in the early eighteenth century, but the change came slowly, and not until the middle of the nineteenth century would the face of the land have assumed the features by which it is recognisable today. But more than a system of farming changed — a people's lifestyle also changed. These pressures of change may be seen at their most extreme where the principles of market farming swept away communities basically geared to subsistence farming (for example, around the Mull of Kintyre, which was stocked with sheep towards the end of the eighteenth century).

In subsistence farming, most of the produce fed the people themselves, and the surplus only — in grain and cattle — was sold to raise the money part of the rent (most of which was paid in produce). But landowners sought increasing profitability from their lands, and encouraged higher rents. The runrig system was abolished, farms were divided, enclosed and drained, and farming methods modernised. The sheep invasion was an early — and momentous — manifestation of the new economic order: it removed, rather than reformed, the old system of farming.

Between 1770 and 1870, encouragement was given to English and Lowland Scottish farmers to settle Kintyre, and in the 1840s Borders shepherds began to arrive. These men were both instruments of change and examples to the native farmers of how the business should be managed. But all this will appear later in the work.

Kintyre was entirely Gaelic in its culture until the first plantation of Lowland stock, in the seventeenth century, and predominantly Gaelic through to the nineteenth century. There is no strict equivalent in Gaelic

1

for the word — or the concept — of English 'farm'. *Baile* — anglicised as 'Bal-', 'Bally-', etc., in Kintyre — serves as an equivalent, but it also serves to describe any settlement.

I use the term 'farm' throughout this book, irrespective of period, but it has to be treated with caution until the nineteenth century. Until the concept of the farm — as an independent agricultural unit, worked by a single tenant — was forced into the frame of Gaelic society, the *baile* was simply a settlement in which the farming was taken for granted, more or less. In other words, the traditional agricultural unit was the communal tenancy township, or joint-farm (as preferred by some scholars: R. A. Gailey points out the 'risk of confusing this use of "township" with its modern legal connotation in a crofting context ...').

The joint-farm was a large unit, usually possessed by a *tacksman*. He generally held the 'tack', or lease, by virtue of his kinship with the chief or of some special status. For example, the bard of Clan Donald in Kintyre, John MacVurich, in 1505 occupied (rent-free, for his services) a multiple holding comprising Brecklate, Gartloskan, Cattadale, Gartvain and Keprigan. A typical tacksman — which MacVurich certainly was not — as described by Andrew McKerral in *Kintyre in the Seventeenth Century*

> ... lived at one of the farms — the principal or home farm — which he probably worked by means of hired servants and cottars or set out in *steelbow* [a system by which he loaned the cattle, horses and implements of farming]. The other farms of his holding were sublet to working tenants ... Although some of the smaller tacksmen may have been working farmers, the class in general were not, but gentlemen whose energies were taken up in the political and military activities of the age.

Runrig

Runrig prevailed in Kintyre down to the middle of the eighteenth century. The joint-farm was worked as a whole by the subtenants who were each allocated parts of it. There were three essential elements to the system: the dwelling, arable, and common pasture. The clustered houses were surrounded by, or stood adjacent to an area of 'infield' land, beyond which lay the detached portions of 'outfield'. Each individual held strips — or rigs (p. 23) — of land, of varying quality, scattered here and there in both infield and outfield. The system is still known and practised beyond Europe. The Dalai Lama's brother, Thubten Jigme Norbu, recalling, in 1954, his childhood in the mountains of Tibet, explained it thus: 'Our farm was made up of separate strips of land situated in different places. This came about by ancient custom, because as the soil was not all good many generations of peasants had divided it up so that each family should till both good and less good patches ...'

These strips — periodically reallocated by drawing lots — were the farmer's arable possessions. His share in the produce of the farm — as also the size of his grazing stock — was proportionate to his share in the tenancy, which in turn determined his share in the rent. In effect, the farm was worked communally. If there were four subtenants, each — in principle — supplied a horse for the common plough, and attended at the ploughing. (In practice, poorer portioners might pair in the ownership of a horse.) This principle John Smith criticised on the ground that 'none would work till all were assembled'.

Smith was writing around 1795, by which time the tacksmen in Kintyre had been half-a-century dispossessed, and their holdings turned over to the working farmers. This must, in its time, have been a remarkable transformation: these subtenants were lifted out of the insecurity of year-by-year occupation and offered leases. They might not have found themselves materially much better off, but at least they had a foothold on the land, hitherto denied them. Into their places, however, stepped the cottar class, and the same pattern of dependence was reproduced.

In Kintyre, the division — and abolition — of the big runrig farms began about the middle of the eighteenth century, and was followed by subdivision which continued into the early nineteenth century (to be countered, ironically, by an amalgamation trend which continues unimpeded to this day). Thus, for example, in 1792 Glenahervy was subdivided into four parts: High, West, South Shore and North-west Shore. John Smith remarked particularly on the effects of subdivision in Southend: 'In no part of the county are possessions more uniformly moderate ... In consequence of this, more waste ground has been of late years improved in this parish than in any other in the county. The yellow corn now waves on the region lately occupied by the heath and moss'.

Population

In a list of 'People upon the Argyll Estate', compiled in 1779, the emergence in Kintyre of the new social structure is apparent. In place of the traditional order of tacksmen, subtenants, and cottars — surviving tenaciously in Mull and Morvern — there were tenants (still, however, described as 'tacksmen'), servants, and a swelling cottar class.

The cottar, as the name implies, occupied a cottage, which was usually a 'wretched hovel' shared with 'the brute creation (p. 153) and held from year to year without security. In the 1840s in Killean and Kilchenzie Parish, rents of £4 and £5 were paid for 'a house kept in bad repair, a small kail garden, the scanty pasture of a cow, and some ground for planting potatoes in the outskirts of the farm'. Aside from a certain number of days' labour given to the farmer — for instance, at seedtime and harvest — the cottar was free to earn at whatever work he could find.

There were, in 1779, 162 farms listed on the Duke of Argyll's Kintyre estate (just one of several estates in Kintyre, though the biggest). These were occupied by 248 tenants and 286 cottars, along with 281 farm-servants. Of these holdings, thirty-three had no cottars attached, being tenanted in the main by only one farmer, for example Innengoich, Glenmurill, Glenrea, Bailinatuine, Arinaschavach and Altantarve. In total, sixty-three farms were single-tenancy. Farms occupied by five to nine families — tenants, servants and cottars together — numbered thirty, and at the top end of the scale there were six farms with ten or more families attached:

	families	tenants	tenants' sons	servants	cottars	totals*
Smerby	15	6	4	11	8	29
Drumlemble	14	2	3	3	10	18
Pollwuline	11	6	7	3	6	22
Killocraw	11	5	4	4	6	19
Beallachgoichan	11	6	3	3	5	17
Torristill	10	6	3	—	3	12

* Excluding all females, and males under the age of 12, who were omitted from the Kintyre census.

Nearly a half of these 162 listed farms have ceased to exist as independent holdings. One of the biggest, Beallachgoichan, near Muasdale, is in ruins. Three farms — Borgadilmore, Innendownan, and Ballinamoile/Ballimaacviccar — were even then unoccupied. These, significantly, were at the Mull of Kintyre, which had been turned over to sheep several years earlier (p. 68).

The statistics for the mining village of 'Coalpits' (near Drumlemble), I removed from the totals, along with the statistics for 'Killean Minister's Glebe' and the mills at Calliburn, Smerby and Machrimore. These were not leased as farms, though some cultivation would have been done on the limited ground attached to them.

The biggest of these settlements was at Machrimore, which retains even now the appearance of a small village, having thirteen occupied houses clustered at the derelict mill. In 1779, on Machrimore Farm, the adult male population comprised three tenants, the son of a tenant, six servants, and two cottars, constituting — together with the unrecorded women and children — five families. At the mill itself, sixteen families lived. There was one tenant — the miller himself — and fifteen cottars, most of whom must have been tradesmen or labourers. In 1841, there were twenty-one occupied houses at the mill and on the adjacent farm. The population of 116 included four tenant-farmers, four weavers, two tailors, two shoemakers, a cartwright, smith, miller and schoolmaster, along with farm-labourers.

Rhunahaorine, north of Tayinloan, has long been insignificant, but in 1841 its thirty-five houses held 144 people. Eight tailors lived there, four handloom weavers, two wrights, two shoemakers, a dressmaker and a schoolmaster.

On the farms of High and Low Margmonagach — lying abandoned on the hill between Barrmains and Killegruar — nineteen houses stood in 1851. Two weavers and a shoemaker were among the predominantly farm-labouring population of ninety-four.

Depopulation

Throughout the nineteenth century the population of rural Kintyre — farmers, cottars, labourers and tradesmen — ebbed away. The evidence is bared in statistics. Between 1831 and 1881, the population of Killean and Kilchenzie Parish dropped from 2866 to 1368; of Saddell and Skipness, from 2152 to 1163, and of Southend, from 2120 to 955. There was a steady movement into Campbeltown for work in distilleries, trades, and at labouring and fishing, but the greatest movement was overseas, to Canada, the United States, Australia and elsewhere.

Emigration from Kintyre certainly did not begin in the nineteenth century, but in that century its full force was released. The subject, in its entirety, has yet to be researched, and a great and rich labour it should be for anyone who will take it on.

There were several powerful forces at work in rural depopulation. Emigration was an effect, but it was also — to some degree that is indeterminable — a cause, for there was willing movement from Kintyre among the more adventurous of the people. The main causes of depopulation were, however, rooted in the land itself and in the economics of farming: increased mechanisation in the nineteenth century, crop failures — of the potato in particular, in the 1840s — and periodic market collapse. In short, the land could not support its swelling population.

A group of prominent Kintyre farmers assembled to say goodbye to one of the Macdonald brothers in East Chiskan — possibly Angus — on his emigration to New Zealand, c. 1907. Top row, L-R: William Cuthbertson, Ballywilline; James Hunter, Machribeg; Peter Clark, Low Peninver; ―― Macdonald; Archibald Mitchell, Clochkeil; Alexander MacLean, Kilmaho; John Gemmell, Dalrioch. Bottom Row, L-R: Archibald Greenlees, Stewarton Store; Archibald MacNair, Moy; Lachlan Clark, Tangy; James B. Mitchell, Aros; David Sommerville, Balloch; Malcolm MacNeill, Amod. Courtesy of Mr Andrew Reid.

In 1783, following the 'disastrous' harvest of the preceding year, English seed corn was sent by the Duke of Argyll to his tenants in Kintyre. In 1820, fifty-two of his tenants in Southend and the Leerside petitioned him for rent deductions following a bad harvest and a drop in grain prices. In 1838, Robert MacLean in Kilypole (now Calliburn) complained to John Lorne Stewart, the Duke of Argyll's chamberlain in Kintyre, of 'the lowness of the markets', and asked to be relieved of the remainder of his lease. He owed a year's rent — £81 16s 9d — and his whole stock was sequestered: seven cows, a bull, five queys, nine stots, five stirks, and six horses. But when the day of the public roup — or auction — of his stock arrived, all that remained were 'two old white mares and one cow'. In 1815, no fewer than 134 farmers on the Duke's Kintyre estate were owing rent.

Eviction and sequestration waited on most failed farmers, and few were as bold as Robert MacLean. At a roup at Bleachfield in 1838, the evicted

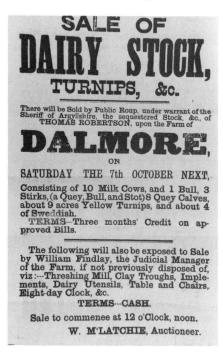
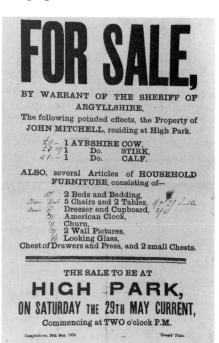

Two bills of roup (public auction), courtesy of Argyll and Bute District Council archive. A. Dalmore, Southend, 1871. The unfortunate farmer, Thomas Robertson, was from Marras, near Irvine, Ayrshire, and got the lease of Dalmore in 1860 at a rent of £160. B. High Park, 1875. The notes on the bill record the prices paid at the auction.

tenant, Humphrey Langlands, lost twenty-one stacks of oats, three stacks of barley, two stacks of beans, eight sacks of oats, potatoes — both stored and in the fields — and a cow, as well as all his household goods. The sum of £244 16s 4d was raised for the Duke of Argyll, and Langlands was left with nothing. The circumstances of his failure are unknown — perhaps he was a bad farmer, perhaps not — but when ruination overtook a farmer his options were few. He could labour to another farmer, as John Algie was forced to do in 1848 (p. 19), he could try another occupation, or he could somehow raise the fare for a passage abroad.

The Leasing System

The system of farm-leasing itself encouraged failure. Farms were generally let for nineteen years; but a year or two before expiry of the lease, the farm would be advertised to let, regardless of whether the sitting tenant wished to remain. Effectively, the farm was being put up for private auction, and in most cases the highest bidder got the lease, providing he had sufficient capital or security to stock the farm. Rents were doubled or tripled at the stroke of a pen, though the bidders knew well that the farm was already heavily enough rented. Frequently these same men would be forced, a few years later, to beg a rent reduction or release from their rash commitment, or would seek to augment the holding by adding another to it, no matter at whose expense or inconvenience. In short, the leasing system encouraged the greedy and ambitious, who frequently had neither the capital nor the skill to succeed. John Smith, in 1795, put the landlords' case: 'They say with some degree of justice, that the tenants only are to blame if they hurt themselves when allowed to make their own rents'. But he added: '. . . They take too much for granted if they think the persons who offer are always better judges than themselves'.

James Malcolm, a land-agent in London, surveyed the Duke of Argyll's Kintyre estate in 1810, and had this advice for his Lordship in the matter of increased rents:

> Have the ideas of the tenants who have given these improved rents been more enlarged and extended in agricultural knowledge in the same ratio? If they have not . . . their stock of corn and cattle will not be increased in value. Their capital being so much lessened by the increased rents, their object will be therefore to get the most they can [out] of the land, regardless of the means, and . . . if by any chance they fail, there is little better than rubbish for you to take possession of . . . If a man farms badly when the land is at a low rent, I should despair of his managing the same land well when that rent is doubled.

Rents were paid, in part, directly out of the produce of the farms and by 'services' — for example, the carting of a specified number of loads of peats and manure for the laird — until the first quarter of the nineteenth century, when money rents became general. Thus, in 1784, Hector MacAlister, joint-tenant in Lagan (Ròaig), paid Skipness Estate £6, a year-old wedder (castrated ram), a stone of cheese, a half-stone of butter, and a pound of lint. Argyll Estate leases generally required payment of quantities of *bear* (p. 44) and oatmeal in addition to cash.

Amalgamation of Holdings

The trend of amalgamation began on the rough margins of the peninsula and on the hilly interior. It continues, so that, even in the choice lowland areas, large farms gobble their neighbours. The introduction of sheep was unquestionably a major factor in that trend, and the land between Ballygroggan and Carskey shows most starkly the effects of depopulation.

Some seventeen known farms lay on that coast, connected by an ancient track, yet only one — Largybaan — is now worked as a (sheep-)farm, while two others — Feorlin and Glemanuill — are dwelling-houses.

On the east side of Kintyre, one can travel from Polliwilline to Kildalloig — a road distance of about seven miles — and pass only two operational farms, Glenahervie and Feochaig. Glenahervie itself expanded to its maximum — 2086 acres at the great auction of the Argyll Estate Kintyre properties in 1955 — by the incorporation of Gartnagerach, Cantaig, Earadale, Succoth and Lonachan (these last two already merged by 1759). On these farms, along with Glenahervie, the population totalled ninety-nine in 1792.

John McInnes — 'Dunaverty' in the *Campbeltown Courier*, which occasionally published articles by him — had this information on Earadale, in 1910: 'I have it on no less authority than the late Mr Peter McKay of Knockstaple, a gentleman who in his day knew the district well, that the heaviest barley ever known to go into Campbeltown was from the farm of Earadale when it was under cultivation'. Such a claim would, of course, be difficult to prove, but it is, for all that, worth noticing.

Farther north on the Leerside, another group of old farms were amalgamated. The first of these to cease as a working farm was evidently Glenmurril (pronounced '-mooril'), close to the head of Balnabraid Glen. It was of the oldest type of stone farm-building found in Kintyre, being entirely unmortared and lacking a chimney. It was constructed in three small compartments under one roof, and there were apparently no outbuildings. Described in 1794 as 'a small muir farm good for summer feeding but [with] no good shelter for winter', it was evidently not a lucky place to be.

Donald MacIlmichael, with his father Hugh, got the usual nineteen-year lease in 1777, at an annual rent of £15 plus a quantity of meal and *bear*. The lease was renewed in 1796 at a straight rent of £20, despite offers from Lachlan MacIsaac in Corphin (£50) and Donald O'Loynachan in Penny-land (£45). In 1800 MacIlmichael became bankrupt, and his brother-in-law, Peter MacConachy in Gartgunnell, took over the remainder of the lease at a rent of £28. When the lease expired in 1815 he was replaced by Lachlan MacIsaac, whose holding marched to the south with Glenmurril, and who had evidently long coveted the smaller farm. The two farms thus effectively became one; but MacIsaac — who got Glenmurril at a rent of £46 — had taken on too much, and four years later he renounced the lease in favour of Donald MacNaughton, Lephenstraw, whose rent, significantly, was reduced by twenty-five per cent. MacNaughton, too, failed with the farm, and in 1823 his stock was sequestrated and the remainder of the 1815

Balnabraid steading in 1986, a sycamore growing through the floor. The fireplace lintel has since collapsed. Photograph by the author.

lease taken over by Malcolm MacKerral at a rent of about £30. MacKerral was also tenant of Balnabraid, which marched to the north with Glenmurril. When the lease expired, in 1834, the tenancy again passed to the tenant (Alexander MacMillan) of a bordering farm, Arinarach in the west. By 1868, Glenmurril was formally leased with Balnabraid.

It is impossible to reckon when the house at Glenmurril ceased to be occupied by a working farmer, but it is doubtful if its occupation on these terms post-dated 1815, when Lachlan MacIsaac took over the lease. But it must have been periodically occupied — probably as a cottar's dwelling — because in 1852 Neil Colquhoun, a pauper there, was getting 4s 6d a month from Southend Parochial Board; yet the house appears to have been unoccupied when the census was taken a year earlier.

Balnabraid (pronounced '-bradj') stands across the glen from Glenmurril. It was associated principally with the MacKerral family — from which, on one of my maternal lines, I am descended — whose tenancy began in 1770 with Hugh and Peter, until then in Kilmashenachan. In the Argyll Estate census of 1792 there were thirteen MacKerrals in Balnabraid.

The lease passed in 1838 to Allan MacDougall, described as a 'cattle dealer' in Campbeltown, who sublet the farm to Lachlan MacNeill. In

1849 the lease was taken over by a stranger, William Brown, who must have introduced a sheep stock, for in the census of 1851 the house was occupied by a 68-year-old shepherd, Colin Campbell, and continued to be occupied by shepherds until the 1870s. In 1868 William Brown lost the lease — he had by then left Kintyre — and it was taken by Alexander Cordiner in Machrimore. In 1879, before Cordiner's lease was due to expire, Balnabraid, with Glenmurril, was advertised as 'an excellent grassing farm carrying about 700 sheep'. By the 1881 census the house had become unoccupied.

Ballinatunie, across the hill from Balnabraid, was leased to the Langlands family from 1775 until about 1856. The lease passed from George Langlands — employed by the Duke of Argyll as a land-surveyor and improver (advising on the division of farms, rotation of crops, etc.) — to his son Matthew in 1818. It is unlikely that George actually worked the farm, which is traditionally associated with the Loynachan (later Lang) family. These Loynachans were certainly there in 1792 — Donald, his wife More MacNaught, and two sons — and were still there in 1811. Matthew Langlands does seem to have worked Ballinatunie. The 1841 census found him there, aged sixty, with his wife, five children, and five farm-servants. In 1851 — mysteriously aged by nineteen years in the intervening decade — he described himself as a 'farmer of 50 acres, employing one man'. By 1861 the place was deserted.

Corphin was tenanted by a family MacIsaac from 1757 to 1856. In 1792 there were twenty people there; in 1841, eighteen; and in 1851, ten. John Spiers of Arran got the lease in 1856, along with that of Auchenhoan and Ballinatunie, and put a shepherd into Corphin. John MacIsaac and his family moved to Dunglas.

Another settlement comes into this survey, but it cannot be located. Blarferne was, by 1757, already leased with Corphin, of which it was a 'pendicle', or subsidiary part.

In 1875, Ballinatunie, Corphin and Blarferne were leased, with Auchenhoan, at an annual rent of £330, to Alexander Cordiner. In 1880 he renounced the lease of Auchenhoan and the others, but these farms were added to his earlier lease of Balnabraid and Glenmurril. Of all these farms, only Auchenhoan has been occupied in this century, and by shepherds only. It and the others are now in Kildalloig Estate. On that mass of land, in and around the scoop of Balnabraid Glen, not a crop grows.

The merging of farms was opposed as far back as the 1790s by John Smith. His arguments, closely reasoned over a score of pages in *The Agriculture of Argyll*, are as sound now as they were nearly two centuries ago:

The occupiers of ... large tracts seldom cultivate many acres. The little meal which they need for themselves and their shepherds is brought from the market, while their fields, rescued from the wilderness by the labour of ages, are allowed to revert to their original state, and to become wilderness again. The same possessions, if in many hands, might be so cultivated and improved as to maintain many families, and even more cattle, and would in a short time be brought to yield a higher rent; so that the public and the proprietors would both be gainers ... That this [present] system, by depopulating the country, is a manifest, perhaps an irreparable loss to the public, is obvious to the most shallow observer.

Agricultural Improvements

Agricultural improvements in Kintyre began tentatively in the eighteenth century, in line with a widespread national trend. The enclosing and draining of land John Smith reckoned to be the 'foundation of all improvements'. On pre-improvement farms, drainage was natural, aided only by ridge-and-furrow cultivation (p. 23). No enclosures existed, unless walled stackyards and kailyards are admitted in that definition. The only extensive walls were the head-dykes separating — not always effectively — infield and outfield arable from the common grazing.

Enclosure evidently began about the mid-eighteenth century, but was largely the concern of lairds who had 'sufficiently enclosed and subdivided the farms in their own hands'. At the end of that century, the general appearance of the countryside was 'still naked and open'. In 1810 James Malcolm complained of 'no draining [and] no enclosures' on the Duke of Argyll's Kintyre farms. That was unquestionably an exaggeration if even a few of the tenants of these same farms had followed instructions, in the 1790s, to 'enclose sufficiently an acre of ground and to have one third of it sown yearly with barley and clover and the other two thirds under clover, to be given green to their cattle in summer'. Yet, in the 1840s, enclosures in Southend were considered inadequate, and, in Killean and Kilchenzie Parish, 'the want of enclosures and subdivisions' was remarked on as 'a great obstacle to a regular rotation of crops'.

The merits of enclosure were several: livestock were kept out of crops; on grazing lands, herds could be dispensed with and the cattle given a change of pasture and clean grass when needed; on some grounds shelter was provided.

Specific directions on draining appear in Argyll Estate leases in Kintyre in 1790, and continue — well into the nineteenth century — to constitute a great part of the improvements programme. The most important result of that programme, however long it took the tenants to put their full weight behind it, was the conversion into arable of tracts of low-lying bogland.

The biggest area claimed by drainage was undoubtedly the Laggan (p. 90), which, in 1795, Smith described as 'an immense moss ... its thousands of acres good for nothing, except furnishing a few peats'.

The transition, obviously, was costly and laborious, and not the accomplishment of a generation. Its results can be seen in the regular patterns of square and rectangular fields which characterise the Laggan, as also the lowland parts of Southend. But, as the lowland bogs were being claimed for cultivation in the nineteenth century, so the hill arable was diminishing with the spread of sheep.

Drainage

In the hills, drainage ditches could almost now be mistaken for burns, were it not for the regularity of their lines. The stipulated breadth of these varied from 9ft to 5ft at the top, and 2½ft to 1½ft at bottom, with depths from 5ft to 3ft. The excavated earth was usually thrown to one side to form a mounded wall, along which thorns or sallies might be planted. That embankment was sometimes faced up with turf or stone. Ditches were frequently incorporated into marches, particularly on boggy moorland which precluded dyke-building.

Down in the earth, unseen, drains that were made in the late eighteenth and early nineteenth centuries still run. Farmers find them when checking or renewing drainage systems. The most substantial type was made with stones. The flattest stones would be laid in the drain bottom, then the sides built carefully, and flat stones fitted on top. Finally, the whole thing would be covered with heather or rushes, or some other pervious material, before filling back the earth. Alternatively, the stones could be fitted to form a triangular drain. Adam MacPhail maintained that 'there's no use o' ye puttin a tile drenn (drain) beside a stone drenn, because the water'll go tae the old drenn. An' ye'll never dry it till ye dig up the stones, an' ye'll need a pick, an' it's hard work'.

If small stones only were available, a simpler drain would be made. These drains were usually 3ft wide at the top, tapered to 1ft at a depth of 3ft. A bottoming of stones, to a depth of 1ft, was laid down, and then the drain was filled in. Adam MacPhail uncovered such drains at Skernish, Barr Glen, and was surprised to find them bottomed with shore gravel — 'as white as the day it went in' — and still running.

When, in 1986, the Fa' Field on Kilkivan Farm was being re-drained with plastic piping, an old drain constructed entirely of discarded sarking was uncovered. Donald Irwin, one of the drainers, described that drain as being box-built in sections approximately 10in square, with the top boards placed on like lids.

On mossy ground, the 'block drain' — as it was locally known — best suited. A tapered trench was dug to a depth of perhaps 3ft, and the 'scraw' (turf) turned upside-down into the bottom of the trench, so that a gap remained to conduct the water. When Donald MacCallum was shepherding on the top of Achnaglach Hill, he would occasionally try his stick in one of these drains, 'an' they wir runnin quite clear in the bottom, for when ye'd get yer stick down ye'd feel it goin right down through this *bose* (hollow)'.

Enclosures

An incalculable mileage of walls was built in Kintyre, during the late eighteenth and the nineteenth centuries, for a variety of purposes: for enclosing fields, defining marches, separating arable from grazing land, lining roadsides, etc. These were built entirely of stone or of *feal* (turf), or of feal and stone in alternate rows. Turf dykes John Smith considered 'so much labour lost' compared with stone dykes. Stones were abundant almost everywhere and labour was cheap. In most places these could be built, in the late eighteenth century, at a shilling the yard. 'This is complete at once; stands, if well built, for a century; and, when it fails, as the materials remain, may be easily repaired.'

The stipulated height of stone dykes was normally 3½ft, but occasionally 4ft, and the stone was invariably capped with two rows of feal. Feal dykes were generally raised to 5ft, tapered from a breadth of 5ft at the base, which great spread on the ground no doubt informed Smith's remark that stone dykes took up less room and saved ground.

Thorn bushes were extensively planted in the late eighteenth and early nineteenth centuries. Until the end of the eighteenth century, Argyll Estate leases in Kintyre often contained a clause binding tenants to the planting and preserving of such thorns as were 'requisite for the improvements'. Later, thorns — as also sallies (shrubby willows) — were prominent in schedules of improvements attached to particular leases. These were used to hedge roadsides and gardens and to line the embankments of march and drainage ditches. Vast numbers of hawthorns must have been planted in Kintyre. In 1789, for example, 150,000 plants were imported from Ireland, 'for the use of his Grace's farms in Kintyre'.

Modern farming notions are not always sympathetic to thorn hedges, because they need caring for; but they are, if maintained, more durable than any other form of fence, and give shelter to stock as well as to birds and other small creatures which have, however, no commercial value.

Shielings

The coming of enclosures undoubtedly contributed to the decline of the shieling system in Kintyre. That system — otherwise, transhumance — had three main functions: it gave the livestock — cattle, sheep and goats — fresh grazing, and in so doing removed them from the unfenced farm environs when the crops were growing; most important, it exploited the lush May-June growth on the coarsest of grazings.

It is hardly possible to walk the hills of Kintyre without seeing the turfy mounds of fallen shielings, if one develops an 'eye' for them. Often, indeed, one can recognise a site a long way off, by the good green grass, dunged in centuries past. There are shielings on Glenramskill Farm, almost within sight of Campbeltown.

In the archaeological survey of Kintyre, published in 1971 by the Royal Commission on the Ancient and Historical Monuments of Scotland, two shieling sites are examined, one at Gartavaich, the other at Talatoll. Some forty-three huts — an unusually large concentration — have been identified at Talatoll. They vary widely in size and shape. Most were single-chambered, and the smallest of these measured about 9ft by 7ft over all. The largest of the three-chambered huts measured about 20ft by 16ft. The average thickness of the turf-and-stone walls appears to have been about 3ft, and the doorways were often formed of upended slabs. Shieling huts in Kintyre were predominantly oval-shaped.

The Gaelic for 'shieling' in Kintyre was *airigh*, which has the English forms 'ari-' and '-ary'. Virtually all the surviving *airigh* names are attached to farms which were established by the conversion of seasonal grazing land into settled arable. When the large runrig holdings were broken up, their hill grazings were parcelled out. There was no longer licence for stock movement on the scale that transhumance sometimes required, involving miles of travel. Farms were given definable boundaries, and these had to be walled or ditched ... and respected. In 1793 the 'common muir called Sleave' was formally divided among the farms of Elerick, Crognagrain, and Arinascavach, and the tenants were bound to their own portions. The creation of sheep-farms closed off greater tracts of mountain and hill land which had been the haunts of the summer herds. The ancient custom of summering stock at the shielings may be accepted as having disappeared, more or less, by the end of the eighteenth century in Kintyre. Consequently, little is known about it in Kintyre.

When spring work was over, the men of the farm went and repaired the shielings, rebuilding the walls and renewing the sod roofs. The shift itself took place at the end of May or the beginning of June, after peats had been cut. All hands were needed, because there was much gear to be carried — bedding, clothing, oatmeal, cooking utensils, dishes, and a range of articles used in making butter and cheese, including milking-stools and a block of iron which was heated until red-hot and placed in the milk to sterilise it. Butter and cheese were the immediate products of the six or seven weeks' stay at the shielings. The women took their distaffs, to spin wool as they moved among their flocks. The women and children generally had the place to themselves — except for an experienced herdsman — because the men returned to the farm and worked there, undisturbed by animals poaching in the open fields.

One end of every dwelling-hut was banked to form a bed, and springy heather-tops were spread on it. A blanket to cover the heather, and another to cover the sleeper sufficed in the summer nights. Meals were mostly eaten outside, and the whole experience had a holiday atmosphere to it. The end of the shieling life must have saddened children most.

CHAPTER 2

Tilling and Fertilising the Soil

Until the late eighteenth century in Kintyre, ploughing was heavy going. Each plough needed four horses, yoked abreast, and at least two men, one to manage the plough and the other to manage the team. A third man might be employed, 'dressing the furrows after the plough', as Peter MacIntosh put it. His job was to follow with a spade, breaking down clods and tidying badly turned strips of furrow. By 1795, some farmers had begun to use only two horses on the plough, and a very few were ploughing without a driver (who walked backwards ahead of the team, leading with the reins and whistling encouragement).

'This', John Smith remarked, 'will be found easier than is commonly imagined. In a very few days the horses come to understand their business, and will give little trouble to direct them by the reins. They also move with greater ease, and make better work, even in cross and irregular lands. It is surprising that such as see so vast a saving and so great an improvement going on before their eyes, are so slow to adopt it.' Soon, he predicted, 'the ploughman who will not do without a driver must ... be considered as unfit to be employed'. By the end of the eighteenth century, the Duke of Argyll was encouraging, with premiums, 'the ploughmen who plow with two horses without a driver'. As Smith reasoned, why keep more horses for the plough than were necessary? 'For every unnecessary horse,' he reckoned, 'the farmer could keep two cows, which would bring him a gain of £5 a year.'

These advances in ploughing methods in Argyll as a whole Smith attributed to Lowland influence, direct and indirect. 'Skilful ploughmen from the Low Country' had been settled in Argyll, and young men who hired their labour in the Lowlands brought back the skills acquired there. Smith also cited the introduction of English farmers into Kintyre by the Duke of Argyll. 'Their skill in ploughing', he judged, 'could not be questioned.' These farmers can be identified in the leases of the Argyll Estate. There were at least ten of them, all from Northumberland and Cumberland, and all were granted leases in either 1775 or 1776. Few appear to have wanted to remain in Kintyre beyond the term of their leases, and one — Thomas Townly — gave up Gartnagerach after three years. John Turner in Tonrioch stayed, as did Robert Makepeace in South

Carrine. He married a local woman, Margaret MacEachran, and his name was Gaelicised to MacPeace — later shortened to Peace — as the records of his children show.

Exact datings in the development of the plough (*beart* in the Gaelic of Kintyre and Gigha) are impossible. Iron ploughshares appeared — in south-east Scotland, at least — during the Romano-British period, from the first to the third centuries AD. Coulters and mouldboards appeared later. At what period these improvements are likely to have reached Kintyre is anybody's guess. It is certain, however, that mouldboards — which turned the furrow as the share (or sock) sliced it — were made of wood until the late eighteenth century. Until then, indeed, ploughs were constructed almost entirely of wood. The main iron parts were the sock and the coulter (the former makes the horizontal cut, the latter the vertical cut). Wooden ploughs were certainly in use in Kintyre until the mid-nineteenth century. In February 1846, A. McNair, blacksmith and farrier in Campbeltown (p. 121), made 'a reist (mouldboard) for a wooden plough' at a cost of 6s 6d, and in January of the following year fitted 'reist of wooden plough' and resteeled the sock and coulter, all for 1s 10d.

Most of these ploughs were made by the farmers themselves, 'in a very rude and clumsy manner, though they affect to say it is after the fashion of the old Scotch plough', as Smith remarked. But even as he wrote, these ploughs — which MacIntosh described as 'very heavy and laborious to work' — had begun to be replaced by light ploughs on the model of James Small's patent of 1767. Small was a Berwickshire farmer's son who adapted the old Scotch plough by incorporating and improving the main features of the English Rotherham plough. The minister of Killean and Kilchenzie, Alexander Stuart, recorded in the 1790s that many farmers in his parish 'instead of the old Scotch plough and 4 horses, use now Small's light plough and only 2 horses, and a few have laid aside the driver'.

The basic form of Small's plough survived until the general adoption of tractors in Kintyre (in 1926 there were still only two). All-iron ploughs had appeared in the early years of the nineteenth century — the first in Scotland was evidently manufactured around 1803 at Uddingston — and progressively found favour. McNair the blacksmith made a new iron plough for Alexander Wilson in Crosshill, in 1846, and charged £4 4s.

Ploughing Matches

Ploughmen enjoyed their skills, and enjoyed displaying them in competition — they still do. Ploughing matches appear to have been

Ploughing *ley* — old pasture — c. 1920. Courtesy of Mrs Annie Gillies.

introduced in Kintyre during the first quarter of the nineteenth century, probably through the influence of the Highland Society (now the Royal Highland and Agricultural Society), and with the encouragement of farmers and landowners, who recognised their value as a stimulus to the improvement of techniques. In one of the historical and genealogical notebooks kept by Archibald McEachran, Kilblaan, are detailed seven successive competitions held in the 1840s.

In 1843 the match was held at Ballegreggan, and 'more than 20 ploughs came forward'. The winner was Daniel Martin, servant with John Paterson, Killeonan. He won again in the following year, on the same ground, and again received a prize of £1 12s.

In 1845, at Dunglas, the winner was John Algie, a native of Renfrewshire, who had lost his tenancy of Cattadale since his appearance in the previous year's match — he was placed second — and become a 'servant at Belloch'.

In 1846 and '47 — at unspecified locations — John MacInnes, servant with William Clark, Gartvain, took first place and a prize of £1.

At Homestone, in 1848, the winner was Edward MacEachen, servant at Kilmichael. In the following year, Hugh MacKerral, son of Dugald in Brunerican, gained first prize of £1 1s, and with it a Highland Society medal.

Among those who were often highly placed, but who failed to take a first place, were Archibald MacKerral, son of Hugh in Brunerican (third in 1843, fifth in '44, second in '45 and '46, and third in '47) and John Stewart, son of Andrew in Peninver (third in 1844, '45 and '46, second in '47, and third in '48).

The most celebrated match took place at Kilkivan on 9 February 1889, to meet a challenge by James Ferguson of Strathbungo to the best of the Kintyre ploughmen. Twelve Kintyre men were picked to meet him, and 'a number of local gentlemen' raised the prize money. The first prize was £10, a lot of money when a year's wage for a married ploughman was £24, with perquisites.

About 2000 spectators gathered though the morning was cold and showery. By the time the competitors had started the second rig, the crowd was thickening at the ends where Ferguson and James MacAulay of Killeonan were ploughing, sensing that 'the battle for the premier prize was to be fought by these two'. And so it was to be. The judges, 'after long and painstaking scrutiny, and many applications of the eye, foot and rule', placed Ferguson first and MacAulay second, with a prize of £6. The other placings were: Duncan MacKay, Drumlemble — £4, Hugh Reid, Auchencorvie — £2, and William MacKerral, Brunerican — £1.

The judges were agreed that 'they never had seen in one field such an aggregation of good ploughing', but remarked on the superiority of Ferguson's plough. Its 'conformity' better served to 'twine' (turn) the furrows. That observation concluded a twenty-one-verse poem written in Scots — and competently at that — to celebrate the event:

> An' still 'tis said, an' mony anes
> Haud it tae be true man,
> That he had but the better ploo
> An' we the better plooman.

There is arable ground in Kintyre that no horse-drawn plough ever broke. The people used hand implements to turn the soil when they could not afford horses or when their plots were too steep or small to let horses work. In such conditions, collective spadework was the answer.

The Cas-Chrom

The *cas-chrom* — technically a plough: it turns a furrow — is unlikely to have been commonly used at any time in Kintyre, because by far the greater part of the arable ground was accessible to horse-drawn ploughs.

The cas-chrom, sketched by 'Cuthbert Bede' and published in his *Glencreggan*. In the background, a harrow is being dragged on the tail of a horse.

Further, unless ground is fairly level, it is next to impossible to use the cas-chrom on lazybeds, and these, in Kintyre, tend to be found on steep ground, suggesting cultivation by spade. Peter MacIntosh — writing in 1857 — ascribed the use of the cas-chrom to 'old times'; yet Edward Bradley ('Cuthbert Bede'), who followed him in most matters, a couple of years later maintained that it was 'even now to be met with here and there'.

The cas-chrom is a long bent shaft tipped with a broad iron blade, and with a wooden footrest. It is especially suited to undercutting turfy ground. One was donated to Campbeltown museum in 1917 and attracted such interest that 'an enterprising allotment holder' in town had a replica made. In May of that year, in a field adjoining Eagle Park on Low Askomil, a Skyeman demonstrated its use. The efficiency of the cas-chrom had been

Single-rigs, revealed by unmelted snow lying in the furrows. Ballygroggan, March 1987. Photograph by the author.

doubted locally, 'the prevailing opinion being that a man could turn over as much ground, or even more, with an ordinary spade'. But although the chosen ground had long been fallow and was heavy-soiled and thickly grassed, it was 'turned up ... with a rapidity which could not have been equalled even by the deftest spadesman'. The interest, however, seems to have been taken no further.

Rigs and Lazybeds

On many upland parts of Kintyre, the scars of plough and spade remain, their patterns set on the landscape. They remain because no modern plough levelled and erased them. These corrugations, whether of regularly ploughed rigs or of patchy lazybeds — made by heaping thin soil into ridges, rather than by digging as such — show best with a thin snowfall on the land or when the low-angled light of morning or evening touches them. There is no trace in Kintyre, to my knowledge, of the 'serpentine' rigs to which John Smith referred in the 1790s. By then, the 'taste' had changed, 'and now new ones are made straight, though the direction of the old cannot easily be altered'. The 'single-rig' (*imir*) was from 5 to 6 yards wide, and the lazybed about 2 yards.

Alexander Fenton, in *Scottish Country Life*, explained how the rigs were made, and how, when improved farming caught on, they were unmade:

> It involved ploughing the land into a series of raised ridges on which the crops were grown, with furrows between that served as ditches for draining surface water. Since the system of underground tile drainage did not become general till well through the nineteenth century, there was really no earlier alternative to the ridge-and-furrow form of cultivation, except in places where the soil was naturally well-drained. But even there, ridge-and-furrow was used, because the ridges were the basic working units of pre-improvement farming, and their width in particular was adapted to suit the needs of sowing grain by hand, and to shearing it with hooks and sickles.
>
> . . . They became permanent fixtures, on which ploughing went on year after year, and since the slices of earth cut by the plough were always turned towards the crown of the ridge, the height gradually increased over a period . . . They had to be levelled and spread — often a task of great difficulty — in the days of improved farming, and once this had been done (or where new land was broken in), it was normal for the new ridges to be split from time to time, so that the positions of ridge and furrow alternated.

One need not leave Campbeltown to see examples of old cultivations — Knock Scalbert and Crosshill bear the scars. There are nice rigs on the north-facing slope of Balnabraid Glen, just over the roadside fence at the Second Waters. Lazybeds are easily enough sighted — the hard walking discounted! — on the steep coast between Machrihanish and the Mull of Kintyre. These communicate, as no book can, the grim struggles of the subsistence farmers. At Innean Beithe, for instance, tiny patches of cultivation lie among the rock outcrops below the fank. Within easy walking distance, there are lazybeds in the small bay between Uisead Point and the old Lifeboathouse at Machrihanish. Four are quite distinct and run to about fifteen yards long.

The rockiness of ground was a great obstacle to cultivation throughout the greater part of Kintyre. Around ruined settlements, stone heaps — set to the sides of fields — evince the great labour of clearing land. The labour was unending — year after year rocks were wrested from the ground and heaved aside, and heap followed heap. That material undoubtedly went to the building of dykes and houses, but much of it remains where it has lain for centuries. James Malcolm, in 1810, plainly believed that greater effort could have been applied to clearing ground and gaining 'larger tracts of fine land for the plough or for pasture'. Probably he underestimated the scale of the labour needed, though his notes on North Kildonnel acknowledge the magnitude of the problem there, at least: 'The land abounds with rocks which unfortunately lie near the surface, and I fear are

Lazybeds above Innean Mòr, the ruins of which may be seen at right, extending into the middle of the photograph. The level sandy-soiled bay was also cultivated, but the traces are indistinct in this photograph, taken by the author in 1986.

both too multitudinous and large to give room to hope that they will ever be removed by the exertions of a tenant'.

Fertilisers

'Artificial' manures — such as sulphate of ammonia and superphosphates (guano: seabird droppings from Chile and Peru) — began to be used in Kintyre during the latter half of the nineteenth century, but these merely supplemented traditional manures. Many farmers, in any case, could not afford to buy fertilisers, and continued to depend mainly on dung and seaweed.

Seaweed

'Wreck' — seaweed, or *feamnach* in the Gaelic of Kintyre and Gigha — was extensively used on farms that were close enough to the coast to make the gathering of it worthwhile. It was mainly used on turnips and potatoes. In a clay soil fertilised by wrack, potatoes tended to be damp, but on sandy-soiled coastal fields a potato crop would do well. John MacKay reckoned that wrack should be spread no later than New Year, otherwise the potatoes took its flavour; but wrack-gathering went on from October until March as long as there were gales to loosen the weed from the seabed and drive it ashore.

The importance of wrack as a fertiliser is evinced on a beautifully detailed map of the coast from Bellochantuy to Machrihanish Bay, surveyed by K. C. Baine of Nairn in 1854. Some of these names — and others omitted here — are probably preserved in no other form:

> Ballochantry Bay — 'Excellent for sea ware in north winds';
> Brand Port — 'One of the best in the Duke's property for sea ware';
> Port na Croch — 'Best upon the shore for sea ware';
> Irish Port — 'Wreck cannot be got out but upon people's backs';
> Big Glen Port — 'Ware must be carried on men's backs'.

When wrack came ashore, competition to get it could be keen. At Port a' Bhorrain, wrack came in with a south wind and was taken back out by an east wind. Work would not begin until 8 a.m., the mutually agreed time. Horses and carts were reversed down to the shore and the *graips* (forks) stuck into the wrack. On the hour, the men would go to work with gusto, 'an' some o' the stronger ones could just about half-fill the cart wi' the first lift', as Neil Littleson remembered. The loads were not transported immediately to the fields, but were tipped above the shore to get as much wrack gathered before a change of wind could remove it.

That practice was the cause of legal action, in 1879, by James M. Hall of Tangy, against a tenant of his own, George Riddell in Tangy Mill and the Tuck Mill Croft. Hall had decided that 'middening' of wrack was 'inconvenient and a cause of dissatisfaction', and told his tenants that the seaweed 'was to be carted away as the carts were filled'. George Riddell ignored the order, was taken to court, defended the action, and lost. Sheriff James Gardiner in Campbeltown found that 'the right to enforce any reasonable rule naturally belongs to the landowner', and that 'the mere right to take wrack cannot be held as carrying with it . . . the further right to occupy part of another tenant's land, for a longer or shorter period, by laying down heaps of seaware upon it'.

At Machrihanish, in the nineteenth century, 7 a.m. was the agreed starting time, and the carts would be assembled at Wreck Cottage, so called. At Bealach a' Chaochain, in the late nineteenth century, the landowner, Robert Colville, charged non-tenants £1 annually for each horse and cart employed at wrack. That was a customary shore for many of the farmers of Muasdale and Barr Glen. Finlay Clark told a story of an incident there many years ago, when Adam MacPhail's cart upset on a boulder concealed by wrack. Adam had not forgotten the mishap either. That was a memorable event in its time. Finlay remembered that three 'rakes' — or loads — could be taken from the shore in the morning, and three in the afternoon. These would be spread on the stubble before the field was ploughed, and in bad years, when the stooks remained in the fields, the wrack would be spread around them.

Archibald Cameron in South Carrine got wrack at Keil and Garadh Dubh, and with an early start could take four or five cartloads each day. 'After a big storm,' he said, 'it wiz birled up an' rowed (rolled) up — ye cou'na tear it apart; but if it came in in wee puckles ye could jeest graip it up loosely.' His father always tried to lay wrack on ground intended for potatoes, but spread as much as he could on turnip ground.

Most farmers used a special 'wreck-graip' for the job. It was long in the shaft, for getting below the weed and for building a high load in the cart. The standard wreck-graip had three iron 'toes' (prongs), each about a foot long and with a 'lift' — or upward turn — to it. In the nineteenth century, the shaft might also be made of iron. Some farmers preferred an ordinary graip.

There was an opinion that wrack was best left rotting for a time before spreading, but, whatever the intention, the wrack was first placed in *coups* (little heaps) in the fields. Sooner or later it would be spread. At New Peninver, one of the girls on the farm would be given the job of 'skailing' (spreading) the wrack. Graham MacKinlay, as a boy at Whitestone, had to follow the plough in a wrack-spread field, clearing weed from the coulter with a pole, to prevent a 'nesty fir' (nasty furrow) being thrown.

One of the farm labourers' grievances heard by Henry Rutherford of the Royal Commission on Labour, when he collected evidence in Kintyre in 1892, was that 'they were expected to gather seaweed on the shore in the late autumn or winter during the early morning, when scarcely daylight, thus floundering in the water and getting wet feet'.

Donald Watson was a firm advocate of seaweed fertiliser. He is dead, but these were his thoughts in 1977: 'Immediately ye came to a portion that there wir no seaweed went on, there's a marked difference in the length o' the crop. An' there still wid be if they wir puttin on seaweed; but they don't seem to now. They get so much artificial, an' of course there's not enough labour on the farms now. There's only two men now where there used to be four'.

A substantial nineteenth-century lime-kiln, at East Skeroblin, 1987. Photograph by the author.

Lime

The use of lime had become general in Kintyre by the end of the eighteenth century, though in many other parts of Argyll 'farmers who have both the lime and the peats to burn it almost at the door ... seldom think of using it'. Small kilns, scooped out and built of stone into the face of a hill, had begun to be considered indispensible. These replaced the temporary turf kilns built in the fields where the lime was to be spread, and John Smith reckoned that, in the improved kilns, only a half of the fuel was needed to burn lime. In Southend, in the 1790s, the only 'draw kiln' there had been built by an English farmer for his own use.

In 1771, however, Donald MacDonald in Achansavil, Southend, had proposed erecting a lime-kiln and storage shed at either Dunaverty or Carskey. He wanted money from the Duke of Argyll: £50 for the building of a 'flat bottomed Boat of about 12 tuns burden to carry Limeston from Irland and Coals from the Low Country'; £5 for building the kiln, and £6 for building the shed. He estimated the costs of handling one cargo at £4 10s: purchase of 12 tons of limestone — 12s; three seamen's wages —

17s; breaking, carrying the stone to the kiln, and burning it — 15s; four tons of coal for burning the stone, all expenses included — £2; 'incidental charges' — 6s. Twelve tons of limestone, MacDonald reckoned, would produce 120 barrels or bolls of lime, which could not be sold at less than 9d a barrel. The proposal presumably came to nothing.

A good deal of limestone was imported from Ireland, particularly to the Southend district. Ireland was closer to Southend than many parts of Kintyre in which limestone was quarried, and it was more economical to ship the stone than to cart it. By 1817, the 'port' of Glenahervie — a 'stone breast-work' built by Colin MacEachran there, to harbour a smack of his — was much used by the tenants round about for bringing in Irish limestone.

As an encouragement to the Duke of Argyll's tenants in Kintyre, Edward MacEachein was obliged to work the quarry at Kilwhipnach in the late eighteenth century, and to have limestone continually available. He was to supply the stone at 2d a cartload — which was 1d cheaper than at any other quarry — and to maintain that differential no matter how low prices went elsewhere. In 1772, Thomas Pennant reported that the Duke granted quantities of burnt lime to those tenants who could 'show the largest and best fallow', and also allowed them a ten per cent reduction in rent.

The conscientious use of lime was evidently considered a good bargaining point when dealing with the Argyll Estate in money matters. In 1784, Peter MacKerall and his son Peter, in Ballinabraid, when making an offer for the renewal of their lease, pointedly mentioned that since they had taken over the farm they had annually purchased and shipped from Askomill enough limestone to 'make four good kilns which they . . . spread upon their ground'. In 1816, their kinsman in Brunerickan, Hugh MacKerral, claimed, when asking a reduction in rent, that he had '. . . burnt and laid out upon his farm during these last 12 months bygone, 197 carts of lime and other years more'.

In Killean and Kilchenzie Parish, by the 1840s, outfield land, after lying two years in lea, was generally manured with a compost of earth and lime or shell-sand (which has a lime content, being calcium carbonate), and sown two years in succession with oats.

Lime-burning was largely abandoned in Kintyre towards the end of the nineteenth century, but the use of lime continued. It was imported ready burnt and required only to be 'slockened' (slaked) and spread on the fields. Disused kilns may be seen throughout the peninsula, for instance at Fort Argyll, Campbeltown — a massive structure — and at Killellan and Kilwhipnach, from the main Southend road.

Sea sand — with little shell content — was spread on moss and clay soils by some Kintyre farmers in Smith's time, and with 'great advantage'. About 1780, John Thomson, Duncan MacGeachy and Charles MacCaog in Beachmore bought a 'Large big Boat in order to be bringing Sand from the Iland of Carra to lay on Land for Mannure'. Six years later, however, MacCaog sublet his holding and 'Began to Irish Trade with the Boat'. His partners were angered and took legal action against him.

Smith was keen to promote the use of the 'astonishing mass' of oyster shells heaped on the shores of West Loch Tarbert, and envisaged a time 'when these shells will be an article of commerce, and be carried at least along the shores of Kintyre'. That time never came.

Dung

Dung has always been the fundamental natural fertiliser. There was a common practice — which had begun to decline towards the close of the eighteenth century — of folding sheep and cattle in the fields that needed dung. Smith condemned it as 'hurtful to the cattle in the extent to which it was carried on, for they were imprisoned there, at night and noon, in all weathers, from May till November, or till the field was dunged'. Yet, he did not wish a total end to the custom, reasoning that many fields were so situated that they could not be manured in any other way.

The lack of regular, compact dungheaps was remarked on in the late eighteenth and early nineteenth centuries. Smith complained that they were 'sometimes placed so near the byre and stable doors, that the cattle must be continually wading through them, to the great injury both of dung and cattle'. Malcolm, in 1810, saw 'no regular dunghills, no extraneous or foreign manures ... no straw yards, indifferent cattle and these left to range about the buildings, poaching the ground, starving themselves, and wasting their essence in the desart (*sic*) air'.

CHAPTER 3

Crops

Oats

Until the mid-eighteenth century, the main food crop in Kintyre was oats, also called *corn*. These were usually the small-grained 'black oats', but by the end of the century that kind had been replaced, except in some 'mountainous farms' of Argyll, where it was grown as winter fodder for outlying cattle. Polish oats were a popular replacement for a few years, but in the 1790s 'Blainsley' oats were the prevalent kind. Coming from a 'poor cold soil', they throve in Kintyre.

Seed was sown from a linen sheet, knotted at the left shoulder and slung below the chest. Originally, the seed was cast with one hand, sowing one side of the rig and then the other (and perhaps laying a sprinkle along the centre of the rig to ensure that the seed cover was complete). By the end of the nineteenth century, manufactured 'sheets' — actually canvas on a wooden frame, with leather shoulder-straps — had been adopted, and double-handed sowing became general. Fields were sown rig by rig, and the mark the sowers worked by, on either side, was the *sgriob bheag* (little furrow) which was made by the ploughman.

The hardest worker at sowing was not the sower himself, but his helper — usually a girl — whose job was to keep replenishing the seed from bags laid in the field. She carried the seed in buckets, one in each hand. The rigs were harrowed behind the sower, to get the seed buried and out of the sight of birds. Harrows with wooden teeth were still being used in Argyll in the 1790s, and in some parts — Gigha for instance — continued to be dragged on the tails of horses (Fig. 5, p. 21). Archibald McEachran, in historical notes written about 1940, mentioned that 'wooden harrows were used in Kilblaan up to about 25 or 30 years ago', but these must have been iron-toothed. He had 'heard about the thorn bush tied to the horse's tail' — a primitive form of harrow — but understood that it was used only on rye-grass fields.

Oats — and all other grain crops — were cut with the sickle (*corran*) until the scythe (*speal*) began to be turned increasingly to that work in the latter part of the nineteenth century. Edward Bradley described a 'picturesque' harvest scene near Glencreggan in August 1859 — the crop was barley —

Reapers, using sickles. A harvest scene near Glencreggan, drawn by Edward Bradley ('Cuthbert Bede') in 1859.

but was evidently more interested in the girls and their clothes than in the operation itself. He did, however, mention that they wore 'coverings' on their feet and ankles to protect themselves from stubble cuts, and that they used the sickle 'as dexterously as did the men'.

Towards the end of the nineteenth century, mechanical reapers began to be adopted on the larger farms. The reaping-machine was a great cost-cutting innovation, eliminating teams of men and women cutting by hand. But manual reaping did not end with that. 'Roads' were scythed around the edges of the field to prevent crop-trampling by the horses. When the field had thus been opened, the reaper could be admitted. Two men were required to operate it — one to drive the horses, and the other to 'put off' the sheaves (*sguaban*) by means of the tilting board mechanism. The sheaves were bound by a team of men and women, using straw bands

A binder at Lephenstrath, c. 1930. Courtesy of Mrs May Barbour.

('straps' in Kintyre). Further labour-saving was achieved with the adoption of string-tying mechanical binders. In the first year of the Great War, scarcity of men was reported as being 'the cause of a good many binders being introduced' in Kintyre. Irish harvest workers had come to Kintyre in great numbers, but by the 1890s the influx had 'decreased by five-sixths'.

The sheaves were brought together and set up; four pairs usually formed the stook (*adag*). The drying time was widely variable, according to weather.

Harvesting usually began about mid-September, but the start could be earlier or later, again depending on weather. In 1921, Will Douglas cut his oat crop at Knockbay on 4 August, which was considered unprecedented in half-a-century. 'It brought his memory back to one harvest 53 years ago when he took part with the late James McNair in the harvesting of the oat crop at Smerby in the first week of August.' Sabbath-breaking began, it seems, in the early years of the present century. In 1908, a few instances were reported, in the *Campbeltown Courier*, of 'leading in' the crop on the last Sunday of September, 'a particularly fine harvest day all over'. But some farmers, having 'qualms of conscience ... waited till midnight when they started work with the aid of lamps. Rain came on, however, about 3.30 a.m. and stopped operations'.

Forking corn sheaves on to a box-cart above the Meadows, Campbeltown, c. 1900. Courtesy of Mr J. D. F. Colville.

In Killean and Kilchenzie Parish, in the 1790s, the average return on oats was reckoned at three-and-a-half seeds; some fifty years later it was reckoned at six seeds. A remarkable stalk of oats, from the crop on Skipness Home Farm in September 1909, carried 142 seeds and was exactly seven feet high.

In 1920, John McInnes regretted the accelerating trend of mechanisation on farms:

> About fifty years ago, it was quite a common occurrence during harvest to see on such farms as Darlochan, Kilkivan, Drumlemble, Tonrioch, Killeonan, Macharioch, and Machribeg about thirty shearers at work, and I question if, with the more improved methods of cutting, more than sixty people are now employed during harvest on these seven farms combined. The old system of harvesting was very hard work, but it was performed with a cheerfulness and good grace that I fear is foreign to the majority of the present generation.

Cailleach

The last sheaf to be cut — even into the time of the reaping-machine — was called the 'Calyach' (*Cailleach*, which is Gaelic for 'old woman'), and the

Women in corn field, Southend, c. 1925. The woman on the left holds a pitchfork. In centre, Janet Ferguson — later Mrs Archibald D. Cameron —and, at right, Katie MacMillan, later Mrs Dan Hamilton. Courtesy of Ms Janet Barbour.

harvester who was able to seize it was considered fortunate. A bunch of that sheaf would be crossed or pleated, dressed with ribbons, and hung on the kitchen wall until New Year, when it was fed to the oldest cow or horse. In a variation of that same custom in Kintyre, before the last swathe was cut the farmer would make a pleat of corn and throw it into the uncut corn. That too brought luck to the harvester who found it in his sheaf, and would be taken home and treated likewise.

The end of harvest was marked on most farms by a 'Harvest Home', also known as a *Cailleach*. The custom was explained in 1855 by various witnesses to a quarrel — at Taychroman, near Tayinloan — which led to an 'assault by biting'. Donald MacMillan, the tenant, said that shearing was finished on 11 September and that he gave his 'servants and the people who

In the stackyard at either Kilirvan or Brecklate, c. 1920. The only possible use for the spades — the one on the right an old-fashioned ditching spade, the other an ordinary garden spade — would have been in beating sheaf-butts into a neat surface (which has not been happening so far to these stacks). The bearded old man on the 'starter stack' is probably Hughie Kelly in Brecklate. Courtesy of Mrs May Barbour.

assisted at the harvest some whisky'. A young helper, John MacMillan in Clachaig, said that in the evening 'the shearers were entertained in MacMillan's house with a supper and some whisky'. James MacDonald, a labourer at Taychroman, described himself as 'one of the party at the "Caelach" or Harvest Home in the MacMillans' house'. On bigger farms, a dance would be held in the barn.

Stacks

The crop was later carted to the steading and built into stacks. The base of the stack (*mulan*) was built on a ring of big stones (*làrach*, and, in Scots, *stale*) which kept it off the ground and ventilated. In the stackyard of Killean Farm, iron-framed stales were in use when Adam MacPhail (b. 1907) was a boy. The stales in the ruinous stackyard of Balinatunie can still be traced on the ground as sunken, overgrown rings of stone.

The most common thatch was rushes (*luachair*), which were scythed, bunched and tied much as oats were, and carted home from the wet portions of fields or the higher hills, where they grew. Adam MacPhail at Skernish required five cartloads of rushes to thatch his corn. Some stack-thatchers pushed the first layer of rushes partly into the eaves (*anainn*, in Scots 'easing') to secure it. Other thatchers did not use these 'steepils' or 'stappils' (staples), but let the thatch overlap the eaves. The thatch was finished with the 'head sheaf', actually a bunch of rushes bound tightly at the cut ends and spread over the peak of the stack, like a pointed cap. A decorative straw shape — Adam MacPhail made diamonds — could be stuck on the very top, and that too was known as the *cailleach*. The thatch was then securely roped with about six vertical lengths — weighted by stones or bricks — and interlaced radially to produce a net-like finish.

Thatch-rope was made on some farms until well into the present century. Indeed, the brothers Duncan and John MacKeith twisted a 'soogan' from hay with the end of a hand-rake shortly before they gave up Kilmichael in 1969. That, however, was an 'emergency' — they ran short of coconut rope — and the implement was improvised. A short rope could be twisted with the thumb (*sùgan ordaig*), but the standard tool was the *corra-shùgain* (Gaelic) or *thraw-crook* (Scots). It varied in design, but was basically a metal hook revolved by a wooden handle. The one that Graham MacKinlay used was made entirely of wood. 'Sprits' — the sharp flowered rush (*juncus acutiflorus*) — were sometimes used in rope-making, but the main material was straw, saved from thrashing. Rope-twisting was usually the work of a day that was unfit for outdoor labour. At Whitestone, the rope was twisted out from the barn to the byre door, and held up on trestles so that the straw did not gather 'rubbish' from the ground. Two men were needed — one to turn the hook, and the other to feed the straw into the lengthening twine. The feeding was the more responsible job, if a strong and regular rope was to materialise. Imported stack-rope eventually eliminated the thraw-crook.

Thrashing and Drying

When oats are thrashed, the grain is separated, leaving straw. For many centuries, the common thrashing tool was the flail (*sùist*). It is unlikely that there is now any native of Kintyre who could use a flail. Duncan MacKeith, who was born in 1887 and died in 1984, was probably the last. The flail was simply enough constructed. The handle (*làmh*) was about 4½ feet long and was fastened to a shorter stick — the *buailtean*, or beater, about 3 feet — by a strip of sheepskin. The sheaves were 'walloped' on a board inside the barn. One side would be thrashed, and the sheaf turned to thrash the other, 'and there winna be a grenn (grain) left on't'.

Winnowing — to separate the 'caff' (chaff), short straw, rubbish and weed seeds from the grain — was done in the through-draught between the facing barn doors. In some smaller barns with only one door, a wall-opening, or winnowing-hole, would be formed opposite the door. (Barns were invariably built across the prevailing wind, and houses end-on to it — useful points in the identification of ruins.) The thrashed grain was thrown and caught in a *wecht*, which was a wooden hoop with sheepskin stretched across its base. A good breeze was needed to blow the useless stuff away, and in the days when food was prepared in small batches, the absence of wind could cause problems. These problems were solved with the invention of 'fanners' — simple winnowing machines — which, in the 1790s, John Smith reported as being 'pretty common'. Thrashing machines, he regretted, were unknown in Argyll; but James Malcolm reported two in 1810, one at Killeonan and the other at South Machrimore ('... among the extraordinaries in the Dead Stock of this farm'). Each was powered by a pair of horses.

Oats cannot be ground unless the very tough husk is separated from the grain. That was done by heating. Most farms had a kiln attached to them for the drying of grain, and in hill places these survive much as they were when the people left. In certain of the bigger settlements — such as Balmacvicar — kiln and barn were conjoined, but in others — for example Craigaig and Inandunan — the kiln was detached. The Inandunan kiln was noted in the Hearth Tax of 1694 against Duncan MacMillan, the tenant. 'Ane *cutag*' — Gaelic for a circular kiln — was also noted at the farms of Amod (Glen Breackerie), Ardnacross, Ballebrenan, Ballmaglack (Balnagleck), Ballimcilchonlie, Drumgarve, Glenahantie, Glenmuclach, Innanmoir, Margmonigach, Muastill, and Ullodell. That kiln at Craigaig is a fine-looking structure, and as sound as the day it was built. It is placed on a slope, and the height varies from 2 feet at the upper end to 8 feet at the lower. It measures 17 feet across, with thick turf-covered stone walls. It is drystone-built with skilfully fitted stones forming the drying chamber, into which the facing flues were led.

The corn-kiln in Kintyre was circular with a conical interior, which formed the drying chamber. A horizontal flue, or flues, fed heat into the chamber from a fireplace which burned peat. The floor of the chamber was sparred and covered with haircloth, according to Peter MacIntosh, who remarked that kilns often caught fire. By the 1790s, in Kintyre, improved kilns had been built '... with brick floors, for drying corn ... and the safety, cleanliness, and convenience of them promise to make them soon more general'.

Craigaig, showing the corn-kiln between the bottom left corner and the main dwellings. In 1779 three families lived there. By 1861, it was deserted. Photograph by the author, 1986.

There were simpler methods of drying oats in small quantities. MacIntosh recorded that, 'If they were at any time very short of meal, they would take in a sheaf of corn from the field, or barn, separate the grain from the straw, dry it in a pot, and grind it with the braidh in a very short time'. The practice of 'graddaning' was also recorded, by Bradley. That quick, but wasteful, device also removed the necessity of thrashing grain. The ears of corn would be set alight to burn away the chaff, and at the right moment — theoretically, anyway — the flames would be beaten out with a stick. The meal itself, from that process, was called *gradan*, and, according to Bradley, was generally preferred in Kintyre for bannocks, brose, porridge and *fuarag* (a mixture of meal and cream or water). Its burnt flavour was central to its appeal.

Hand-Milling

The 'braigh' — usually *brà* — to which MacIntosh referred was the hand-mill or quern. It was simply a round stone turned, by a wooden handle, upon a lower stone, while grain was fed into it through a central hole. The meal was caught on a cloth spread under the quern. The use of

The quern in use, from R. R. McIan's *Highlanders at Home* (1848), courtesy of the Scottish Ethnological Archive, National Museums of Scotland. The stones found in Kintyre are much thicker, and roughly hewn.

querns continued, in Kintyre, until about the end of the eighteenth century, and perhaps — in remote places — into the nineteenth, despite the opposition of feudal authorities, determined that corn be ground in official mills (p. 123), and dues paid accordingly.

As the querns became obsolete, they were left lying around the settlements. Some, no doubt, remain there, covered by the earth, but many were removed and can be seen throughout Kintyre in gardens and at doors, transformed from tools into curios and ornaments. Still others were built into walls. At Sunadale Farm, a quern was lodged on the top of a dyke, and Duncan MacKeith later confessed to being 'spited' that he had not removed it when the family left to farm Kilmichael. That quern had probably been worked by his ancestors, for he was the fourth generation in Sunadale. Bradley, in the mid-nineteenth century, noticed a quern 'built into a wall by the roadside near Glenbreckrey', and another in the pavement 'in front of a fisherman's cottage at Bealochintie'. A third he saw on the site of Kilkerran Castle, Campbeltown. Neil Thomson, as a boy in Muasdale, heard a story — *ùr-sgeul* — from his grandfather about a quern at Creagruadh which could be heard, at nights, working without anyone being near it.

Daniel Docherty 'grubbing' potatoes, to slacken the soil and kill weeds. High Ballivain, c. 1910. Courtesy of Mr Donald Irwin.

Potatoes

In 1795, John Smith remarked that potatoes had been 'long, and much cultivated in this country'. This hardly seems sensible, because potatoes were evidently only becoming a general element in the Highland diet about 1750. The potatoes most commonly planted in Argyll at the time Smith was writing were 'the Scotch-grey, the lady-white, and pink-eye', types which are now unidentifiable.

Potatoes, he wrote, were most commonly planted on poor ground, after a crop of oats. The ground was ploughed twice: in winter or early spring, and again shortly before planting. It was also harrowed twice, in the intervals. Before planting, the ground was formed into drills, from 30 to 36 inches apart, and manure spread in the furrows, usually over, but sometimes under the sets, which were placed at 6 to 8 inch intervals in the furrows. The drills were then split to either side, and new drills formed over the potatoes where the furrows were before. About three weeks later, the ground was harrowed across the drills. After the plants had emerged, the earth was put up to them with the plough. The ground was later hoed twice, weeding and building up the soil about the plants.

Poor folk, without horse or plough, and farmers cultivating steep and stony parts of their land, would raise their potatoes in lazybeds (p. 23). On plots of potato ground, a spade with a pointed end — in Gigha *caibe-biorach* or *caibe-stobaidh* — could be used for dibbling the seed.

The largest potatoes, generally, were selected for seed, and split with at least one eye to every set. Planting took place at the end of April or beginning of May. Smith reckoned the yield, per set, at 9 to 12 potatoes, and, rarely, 15 or 16. In the 1790s, in Killean and Kilchenzie Parish, the average return was 12 to 15 potatoes; about fifty years on, in 1845, it was 16 to 20 potatoes.

In Kintyre, at the end of the eighteenth century, working horses were generally fed once a day on potatoes. Smith reckoned that from 15 to 18 lbs made a 'good and cheap meal for a horse', and that about the same quantity, morning and evening with a little straw, would maintain a milk cow.

Lifting the Crop

The main potato crops were lifted in October and November. When, in the nineteenth century, the crop became commercially important, squads of workers were required to lift it. Mary Armour was born in 1888 at New Peninver, daughter of James McNair, farmer there. The Peninver earlies, grown in fields that have become a caravan site, were among the first crops that 'went intae town', she said, and were usually exhausted by the end of July. A merchant in Campbeltown would buy the entire acreage of potato ground, and, when the crop was ready for lifting, a squad would be sent from Campbeltown, accompanied by a foreman who lodged with the McNairs in the farmhouse. The squad — generally two men and two women — was accommodated in an old stable and slept on straw. A grate had been installed, and the smoke from the fire went out through a hole in the wall. They lived on boiled potatoes, supplemented by milk from the farm and rabbits.

The squad would arrive early in July. The men dug the potatoes with a *graip*, the women gathered them into baskets, and the foreman filled them into barrels for carting to Campbeltown. During Glasgow Fair — the second fortnight in July, when the population of the town almost doubled — two loads would be driven, one in the morning to catch the shops opening at eight o'clock, and another in the afternoon. When the New Peninver crop had been lifted, the squad would shift to another farm, usually Low Peninver; thence to Southend. The 'worthies' who formed these squads included the piper 'China' (John Galbraith) and the celebrated 'Sailor Jeck' (Agnes Morrison), who had the physique of a man

An Irish potato squad at Lephenstrath, Southend, c. 1920. The crop — which is being dug
with graips — was probably shipped in barrels to Glasgow. Archibald MacKay, the farmer
— bearded and wearing a dark waistcoat — is carrying a basketful of potatoes. Courtesy of
Mrs May Barbour.

and preferred men's work. She died on a Southend farm — Pennyseorach
— while engaged as a potato-lifter. She was found dead in bed on 1 October
1909, at the age of 52. Heart failure and asthma finished her.

Potato-baskets continued to be made on some farms until about the
beginning of the present century. Duncan MacKeith himself made several
at Sunadale. The oval mouth was first formed with a spliced wand, then
five or six curved ribs were secured to the mouth; finally, the skin of the
basket was woven with twigs, leaving gaps for the handles. Willows were
preferred because they made a finer basket, but hazel also served. Baskets
had to be stored dry after the potato harvest to ensure their preservation.

In Largieside, four 'digging machines' were introduced in 1868. These
were no doubt potato-ploughs — developed by the mid-nineteenth
century — which lifted and spread the tubers.

Storage

Potatoes were kept through the winter in hut-shaped stacks called *pits*. The
actual pit — generally less than a foot deep — would be dug in the field, and
the potatoes piled into it and covered with rushes or (less commonly) straw.
After the potatoes were judged to be dry, earth would be packed over the

rushes to a depth of about six inches. Some farmers, such as Donald Watson in North Muasdale, inserted draining tiles into the stack, some 18 inches from ground level, to help ventilate the potatoes; but these tiles encouraged the entry of rats.

On some farms — for example, Glenramskill in 1810 (p. 144) — outbuildings were erected for storing potatoes. The MacKinlays at Whitestone had two stone-built 'potato houses' — which may still be seen — on the shore. These were for the convenient shipping of potatoes from an adjacent 'quay', actually a jutting rock with additional stonework to improve it as a breakwater. The potato business was conducted with Matthew MacDougall of Carradale, a relative of the MacKinlays. MacDougall was a fisherman who had turned to boatbuilding. One of a succession of boats built by him was the *Mary and Agnes*, a half-decked lugger. She was launched in 1877 and remained in his possession until 1901, when sold to Tarbert. She was the vessel MacDougall used for carrying Whitestone potatoes to Ireland. In favourable seasons, he would fish from Howth and return with a cargo of salt herring.

Markets

The bulk of the Kintyre exportable potato crop — upwards of 50,000 bolls (approximately 3,125 tons, or 3,175 tonnes) annually in the 1840s — was probably shipped to Ireland. Particularly during and after the famine years, 1845–48, there was a great demand in Ireland for seed potatoes. The Kintyre farmers were said, in 1843, to 'excel any other division of Scotland' in the cultivation of potatoes, and to 'chiefly depend upon them for payment of their rents'. The frequency of Irish potato smacks on the coasts of Kintyre is remembered in oral tradition, and the final phase of the trade was recorded in the *Campbeltown Courier*. For example, a report of 14 March 1874:

> 460 tons of rock potatoes, besides a good many tons of kemps, were shipped at our shores this year, and Mr May, Dublin, who bought almost all the potatoes in this district, is on the look out for the arrival of vessels to convey to Dublin the remainder of his purchases; while Captain Ryan, *Fairy Queen* of Dublin, is just now at our shores for another cargo, which he purchased previous to leaving with his last cargo for Dublin. The prices were — £4 10s for kemps, and £2 15s to £3 for rocks, per ton.

There is quite a story attached to a certain shipment of potatoes from Gigha in 1838. Donald and Hugh (surname omitted) had a smack, the *John Bull*, and in March of that year loaded her with 32 tons of potatoes, one half belonging to their brothers Archibald and Neil, and the other to David

Smith, Kinerarach, Gigha. The parties debated where they should sell the cargo, and Glasgow, Liverpool and Dublin were discussed. The price in Glasgow market was considered too low, at 30s the ton. The brothers opted for Dublin and sold the cargo there through a 'potato broker, who [was] generally employed to sell Scotch potatoes, particularly from the Highlands'. After deduction of brokerage and various other dues, the sum remaining was £50 7s, which was paid to them in silver and gold. Three days out of Dublin, on 9 April, the *John Bull* grounded in fog on a Solway Firth sandbank, and broke up. The money, which had been hidden under the bed in Donald's cabin, had to be abandoned when he and Hugh took to the small boat. That was the story told by the brothers when they returned to the island. David Smith was incensed and refused to believe the story. He took the brothers to court, for the sum of £27 with interest, but the result of his action is unknown.

For as long as I can remember, I have listened to older folk complaining about potatoes — which are not as dry as they used to be, or as tasty, and so on — and have, myself, begun complaining (though I fear that it forewarns of old age!). '. . . Potatoes selling just now are as a rule not good value for the money paid for them. It seems as if the days of dry wholesome potatoes are past and gone like many other good things.' These remarks encapsulate the matter . . . but they were published, in the *Campbeltown Courier*, on 22 September 1877!

Bear and Barley

Bear, or *bigg*, was an early type of barley, from which it is quite distinct. John Smith noted in 1795 that it was 'improperly called barley', but James Malcolm in 1810 persistently refers to barley when — if he would satisfy the native pedantry — he obviously meant bear. Bear had four rows of grain on it, while barley had two; but the barley grains were tighter in the row, and bigger, which more than compensated.

In the period from the mid-eighteenth to the mid-nineteenth centuries, the evidence suggests that bear was probably the main grain crop in Kintyre, surpassing even oats. Pennant reported in 1772 that 'much bear' was grown, yet there was 'often a sort of dearth, the inhabitants being mad enough to convert their bread into poison, distilling annually 6000 bolls of grain into whisky'. John Smith complained at greater length about 'this enormous and increasing evil' (p. 99). 'The great object of the farmer,' he wrote, 'is to raise as much of this grain as he can, as it always finds a ready market for the use of the distiller.'

John MacMillan scything a barley crop on Kilkerran Farm, c. 1920. The comb-like device is a 'bow' or 'cradle', which helps collect and lay long-strawed grain for the lifters. Courtesy of Mrs Barbara Wilkie.

Until about 1828, in Killean and Kilchenzie Parish — and no doubt elsewhere in Kintyre — the tenants who had not, by rent day, 'converted a particle of the produce of their farms into cash', were forced to seek an advance of money from Campbeltown maltsters (p. 105), to whom they committed all their bear. No particular price would be agreed, and the maltsters generally fixed a price among themselves later. That racket ended with the increase of legal distilleries in Campbeltown, which created a competitive market. In the 1790s, of some 20,000 bolls of bear annually converted into whisky in Argyll, almost 8000 bolls were distilled in Campbeltown Parish alone.

The distilling market tempted farmers to sow bear on land so poor that the yield was meagre. Smith, and others, were anxious that oats should supplant bear — 'the land that will not give five returns of bear, would give more than seven of oats' — and that such bear as was grown should be milled rather than distilled. Yet, a deterrent to the milling of bear was the multure (p. 123) — the miller often took a twelfth part of the bearmeal compared with a twentieth part of oatmeal. In his eagerness to promote the 'wholesome and palatable' bear-bread, Smith resorted to a bit of Roman history — it was 'the food of gladiators, to give them strength'. Unfortunately, for Smith and good men of his kind, the people had a stronger taste for whisky.

The Turnip

Turnips were known in Scotland from at least the fifteenth century — the poet Robert Henryson refers to the 'neep' — but not until towards the middle of the nineteenth century did they begin to take their place in the crop rotations of Kintyre farmers. Turnip cultivation in Kintyre began experimentally around 1770, on the initiative of certain lairds. In the 1790s, a few farmers, particularly in northern Kintyre, began to try turnips; but the greatest quantity grown in Argyll during the eighteenth century was on a farm near Campbeltown about 1794. The farmer, W. Kerr, raised four acres of the crop and received a premium from the Highland Society for his effort, but I have been unable to identify the farm. One of the main deterrents to turnip-growing was undoubtedly lack of enclosures. In the 1790s, a few farmers in Killean and Kilchenzie Parish had grown turnips, 'and no doubt many would do so if the lands were enclosed'. In 1843 turnips were listed with the 'principal exports' from Campbeltown.

The main value of the turnip, however, was as winter fodder for sheep and cattle. Cattle fodder, until the early twentieth century, was generally boiled, but the practice was believed to cause colic in stock. The Watsons in North Muasdale filled a 100-gallon boiler with turnips and chaff each morning throughout winter, and a lot of peat was needed to fuel that boiler. In William Watson's time, turnips would be drilled during the first fortnight in May, after which, if possible, the peats would be carted home. Turnip thinning, or singling, began in June, and much casual labour was needed: tinkers, schoolchildren, and the unemployed and poor of Campbeltown.

John Campbell — the Campbeltown folk-historian and storyteller —

'jobbed' on farms as a young man, in the years immediately after the First World War. The thinning squad was collected by charabanc at 8 a.m. and driven to whichever farm was on the schedule, a routine which continued for four or five weeks until the season ended. Each journey was 'a concert in itsel' ', the wits and singers of the company keeping up the entertainment. The workers took with them 'pieces' (sandwiches), sugar and mugs, but the farmers provided tea, brewed in big kettles. The men wore sacks tied around their legs as they crawled in the fields, scraping out the seedling tufts by hand to leave the chosen one. The women wore 'bratties' (aprons) of heavy sackcloth to protect their legs. The first summer that John Campbell thinned turnips there was a heatwave: 'Oh, an' the bleezin heat. Oh, the heat we had that summer. The back o' yer neck there wiz burned, jeest hittin ye aa' (all) the time. Har'ly an err (air) o' win' in't'.

In Archibald McEachran's farming diary, he noted on 6 July 1932 the completion of turnip-thinning at Kilblaan that afternoon. He computed that he himself had thinned about 20,000 yards (11.3 miles). In the following year, he paid off his two thinners on 10 June — having earned, between them, £3 15s 10d at the rate of 4d per 100 yards — and finished the work himself on 21 June. He reckoned that he had thinned about 16,300 yards (9.25 miles) that year, over a period of nine days.

Turnips were thinned by hoeing on some farms, but most thinners worked on their knees. Margaret Littleson remarked: 'If ye had started [young] thinnin wi' the hoe, ye wir all right, but if ye dinna start wi' the hoe ye wid rather do it wi' yer han's an' crawlin on the ground. I believe ye made a better job wi' yer han's'.

Possibly the greatest concentration of turnip-thinners that ever worked a single field in Kintyre assembled on Killean Farm in mid-June of 1931. The farmer there, Gilbert Black, brought some sixty thinners from Campbeltown in two buses, and the twenty-acre field was finished in a day.

Turnip cultivation has been reduced to insignificance owing to its costly labour-intensiveness and to altered feeding systems. Seldom may be seen, in the winter fields, farm-workers slicing off roots and leaves with the distinctive hook-bladed 'snedder'.

Wheat was grown in Kintyre — mainly around Campbeltown — in the eighteenth century, but was evidently not persevered with. Pennant, in 1772, claimed that little of it was grown 'for want of mills to grind it'. Such wheat as was grown was milled in Ayrshire, and that flour was supplemented by supplies from England. John Smith, in 1795, dismissed both the excuse that flour mills were lacking and that more enclosures were needed. 'Good spring-wheat,' he wrote, had 'been raised on fields entirely open; and if the grain should be raised to a sufficient quantity, it would always find a mill. A little addition to the machinery of the present mill would serve.' He added: 'The true reason is that the demand for bear to make whisky is greater than even that for bread to eat; and the distillers have a brisker trade and more ready cash than the bakers'.

John Turner in Tonrioch — significantly an English settler, from Cumberland (p. 10) — grew wheat in the late eighteenth century. A crop of eight or nine acres brought him, one year, more than £100, and a crop of four acres, another year, realised £50. Kintyre wheat, at that time, was occasionally sold to Ayr and Glasgow, and, according to Smith, 'fetched the highest price in the market'. The crop was also tried in Southend — by Richard Thompson in Ballybrenan, for one; he too was an Englishman — but without success.

Flax — or lint — was grown on many farms until the latter half of the nineteenth century. James Malcolm's survey in 1810 specifically mentions flax crops on the Leerside farms of West Glenaharvy and Gartnacorrach, but these were certainly incidental references. There was, however, little commercial interest in flax, and it is unlikely that much of it would have been grown on any holding. The processing of the crop is discussed on p.

Rye was tried in the eighteenth century, but is nowhere mentioned in the nineteenth. According to Smith, the cultivation of it was 'so inconsiderable as hardly to merit any notice'. It was grown on 'some light sandy soils on the shores of Kintyre', but nowhere else in Argyll. The Old Statistical Account for Southend mentioned 'some rye cultivated in the parish'.

Beans were commonly grown from the eighteenth to the twentieth centuries in Kintyre. Sixteen farms in Malcolm's survey of 1810 have crops listed against them. Potatoes, oats and 'barley' (i.e. bear) predominated, of course, but on eight of these farms — Kilmichael (in its divisions), Balegregan, West Glenaharvy, South Kildonnel, South Bellochgare, Laigh Peninver, Newtown Peninver, and High Smerby — beans were grown. These were sown in late March, generally on 'poor oat stubble', and ploughed down; but sometimes the ground was first ploughed, and the seeds were harrowed in afterwards. In 1821, the Campbeltown maltster John Colville (p. 105) bought a boll of beans from John Campbell in Gartgruillan and almost three bolls from Duncan Stewart in Peninver. In 1838, David Smith in Kinerarach, Gigha (p. 44), 'happened to have some beans to sell', and took them to market in Glasgow. Beans were among the main exports from Campbeltown in the 1840s.

Peas were less commonly grown. Some farmers sowed them along with beans. Malcolm mentioned 'a few pease' growing at West Glenaharvy.

Kail in the eighteenth century had not yet become a field crop, and its cultivation was generally confined to gardens. It was widely grown as a green food, being the only brassica which will produce a crop from any kind of ground.

Hay

Until the nineteenth century, hay-making was neglected to a surprising degree. The natural meadows were, in general, neither drained nor enclosed, and got no manure 'but what chance bestows upon [them]'. Where hay was cropped, the work was left until 'late in the harvest', by which time the hay was 'so much withered as to be more fit for litter than for food'. Hay-making, in the late eighteenth century, as John Smith described it, involved 'spreading it and turning it through the day, and gathering it into small coils at night'. He maintained that hay was often 'more than made', by being dried excessively. At that time farmers scarcely used grass seeds. Clover and rye-grass were grown, but, according to Smith, 'in no great quantities'. In 1810, some twenty-five years on, James Malcolm was complaining that he had found in Kintyre '... no rye [grass] ... but little clover, and less of the other artificial grasses'. Yet, in the Old Statistical Accounts of the 1790s there had been indications that artificial grasses were gaining ground. In Killean and Kilchenzie, farmers were 'beginning to find the advantage of having some clover and rye-grass'. Some fifty years later, in that parish, these grasses had been incorporated in the crop rotation of the more advanced farmers: 1. potatoes; 2. bear; 3. clover and rye-grass; 4. oats without manure, or bear well manured with seaweed; 5. potatoes, etc.

In the 1790s, Smith had remarked on the common practice in Kintyre of farmers growing 'a patch of clover or green kail in their gardens, to feed their cows when they are housed at noon'. In most other parts of Argyll, the cattle were 'folded and allowed to fast; the consequence is, that a cow in Kintyre gives generally a third more milk'.

Hay was cut with scythes, but in the latter half of the nineteenth century horse-drawn mowers began to come into use on the larger farms. These brought the necessity of stone clearing in the hay fields, to protect the blades of the machine. The children of the farms would be sent out to 'stone clover'. They gathered fist-sized stones and heaped them in the fields for carting away. Fields were also rolled, but there were always stones that did not go into the ground.

Mown hay, in good drying weather, would be left a day or two in the

Archibald MacKay cutting hay at Lephenstrath, c. 1920. This photograph was probably 'posed' — there was no need for two men on a mower. The hay is noticeably weed-infested. Courtesy of Mrs May Barbour.

swathe. After raking and turning, it could be heaped into *rucks* or *ricks* (*trampachan* in the Gaelic of Gigha and Kintyre). Often, however, it was first gathered into small mounds, called *coils*, before rucking. A coil in Kintyre Gaelic was *cuarag*, and in Gigha Gaelic *ruc*. In damp weather, hay would certainly be coiled, and, when a dry spell came, shaken out again, and the process of coiling and scattering repeated until the hay was ready for rucking. In very wet weather, hay would be rucked regardless, but with a plan to have it making in the rucks. Each ruck would be built on a tripod of 'pailin-stabs' (fencing-posts), tightly roped at the point. A hay-filled chaff-bag was stuffed between the legs of the tripod, and, when the ruck had been built, the bag was removed leaving a vent.

Before the hay was rucked it had to be concentrated in quantities convenient for handling. That, originally, was done with hand-rakes, but, on bigger farms, a stout plank could be horse-drawn in the field with a man or boy standing on the plank to keep it to the ground and gathering. That crude and risky method never became general, and was replaced, again on large farms, by a horse-drawn sweep, the *Tumblin Tom*, which worked on a principle introduced to Scotland from America in 1828.

Hay was generally 'led' in August. The building of the hay on to carts was a skilful job. In the late 1880s, ricks began to be transported entire from the fields to the steading. The tripod rick-lifter was invented and

Building a hay-stack at Kilkerran Farm, c. 1910. The man on the stack, pitchfork in hand, is tramping the head. Courtesy of Mrs Barbara Wilkie.

marketed by Peter MacKay, who was born c. 1838 on the Leerside farm of Earadale. He served his apprenticeship as a wheelwright with John White at Dalbuie, then worked some years in Glasgow. Returning to Kintyre, he set up for himself and eventually owned a business in Glebe Street, Campbeltown, with workshops for coachbuilders, joiners and blacksmiths.

The rick-lifter — which, MacKay claimed, could be assembled by 'ordinary farm hands in about ten minutes' — was capable of lifting a load of 15 cwts. A wire rope was connected to three chains, which in turn were each connected to an angle-iron. These irons were slipped below the rick. The rope, led through a pulley on a leg of the lifter, was attached to a horse, and as the horse drew forward the rick was raised and a cart backed under it. The rick could then be lowered on to the cart, and the lifter wheeled to the next rick. At a trial of the apparatus, twenty-eight cartloads were managed in sixty-two minutes. The prototype was tried by John Douglas, Christlach, in September 1888, and by 1899 more than 150 of MacKay's rick-lifters were in use in Scotland. But on most farms the preferred method was to carry the rick on a special horse-drawn *bogie* — a small, flat cart with tackle for hauling the whole rick on board — and deposit it in the stackyard, where it was then forked into stacks.

Hay-stacks were thatched and roped just as corn-stacks were. There was a linguistic difference in the Gaelic for the two forms of hay-stack. The smaller, rounded one was *mulan,* while *cruach* was given to 'the big square hay-stack, just like a house'. Sprits (p. 36) were also cut and stacked for winter fodder. They often grew on outlying parts of hay meadows.

Silage is now standard winter cattle-fodder, but that method of grass preservation was not adopted generally in Kintyre until the present century. The first experiment with silage was conducted at Limecraigs, Campbeltown, by David McGibbon, the Duke of Argyll's chamberlain, in 1883. In December of that year, some six months after laying down the grass, McGibbon opened the silo to test the contents and 'found that even on the surface, where the air could to some extent penetrate, the fodder was in good preservation; while about six inches from the surface it was as fresh and juicy as on the day it was put in. Some of it on being thrown on the ground was eaten by the cattle with evident relish'.

CHAPTER 4

Cattle and Horses

Cattle in Kintyre were the old Highland breed, usually termed 'black cattle'. Smith described them as 'a small hardy breed', seldom polled, but generally small in the horn anyway. Kintyre cattle were evidently poor specimens. Smith considered them 'generally less handsome than in other parts of the county', and the writers of the New Statistical Accounts were no less critical. In 1843 Donald MacDonald, minister of Killean and Kilchenzie Parish, described them as a 'uniformly ... ill-shaped, small-boned breed of the Highland species, always housed at night, and of course not in such repute for the market as those outliers reared in the upper districts of the county'. Daniel Kelly, minister of Southend, also regarded them as being 'of inferior description to those in the upper part of the county'. They had, he wrote, 'merely a faint resemblance to the original breed of Highland cattle'. He attributed that degeneracy to their being 'a cross between the Irish and West Highland'. There was, no doubt, a measure of truth in his remarks, for there was extensive trade between Southend and the Glens of Antrim, and in 1790 the author of the Old Statistical Account of Southend had noted that 'the Irish bring over some black cattle, and carry back small horses in return'. In 1809, more than 150 vessels crossed to Ireland from Southend, 'carrying, along with passengers and goods, 1800 horses'. That traffic was computed only from the records that were kept.

Cattle-trading from Kintyre was carried on from at least the sixteenth century. In 1565 and '66, inhabitants of 'Ergile, Lorne, Braidalbane, Kintyre and the Ilis' complained that they were afraid to go to the Lowlands and risk the confiscation of their cattle. *Marts* — fattened cattle — were important elements in the old produce rents. In the sixteeth century, when the lands of Kintyre were held by the Crown, the King's marts were driven overland and delivered at Stirling Castle, under supervision of the parish clerk at Kilkerran (Campbeltown), who had rent-free land for performing that service.

The droving of cattle from Kintyre to the great tryst at Falkirk ended at some time in the latter half of the nineteenth century. Archibald Cameron, father of Archibald D. Cameron, drove cattle from Keromenach in Strone Glen to Falkirk, subsisting on 'stir-up' (oatmeal and cold water mixed) during the long tramp. Duncan Clerk, discussing markets in his 'Agriculture of the County of Argyll' in 1878, wrote:

> In the end of the year, old cows from Argyllshire are disposed of in large numbers; and at Falkirk Tryst of September and October droves of heifers from this county make up a large proportion of the stock shown, and often formed the most attractive feature in the market. Dealers from England, and all who are in search of superior West Highland cattle, attend the Falkirk Tryst, where they are sure of finding the kind of stock they require.

Small-scale droving continued beyond that period, to Oban, and, until well into the present century, to Tarbert and Campbeltown. William Watson, born in 1911, walked cattle from Muasdale to Tarbert market, and to Campbeltown for shipment to Stranraer. That journey to Campbeltown was usually made on 11 November (Martinmas — p. 179). The neighbouring farmers around Muasdale would meet, each with his two or three cows, and they would drive the cattle in company. The fifteen-mile drove generally took no longer than five hours.

Smith conceded that the Kintyre cattle, for all their defects, were good milkers. This attribute he explained by their 'having less distance to travel for their food, to their being comfortably housed at noon and night, and to their having, on these occasions, a handful of food'. In most other parts of Argyll, cattle were driven daily over the greater part of the farm, 'instead of making them eat alternately in patches, and giving them clean grass in succession'. Enclosures, he suggested, would be 'of the greatest benefit' in reducing the custom.

A similar argument was advanced by Archibald Campbell, laird of Knockbuy on Lochfyneside, and one of the earliest 'improvers' in Argyll. In a letter to the Duke of Argyll, in 1744, he maintained that it would be necessary to 'improve the county by enclosures' before cattle could be improved and their weight increased. He advocated the replacement of the customary turf dykes with stone dykes.

Herding Cattle

The absence of enclosures, over the greater part of Kintyre, required the herding of livestock, to keep them within the bounds of their own ground, and out of mischief. Herding was the work of cottagers, the sons and daughters of the tenants, and — perhaps the unhappiest class of all — hired children. The earliest censuses — of 1841 and '51 — record many of these hired children, some of them far from home. The following selection —

from 1851, and listed north to south — supplies place of origin whenever that differs from the locality of service:

Corputachan — Archibald Campbell (12), Dalavich;
Belachantuy — Hugh MacMillan (13), Campbeltown;
Killaraw — John MacLeod (12), Islay;
Ballivain — Duncan MacSporran (12);
Tirfergus — John Campbell (11);
Achencorvie — Neill MacNeill (12), Ireland;
Lailt — Neil MacNaught (13).

Archibald Gilchrist was born in High Street, Glasgow, about 1838. His mother died, and he was sent to Killean Parish to be reared by his grandfather. When his grandfather died, Archibald 'went as a servant' to several farms. In 1851, at the age of fifteen, and while he was herd with Robert Donald in Largybeg, he contracted typhoid. Donald sent him to a relative in Campbeltown, who promptly returned him to Largybeg. 'As soon as he went there his master ordered his servant to put [the boy] into a cart and leave him on the streets of Campbeltown. At that time he was five days advanced in Fever. The servant, as ordered, left him upon the streets, in a cold wet night, and there was no person to look to him.' Fortunately, he was admitted to the Poorhouse and successfully treated. The inspector there complained, to the procurator-fiscal, of Donald's 'cruelty'. The complaint was investigated, but no prosecution followed.

In his logbook on 27 March 1874, the schoolmaster at Rhunahaorine noted that 'five of the children ... have engaged with farmers in this district as cow-herds'.

Edward Bradley encountered, in 1859, a girl herding on the moors above Glencreggan. Her name was Jenny MacCallum and she obviously took his fancy because he described her lavishly and sketched her looking over the moors. She was barefoot and wore 'a loose bonnet of white calico, a looser jacket of pink calico, and a dark petticoat'. She could neither read nor write, and spent her days tending some thirty cows and three bulls, 'great swarthy long-haired fellows, with sharp horns and wicked eyes'. Bradley had no mind to approach the bulls, but Jenny did not fear them, and when one '... was evidencing a tendency to roam to further pasture, the lassie speedily ran after him, and with voice and action, but above all with hearty thwacks of her oaken staff, compelled him to return to his appointed spot'. Her day Bradley described thus: 'Hither to some part of the moor, where there were irregular patches of grazing-ground amid the heather, she brought her beasts at early morn; and here, through the long day, she kept them together, and then at dewy eve took them back to their farmstead'.

The cattle, as Bradley described them, were '... of the small Highland

Jenny MacCallum herding cattle. Sketched by Edward Bradley in 1859.

breed [which] in their rough, shaggy coats looked like so many door-mats or carriage-rugs'. He remarked on their diversity of colour, 'every possible variety of hue that can be made up of white, black, red, brown, grey, and yellow ochre ... in singular harmony with the moorland landscapes'.

Already, however, their time was running out. An increasing interest in commercial cheesemaking on a large scale brought into favour the Ayrshire breed of cattle. The chamberlain of Kintyre, John Lorne Stewart, was instrumental in that trend. Around 1840, he 'established a dairy of forty-five low country cows upon one of his own farms, as an example to the inhabitants of the district to excite them to pay more attention to that breed'. He was also selling 'imitation English cheese' in the Glasgow market, and receiving there 'the highest English price'.

The last farmer in Kintyre with a herd of native cattle was evidently Lachlan Clark in Tangy (Fig. 1, p. 6). He sold these about 1867, but by 1895 had still one black and white cow descended from the old stock. She was described, in an issue of *The Scottish Farmer* of that year, as 'one of the nicest in the dairy herd, and a right useful looking dairy cow'. In 1895 Tangy carried a stock of 40 Ayrshire cows, along with about 1000 sheep, 300 of them black-faced breeding ewes. The cattle were all bred 'with a special eye to the production of a plentiful supply of milk for cheese-making'. Clark was rearing, that year, twenty-three calves — more than the usual number. His general practice was to bring in ten to twelve young cows each year, and sell the surplus when in calf. Some of these were purchased by dealers for sale in the Rhinns of Galloway. His system of farming was to let the stock consume all that was grown on the farm, selling only cast cows, surplus queys, sheep and cheese.

There was a good deal of resistance, initially, to the transition from beef to dairy farming, the native farmers having 'grave doubts as to the wisdom of attempting to make a rent and a living out of the sale of cheese'. But an influx of Ayrshire farmers, principally to Southend, in the mid-eighteenth century, settled the issue — the system was seen to work. Two of the earliest of these Ayrshire farmers were James Dunlop in Ballyshear and William Hunter in Machribeg. Many of the names that arrived with these settlers — Robertson, Caldwell, Smellie, Gibson, and Ramsay among them — have disappeared from the farming community in Southend, but others — notably Galbraith and Ronald — are prominent.

Cattle-Stealing

Cattle-raiding was a fundamental trait of Gaelic society throughout the clan period. Cattle were wealth and therefore prestige, and these assets were transferable then no less than now. Peter MacIntosh, in his eccentric but interesting *History of Kintyre,* was apologetic about the tradition of cattle-thieving. It vexed his Christian belief, and he tried to explain it: 'No doubt the example of the times had a strong effect, and, considering the mountains as common property, they thought it as little crime to supply themselves with a fat ox or cow, as a poacher would of killing a hare or a moorhen'. The following is one of his stories.

Three men who lived in a remote glen of Kintyre had a habit of

This bull has been identified, with reasonable certainty, as a Welsh Black — a rare breed in Kintyre — and was possibly being travelled within the district to serve females as required, though bulls, unlike stallions, were never taken over long distances. The photograph was taken about 1910 at Tayinloan Store. The storekeeper, Dugald MacFater, looks on from his seat on a crate. Courtesy of Mrs Barbara Wilkie.

supplying themselves with *feòil-gheamhraidh* (winter beef) by going out on the mountains for a fat beast belonging to somebody else. One of them died, and when the other two set off as usual the poor widow began to weep and complain that she had no one now to supply her beef. Her son, a boy of twelve years, was affected by this and took an old gun that had belonged to his father, put some powder into it, and hid himself near the road his neighbours would take coming home. He waited in the darkness, and, when they passed with a fat cow, he fired the gun. They fled and left the cow, which he led home by another way, thus assuring his family of their winter beef.

There is record of the theft of a *quey* (heifer), in 1840, but there appears to be no conclusion to the case, because the accused man, John MacGeachy of Clachaig, fled to Glasgow as soon as the investigation began. He was unfortunate in his conduct. He had maintained, to acquaintances, that he simply took the quey to settle a debt of £3 10s. Not only did he (presumably) lose his money, but he also (inevitably) lost the quey, and lost, in the end, both his home and his livelihood, which was precarious enough. He had a cow and a quey of his own grazing on Clachaig, which was farmed by an uncle, Duncan MacGeachy. He 'got his meat' there, but no wages, and occasionally 'wrought to other people, by which means he provided himself with clothes'.

He claimed that the money was owed to him by Donald MacAllister Jr., a cottar in Achadubh (also given as Monebeg), which was a pendicle of Achadadunan, farmed by Archibald MacDougall. MacAllister had a 'cot house and cow's grass' there, for which he paid £4 annual rent. He seems to have had trouble surviving by his own resources. Two years previous, unable to pay his rent, he was given £3 10s by his sister Catherine, who, in return, became owner of his cow's red quey calf. After a year, the calf was taken from its mother and sent to graze on the farm of Talabhtoll, tenanted by Angus MacKeich. Catherine, in the interval, had gone to Ayrshire as a farm-servant, but she paid MacKeich the calf's 'grassmail' (grazing rent) for the year 1839. The calf was removed to Achadubh for the winter, and in February 1840 was returned, 'in very good condition', to Talabhtoll.

On 28 March, one of Angus MacKeich's female servants informed Donald MacAllister Sr. that the calf was missing. Next day, MacAllister went to Talabhtoll and spoke with MacKeich, whose fear was that the calf had 'fallen into a hole'; but a search of the farm produced no carcass. Then information reached MacAllister that John MacGeachy had been seen driving the quey south from Talabhtoll. Donald Jr., with his brother Alexander (of Knockanabuaichail, a pendicle of Stewartfield) and three others, set off for Clachaig and found MacGeachy harrowing a field near his house. Seeing them approach, MacGeachy 'deserted the horses and harrows and ran away'.

MacGeachy's cousin, Duncan MacGeachy, who had been sowing a field, was left to argue with the visitors. The MacAllisters decided to have John MacGeachy's cow as security, and had begun to drive her away when Duncan intercepted them and turned the cow back. While the dispute was going on, John MacGeachy appeared, admitted that he had taken away the quey, and offered to restore her when the debt had been paid. Donald MacAllister denied owing MacGeachy £3 10s, but admitted that he was 'due something'.

Donald MacAllister Sr. spent two weeks 'searching through the country' for the red quey, and finally found her in a roadside field on the farm of Barr. The herd-girl, Anne Colville, would tell him nothing but that the quey had not been long in Barr. He took the quey away and drove her home to Achadubh.

Horses

In 1797–8 there were 1304 horse on Kintyre farms. That was according to a survey for the levying of tax on work-horses — 2s for each one — and it hardly seems necessary to suggest that some evasion could have gone on. Whatever the deficiencies of the survey, it contains much useful information on the distribution of horses. There are 399 names in the survey, listed against their holdings. The statistical break-down is as follows:

horses owned	tenants
1	31
2	109
3	90
4	109
5	32
6	19
7	3
8	3
9	1
10	1
11	1

Plainly, the great majority of farmers — 339 in 399, or 85 per cent — owned fewer than five horses. Of the total of 1304 horses, 302 — or 23 per cent — were, for whatever reasons, not classed as work-horses and escaped taxation. Most one-horse owners were in joint-tenancy or held parts of subdivided farms. In effect, then, these holdings had more than one horse attached to them. For example, in Garvachy, James MacLarty and Donald MacMillan had a horse each. In Auchencorvie, Donald MacNeillage had one horse to Duncan Arnot's two. In Loup, John MacVannel, Peter MacVannel, Nathaniel MacCallum and Donald Blair had a horse apiece. In Drummore, John Sillars had one, while John Johnston had nine, William Ferguson five, Donald Brolichan three, and Robert Colvel two. Five single-tenant holdings had only one horse: Glenegadel (Glenadale), Lossit Mill, Shirdum, Dumnaleck and Blarie. These tenants no doubt got the use of additional horses when needed.

The greatest concentration of horses on a single holding was twenty-two in Kildavie. Alexander Picken and David, Matthew, and John Reid each had four, while Peter and John Hughie (Huie) each had three. Considering the Leerside holdings which merged into the three farms of Auchenhoan, Feochaig and Glenahervie (p. 9) in the nineteenth century, only Glenmurrel of the northern cluster appears in the survey. Donald and John Carmichael (also MacIlmichael, the older form) each had two horses there. In Feochaig, Angus MacIsaac had two, Donald MacIsaac three, and Archibald Loinachan three. In Glenahervie, Colin MacEachern, Robert Hall and Donald Loinachan each had four, and John MacEachern three. Of the smaller farms which were incorporated into Glenahervie, two appear in the survey: Cantaig (Neil Conly, three horses) and Eridle (Archibald MacKay, four).

There are many surprising omissions from the survey — Auchenhoan, Balinatunie, Balnabraid and Corphin among them — which must call into question its comprehensiveness. None of the coastal farms between Carskey and Ballygroggan is included. The explanation should simply be that these were exclusively grazing farms, but the dispute between rival sheep-graziers in 1818 (the Moil Company against MacNeill of Carskey and others, p. 69) concerned the very issue of whether sheep farms should be cultivated at all. The Moil Company's interpretation of the leases was that 'the tenants were to occupy the lands ... entirely with a sheep stock'; but the defending parties were tilling parts of their holdings, and cited their predecessors' keeping 'no small number of black cattle and horses on the ground'.

The native horses in Kintyre were described, towards the end of the eighteenth century, as 'long-bodied, long-legged, hard and high in the bone, and ill to support ... They are not in general wanting in size, but very much so in shape'. Some farmers, about that time, had 'joined in buying one or two large stallions of the low country kind, but whether any great advantage will result from this cross, is yet doubtful'. In 1843, the Rev. Donald MacDonald in Killean and Kilchenzie reported that the farmers there had been 'indefatigable in improving their breed of horses'. Their faith remained with Lowland stallions, and they had 'succeeded well in rearing powerful and large draught horses well adapted for farming operations'. In the end, the native horse was entirely replaced by the Lanarkshire breed of Clydesdale, and became — like the native sheep and cattle — extinct.

Clydesdales

The first notable horse of the Clydesdale breed brought to Kintyre was evidently a black stallion acquired by Sir Charles Lockhart of Largie about 1820. Charles Brown in Low Machrimore — then reputed to have 'about the best stock of farm horses in the district' — had his choice mare, 'Darling', served by the Lockhart stallion, and the produce was considered 'one of the best entire [uncastrated] horses that travelled Kintyre':

... A fine square-built, clean, flat-boned, upstanding black horse with white points, [he] left his mark on Kintyre, which remains to this day (1877). On several farms in Kintyre a fine class of Clydesdale mare has been bred, no doubt descending from Charles Brown's horse ... Since then, Mr Alex Campbell deserves credit for keeping the district supplied with the best-bred Clydesdales, from old 'Rob Roy' down to the present 'Prince David', who claims the highest pedigree known, direct from 'Prince of Wales' and his dam, 'Peggy'.

Notices advertising the services of travelling stallions were annual features in the columns of local newspapers. In the *Argyllshire Herald* of 17 August 1895, for instance, three studs were competing for business — 'Prince of Kintyre', bred by Alexander Cordiner, Machrimore, and 'King of the Ridge' and 'Rosedale', both owned by William Taylor, Park Mains, Renfrewshire — in addition to the Duke of Argyll's 'premium stallions for 1895'.

Itineraries varied — some stallions were led through every parish of Kintyre, while others remained in south Kintyre. In 1869, 'Sir William Wallace' — owned by Thomas Wallace of Torchollean — was at Barr on Monday evenings, Tayinloan on Tuesday nights, Putchachan on Wednesday nights, Ardnacross on Thursdays at midday, Campbeltown — the Commercial Inn — on Thursday nights, Southend on Fridays, and at home on Saturdays. Three years later, in 1872, that 'favourite and well-known horse' was still doing the same rounds. William Taylor's 'Lord Derwent' — advertised with the particulars of his splendid pedigree — did not leave south Kintyre in 1907. On the nights of Monday and Tuesday he was at the Southend farms of Dalbhradden and Machribeg respectively; on Wednesday, Drumlemble; Thursday, Drum; Friday, Ardnacross, and from Saturday until Monday, at Moy. The terms were £1 at service and £4 'when Mare proves in Foal', with 2s 6d for the groom. Twenty-five years earlier, the groom of 'Young Doncaster' — owned by John Bicket in Ugadale — had his 2s 6d 'at service', but the other charges were much less — 10s at the end of the travelling season, and £1 when the mare proved in foal.

Dr Duncan McEachran

Kintyre-bred Clydesdales had a substantial reputation, which must, in some measure, be attributed to the interest of Dr Duncan McEachran, whose achievements are esteemed in Canada, but practically forgotten in his native Kintyre. He was born in Campbeltown in 1841, graduated in veterinary surgery at Edinburgh University in 1861, and emigrated to

Canada in 1862. To his influence, 'veterinary surgery owed its elevation from the status of a trade to that of a profession and subject of university standing in Canada'. He became Dean of the Faculty of Comparative Medicine and Veterinary Science at McGill University, was veterinary adviser to the Canadian government, and wrote *The Canadian Horse and his Diseases*.

He was also a pioneering rancher in the Western Plains of Canada and became Chief Akotas of the Piegan tribe of Blackfeet, a period of his life which he recollected in an article in the *Campbeltown Courier* of 20 August 1924, less than two months before his death. An avid breeder of horses, when he retired to his stock-farm near Ormstown, Quebec, he 'surrounded himself with the very best of Clydesdale breeding stock, selected and imported by himself'.

He did not forget the horses of his native Kintyre, and, in one year alone — 1910 — eleven Clydesdales were purchased for him by William Smith, Largiebeg, and shipped in October. These horses were bought from: J. M. Hall, Killean; Hugh Johnston, Killocraw; J. Harvey, Park; A. Cameron, Carrine; A. Ronald, Pennyseorach (two); W. Russell, Ballymenach; R. Smith, Langa; J. Gemmell, Dalrioch; A. Johnston, Uigle, and A. Stewart, Parkfergus.

That the name MacEachran is popularly believed to derive from Gaelic *Mac Each-thighearna* ('son of the horse-lord') is a fitting conclusion to this brief account of a remarkable man.

Carts

Wheeled farm-carts were evidently unknown in Kintyre before the mid-eighteenth century. The first in Southend, according to Archie McEachran's notes from oral tradition, was 'brought in' by one of the Duke of Argyll's English tenants, Christopher Thompson, who took the lease of Dalabhraddan in 1775. Certainly, wheelwrights were working in Campbeltown in 1767, and in Campbeltown Parish in 1798 there were 94 horses and carts, 34 of them owned in the town itself. In Largieside, in the 1860s, there was an old man who claimed to remember the first cart coming to the district. 'People flocked from all quarters to get a sight of it,' he said. The proud owner, to safeguard his cart, habitually dismantled it and stored the box, wheels and axle until again needed.

Prior to the introduction of carts, loads were carried in creels slung on the horses' backs, or in *slipes*. The slipe — or slide-car — was simply a pair of shafts with a horse yoked at one end and a framework of some

Duncan MacCallum — who later worked one of the Tomaig smallholdings — with 'Jean' and 'Polly' hitched to carts at Knockstapple, c. 1930. Courtesy of Mrs Annie Gillies.

description fixed at the other, for containing the load. The shafts might have runners attached, or might simply be dragged along with the ends on the ground. In these slipes, manure was taken out to the fields and the harvest brought in.

CHAPTER 5

Sheep

Native Sheep

Before the advent of intensive sheep stocking in Kintyre, the native breed alone was reared, almost exclusively for domestic use. There was little external demand for the wool or mutton of Kintyre sheep. The breed was mainly white-faced, but many individuals were black or grey in the fleece, which colours were preferred to white, 'as they saved the trouble of dyeing the wool'. The fleece, like the carcass, was small, but 'fine, close, and matted'. Their main weaknesses — contrasted with the black-faced breed which largely replaced them — was that they required superior grazing, and shelter in the winter.

These sheep — which are today represented by such types as the Soay and the Shetland — were, according to John Smith, 'under the most barbarous management':

> Their pasture was poor, and often at great distance. They were folded in summer and harvest, and housed in winter and spring. No attention was paid to the change or choice of rams, and they were often left to their own discretion as to the season of breeding. The consequence was, that the lambs came before the grass, and of course they were all stinted, and many of them starved.

The main value of the sheep was their wool, for clothing, but they were also milked. Some of the milk was converted into cheese and butter (the latter used for *smearing* — p. 73), practices which gradually ended with the introduction of southern breeds. A ewe would yield about a pint of milk, which was thicker than that of cows'.

From the middle of May the lambs were deprived of half of the milk, by separating them at night from their mothers, which were milked in the morning. About the end of June the lambs were weaned, sometimes by tying a small stick across their mouths, which not only prevented them from suckling, but also from grazing easily. After that, the ewe continued to be milked, morning and evening, until September. 'It is unnecessary to add,' Smith added, 'that the flock did not thrive.'

'It is rather a wonder,' he remarked, 'that the species did not become altogether extinct. Nothing but their remarkable hardiness could save them from utter perdition under such wretched management. They became, however, small and ill-shaped; but, in general, they still retained a fine pile of wool.' Smith, a vigorous advocate of the native breed, believed that, if better managed, it could prove 'a much more valuable stock than the black-faced kind'. He suggested that, in time, the native sheep 'might probably be brought to an equal size'.

The quality of its meat was, by all accounts, superior, and he referred to a sheep-farmer whose habit, whenever he wanted very fat mutton, was to kill one of the few native wedders he kept in his stock. At the time of Smith's writing — about 1795 — the wool of native sheep had frequently sold for 16s a stone (a variable measure, but probably 24lb in Kintyre then) against 7s or 8s for other wools.

He cited the mixing, about 1780, of a black-faced stock with 'considerable parcels of the old Highland breed' on the Mull of Kintyre. That cross-breeding, of black-faced rams with white-faced ewes, did not noticeably diminish size, and the wool was much improved.

For experiments in the breeding of fine-woolled sheep, a Spanish ram and a Herefordshire ram and two ewes were supplied, in 1791, to Kintyre members of the British Wool Society by Sir John Sinclair of Ulbster, a noted improver. The Spanish ram was immediately put with nine 'fine Woold sheep, natives of Kintyre', and six lambs resulted. In the following year, the ram and ewes were confined on Sheep Island, off Sanda, to discover 'how far the progeny of the Spanish Ram would Stand the Winter Weather of our Climate'. The trial was successful — all the ewes produced lambs which throve. The Herefordshire stock also survived, and the cross-breeding of the ram with native ewes was projected in 1793.

The main experimenters were Peter Brolochan Sr., 'grazier' (p. 69), Duncan Campbell, sheriff-substitute of Kintyre, and William Langlands, 'improver'. In July 1793 they applied to the Duke of Argyll for a lease of Ballygroggan — then in two divisions — together with Craigaig. They stressed the need for enclosures to separate experimental stock from other stocks, and proposed erecting stone dykes to the value of £200, on condition that the lease ran to thirty years. But their application failed, and the outcome of the project is unknown.

John Smith was more concerned with the preservation of the pure native strain. 'Upon the whole,' he wrote, 'there is every reason to cherish this breed, which has been for ages naturalized to the soil and climate. If any one would take the trouble to collect what would stock a farm of them, and pay them proper attention, he would in a few years have an immense advantage over those who have the other kind. If the breed shall continue to be neglected till they become altogether extinct, the loss may be regretted when it cannot be repaired.' Tragically, Smith's plea was not heeded. It is doubtful, anyway, if many copies of his book would have been read by the men whose practical influence might have saved the old native breed. 'Progress' has little patience with either sentiment or commonsense.

The disappearance of the native sheep is recorded in the Statistical Accounts. The information is sketchy, but all of it tends towards a common conclusion. In Killean and Kilchenzie Parish, in the 1790s, there was 'only one considerable sheep-flock ... in a mountainous farm', but all of the other farmers kept a few sheep for their own use. These were 'of the old small white-faced kind, which have more delicate flesh and finer wool'. Less than fifty years later, in that parish, the breed had become 'extinct', and 'the prevailing stock consists of a black-faced breed, said to be originally imported from Moffat'.

In Southend, in 1843, the sheep stock was mixed. The main breed was the black-faced, or Linton, 'introduced by store-masters from the south'. Native sheep did survive, but were being 'improved' by cross-breeding with black-faced tups, apparently — and curiously — a continuation of the experiments that had been going on in the same area sixty years earlier. Leicester sheep were also being reared, for domestic use, by several of the better-off tenants in low-lying farms. These were allowed to graze with the black cattle, and in winter, 'from the dampness of the climate', were housed.

The Sheep Invasion

There is apparently no evidence that evictions were carried out in Kintyre to free land for sheep stocks. A great part of Kintyre was held by the Argyll Estate — the powerful Campbell dukedom — which opened hill farms to graziers within the leasing system. In 1776, for instance, Colin MacEachran and Colin and John Campbell — described as 'shepherds' — offered £18 rent for Balemontgomery, which was accepted. There is a tradition that Ballochroy Glen was 'cleared' for sheep, but documentary proof is, so far, lacking. Peter MacIntosh, in his *History of Kintyre*, first published in 1857, complained that 'a good many inhabitants resided in it fifty years back, but at present it is almost depopulated, in order to leave space enough for the sheep and heather fowl'. That humane and wise scholar, John Smith, had grave reservations about the trend towards sheep stocking. He predicted: 'The ground rescued from the heath and wildness by the labour of ages, is in the way of becoming a heath and wilderness again'. That prediction has been fulfilled, and large-scale afforestation in this century has, in its turn, wasted much of the old arable land that lay out in the hills. 'Let sheep be encouraged, but let the people be cherished also', Smith pleaded.

The Rev. Daniel Kelly in Southend echoed him in 1843: 'Cottagers ought to be more encouraged. The Mull of Kintyre has been converted into an immense sheep-walk, under one company, and is now occupied by 6000 sheep. This was, half a century ago, a great pastoral country [i.e. under cattle], which then reared and supported thirty or forty families, whose ancestors had occupied that remote and extensive region for ages'.

The area about the Mull — hill and moorland characterised by marginal farming — was one of the first, if not the first, in Kintyre to go under sheep. That gradual transformation of a string of hill farms into one extensive sheep-farm began in 1771, and almost fifty years later (in 1818) was reviewed thus:

> The Moil lands ... were in detached possessions or small farms and possessed by small tenants who all ploughed and sowed as much of the ground as was sufficient to maintain themselves and their families, and sheep stock being then in its infancy in this part of the country, the Duke of Argyll and his doers seeing the Moil lands more suitable for a sheep stock than for small tenants, wished to give every reasonable encouragement to a set of people who then offered to take them under the name and form of a company, as a joint concern ...

The initiative appears to have been taken by a partnership of local men, Colin and John Campbell, and Colin MacEachran. In 1775, they were granted a nineteen-year lease of Inendunan, along with the neighbouring farm, Inencocallach. Described as 'graziers in Kintyre', they were bound by the lease to 'occupy the lands entirely with a sheep stock', and not to export to Ireland, or anywhere else, the wool that was produced. In the following year, 1776, Ballimacviccar — immediately south of Inendunan, and marching with it — was taken over by them, under the same conditions. In 1777, Balimontgomery came into their possession, and — completing the sweep south — Balimaconolly in 1780. (That last lease, being for sixteen years rather than the usual nineteen, was probably granted three years subsequent to the actual taking of the farm, noted as 'presently possessed' by Campbell, MacEachran and Brolochan.)

By 1780, John Campbell had evidently given up his interest in the business — or, at least, had decided not to involve himself in the leasing of another farm. He was replaced by Peter Brolochan, who had also an interest in the conjoined farms of Borgadilmore, Borgadilbeg, and Glenmanuilt. These, in 1775, were granted on a fifteen-year lease to John

Stevenson, Duncan Brolochan, and Peter Brolochan, at an annual rent of £42. Stevenson was described as a 'sheep grazier in Glenmanuilt', and, judging by his name, was probably from the Lowlands of Scotland. The Brolochans were Campbeltown businessmen — Duncan a merchant and Peter a butcher — and would have had little or no practical involvement in the management of the sheep stock.

The above three farms had been effectively given over to sheep in 1771, the earliest such record. Significantly, perhaps, the lease was taken by the Duke of Argyll's chamberlain, Captain James Campbell of Inveraray, who must have employed a manager for the farms. By the conditions of that lease, sheep only were to be kept, with twelve cows allowed for 'victualling his servants'. Four years later, in 1775, Campbell relinquished the lease, which was then taken over by Stevenson and the Brolochans. In 1798, Robert Colville, son of William in Trodigall, was granted a nineteen-year lease on the farms, at an increased rent of £100.

In a mere decade, between 1770 and 1780, a sizeable chunk of land, extending north and east of the Mull of Kintyre, had gone under sheep. In 1818, amid litigation and counter-litigation, a new consortium — the Moil Company — was poised to move in. In that year, the Mull sheep-farms were leased thus:

> Glemmenuilt and Borgadale — Robert Colville;
> Balinamoil and Balimontgomery — Lieut.-col. Malcolm MacNeill of Cariskey;
> Strone, Ballimacviccar and Inendunan — Alexander, Donald and Dugald Campbell;
> Inengaich, Inenbea and Inencocaillach — George, William and James Campbell;
> Inens more and beg — Thomas Train.

The Moil Company — Captain Charles Campbell, Dalintober; Hugh Stevenson, William Watson Jr., and John Beith, merchants; and Nathaniel Harvey, 'writer', all of Campbeltown — was preparing to enter that massive amalgamated holding on Whitsunday of 1819. But the outgoing tenants were threatening to plough and plant parts of their holdings in that final year, and the Moil Company was intent on preventing that action, which it considered a blatant breach of lease. The dispute, which went to law, concerned the issue of whether or not the Mull farms had been leased entirely as sheep-grazing lands (p. 61).

The trend of turning upland farms over to sheep continued beyond the mid-nineteenth century and brought, increasingly, an infusion of shepherds from other parts of Scotland. After the publication of John Smith's work in 1805, and the Statistical Accounts of 1843, there was very little published material about sheep and shepherding in Kintyre. The survival, therefore, of two nineteenth-century precognitions concerning sheep-stealing is fortunate, because these contain enough practical information to justify careful examination. The first case occurred in 1820, the second in 1837; in both cases, the accused were themselves herds.

Sheep-Stealing

John Campbell, the first accused, had for three years been a cottar at Auchavraulladle on Largie Estate, prior to which he was tenant there. He was hired as herd of the 'Common Muir of Largie' in June 1820, and 'went to live at the Muir house, the usual place of herds'. The Muir was jointly possessed by Campbell himself and six others. He had in his charge black cattle, sheep, and horses, including about ninety sheep which had belonged to his son Archibald — drowned the year before — four cows and three stirks belonging to his daughter Barbara, and a horse of his own. The ear-marks of his dead son's sheep were, part of the right one cropped, and the left with a spade shaft at the top, on the side next to the horn. The letter 'Z' was marked above the nose, which mark he had used for more than twenty years.

John MacCallum (46) had been herd at Lagloskin for fourteen years. The tenants there were Thomas MacMurchy, Lenagboyach, and John MacEachran, Auchindrain. For the past year MacCallum had been 'missing sheep from his flock', and suspected theft. On 29 August, he noticed that two sheep were missing from a batch of thirty-seven 'strange ones' that had been brought to the farm and were kept on 'low grounds', possibly a reference — but nowhere made explicit — to southern stock. He had been 'in the habit of counting them every day'.

The marks on the missing sheep were, a 'small bit cut off the top of the near lug, and a hole through the middle of the far off lug'. The letter 'A' had been branded on the nose and a stripe of tar laid across the middle of the back. The suspect head and skin corresponded exactly with these marks, except that the far off lug had been entirely removed and that a half of the near lug had been cut off, 'leaving what remains nearly in the form of a spade shaft', but with the previous mark still distinguishable.

Donald MacEachran (36), farmer in Auchindrain with his brother John, said that his late father, Archibald, and Archibald MacMurchy at Lenagboyach were for many years tenants of the farm of Lagloskin. On the death of his father, Donald and his brother got one half of the farm and stock between them, while Archibald MacMurchy, being an old man, gave his half to his sons Thomas and John. Both old men being Archibald, the brand which they used on the Lagloskin sheep was the letter 'A', which their sons had continued. The tar mark, placed on the back, had also been

'A', but, being 'troublesome to make', was changed to 'Ⱶ', which none of their neighbours shared.

John MacMurchy (42), in Lenagboyach, stated that, on the suspect head, the 'far off' — or right — lug had been cropped, 'which is commonly called the "thief's mark" '.

That head had been found at the house of Neil MacKinven (or MacKinnon), ferryman at Tayinloan, on the third day of a house-by-house search of the district, involving two constables as well as the aggrieved farmers. John Campbell had left the sheep in MacKinven's house at midnight, and the animal was killed the following morning. MacKinven maintained that he 'had a debt against Campbell', who had 'promised to give him a sheep for it'.

(At the time of the stir, the Tayinloan ferry-house was packed with emigrants waiting for a ship to take them to Wilmington, North Carolina. The MacBride family had been lodged there more than a month, having given up the farm of Auchaloskin, and had a sheep of their own killed and salted — the head too — as provision for the passage.)

The accused, in the second case, was Hugh MacIntyre, shepherd to Dugald MacMath and others in Margymonygach. He had been seen on the brae of Bellochantuy by a party of five men going home after midnight on 20 May 1837 from the public-house at Drumore na Bodach. MacIntyre had previously been suspected of sheep-stealing, and the men were anxious to see what was in the bundle he carried on his back. He escaped from them, but had to abandon his load, which proved to be a sheep carcass, three skins, and two heads, all wrapped inside a 'black and white small checked' shepherd's plaid. MacIntyre got out of Kintyre by persuading the boatman at Skipness to ferry him immediately. He gave him a story that he had 'given a beating to an Excise officer who was taking smuggled goods from him'.

Thomas Greenlees (40), son of John Greenlees, tenant in Putechan, said in his evidence that there were 'between three and four score of sheep grazing on the hill . . . of Putechan'. These sheep were marked with a spade haft on the left lug, the right lug being left whole, and branded on the left side of the nose with an inverted 'T'. He identified, from remains shown to him, a skin and a head from his father's sheep stock, which had suffered the loss of six animals eight days before.

Lachlan Clark (27), son of John Clark, tenant in Tangy, stated that his father had a stock of sheep on Tangy and another on Gartgunnel. Both stocks were marked with a swallow tail on the near lug and a crop on the far lug, and branded with a half-moon across the nose. At Martinmas last, Clark had bought four tups from Malcolm MacMillan in Gartavaigh,

Southend, two of them reared by MacMillan himself and the others purchased at Linton. Clark had not examined the marks on these tups, but the horns of the Lintons had been cut before he got them, and he cut them again that winter to stop them 'approaching too near the head'. When Clark heard that the horns of a ram's head found in MacIntyre's possession were cut, he checked his own flock and discovered one of the tups missing. He went to Campbeltown to examine the head, 'as there were no sheep in the neighbourhood with cut horns except [his] Linton sheep', and was sure it was that of the missing ram.

It is worth noticing that in the 1820 case there were 'herds', and in the 1837 case 'shepherds'. The distinction may be linguistic only, but more likely the increasing concentration on sheep necessitated herds who were capable of tending a big stock in a big area. John Campbell, in 1820, had charge of cattle and horses as well as sheep, and was employed by an aggregation of farmers with grazing rights to the Muir of Largie. Hugh MacIntyre, in 1837, did not wait around to benefit social historians with an account of his circumstances, but he was described specifically as a shepherd, and so was Peter Blackstock. Blackstock has not been mentioned until now — his evidence merely confirmed that of Lachlan Clark — but he was born about 1800 in Skipness Parish, and was shepherd at Gartgunnel for John Clark in Tangy. He was still at Gartgunnel in 1851, and there are still Blackstocks in Kintyre.

There is record of the trial and execution, in 1710, of John 'Bocan' Weir, described, in the indictment, as 'ane habitual Thief and Picker' (petty thief). He lived at Inanmore, and his accomplice Neil MacIlglash lived at Inanbeg, across the glen. In October 1709, they set off 'under cloud of night' to Garvachie (formerly a farm between Oatfield and Uigle), and drove thirteen sheep, belonging to William Fleeming, back to Inanmore 'by the mountain way that [they] might not be discovered'. On the following night, Weir killed two of the sheep half-a-mile from his house. Three more sheep were hidden alive in 'a hole upon the lands of Inanmore'. The rest were not accounted for.

About Lammas, 1709, Weir had gone to Coalhill and stole 'ane Coll Seck' (coal sack), in which he carried home a number of kail plants taken from the kailyard of a Drumlemmil weaver, James Raeside.

The verdict of the jury of fifteen gentlemen and farmers was heard on 23 June 1710 in Campbeltown, and it was one of 'guilty'. The sentence was recorded thus: ' ... The said John Weir alias Bocan to be taken to the ordinary place of execution on Friday the fifteenth day of September next betwixt two and five o'clock in the afternoon and then and there to be hanged on ane gibbet till he be dead'.

Borderers

Many shepherds came to Kintyre from other parts of Argyll and from the farther Highlands, but a sizeable number of them were Borderers, notably Todds and Beatties. The Todds originated in Dumfriesshire, but were not typical of Borders stock in Kintyre, having become Gaelic-speaking during an intermediate settlement in Mid-Argyll. The first was George Todd — born in the parish of Glassary about 1805 — who arrived in 1844 as shepherd at Allt an Tairbh (by then merged with Stramollach and Mulbuy as a single sheep farm). The family name has died out in Kintyre.

The Beattie brothers, James and Walter, arrived in the late 1850s. In the census of 1861, James (38) was in Ballegroggan, and Walter (33) in Glemanuillt. Walter died there two years later, in July 1863, of tuberculosis. The Beattie line in Kintyre issued from him, James and his wife apparently being childless. The Beatties were also of Dumfriesshire origin: Westerkirk. I had the pleasure, in 1977, of meeting and tape-recording the last of the Beattie family in Kintyre, Alistair, shortly before his death.

The Borthwicks were another Dumfriesshire family which came to Kintyre — about 1863 — and stayed. Alexander Borthwick and his family were at High Lossit in 1863, and at Kylipole in 1871. That family is still securely represented in Kintyre, though none of its branches has maintained the shepherding tradition.

George Jackson, from Westerkirk, arrived in 1855 with his wife Ann and an infant daughter born in Eskdalemuir. They were at Strone in 1861, with five more children and his shepherd brother John (18). George died at Balinamoil in 1894, aged 62, and the name has disappeared.

There were other Borders families which stayed only briefly in Kintyre and left little or no trace in the genealogical record.

There is too much involved in the work of shepherds to put into a chapter of a book. Most shepherds that I have known would need a book to themselves, and a big one at that. What follows, therefore, is simply a series of brief accounts of the main duties in the lives of shepherds, set against a sketchy historical background.

Smearing

Before the introduction of dips, the customary scab and vermin preventative was a mixture of Archangel (Russian) tar and butter. The 'smearing' was done at the 'back end' of the year, October or November.

The shepherd sat astride the special 'smearing-stool', with a dish of the mixture beside him, and by repeated dipping of forefinger and second finger, together, into the dish, applied the mixture as he shed the wool in a strip. A shed along the ridge of the back, and two or three on each side of the sheep evidently sufficed, for the heat of the animal's skin would naturally melt and spread the stuff. Estimates of up to twenty sheep smeared per day by individual shepherds were offered, but not even the oldest shepherds with whom I spoke had ever seen the practice. Donald MacCallum understood that 'it wiz a tedious job an' very sore on the hands. I used tae hear them sayin their fingers wid jeest be aboot burnt through'. The fingertips were liable to 'beel' (fester) and the nails to cast.

Smith described smearing as 'a general practice' in Argyll. 'All,' he wrote, 'smear the lambs and tups, and some smear all except the old wedders. The purpose of it is to defend from the cold, scab, and vermin; and to increase the quantity, and mend the quality of the wool.' Calum Bannatyne subscribed to these theories: 'It wiz tae keep them dry an' warm in the wintertim'. An' then it grew wool forbye, heavy heavy wool.' Smith suggested three to four pounds of butter to a Scotch pint of tar as a 'proper allowance' for the treatment of nine or ten sheep.

As smearing was done towards the end of the year, the work would often have taken place under shelter. Alistair Beattie was shown an old building by the road at Glemanuill, which, he was told, had been used for smearing. The smearing-sheds were lit by cruisie lamps (p. 162). When, in 1860, John Symington of Ayrshire applied (unsuccessfully) for the lease of Cairnmore, Cairnbeg, and Altnaboduy, he stated that a shepherd's house and a 'smearing house' needed to be built there.

Special 'smearing-stools' — sometimes made by the shepherds themselves — were used. These were cross-sparred, so that the legs of the sheep could be dropped through the gaps and thus immobilised.

Bone grease and other substitutes for butter became common in the mid-nineteenth century, and about 1868 dipping began to be adopted. In 1875, in Campbeltown, a variety of 'sheep dips' were being advertised to 'flockmasters' alongside 'smearing material'. 'One thing likely to turn the scale in favour of dipping,' remarked Duncan Clerk in 1878, 'is that there is much difficulty in getting sufficient hands for smearing.'

Clipping

Clipping could be performed on the ground, with the legs of the sheep tied; but that practice was hardly encountered in Kintyre by the beginning of the present century. Stools of either turf or wood allowed the work to be done with greater comfort to both sheep and shepherd. Turf-stools were in use, in some parts of Kintyre, until well into the present century. These were built at the fanks, with strips of turf usually cut to the full length of about four feet and tapered at one end. The turf was cut, carried to the fank in rolls, and built to a height of about two feet. Some stools were built on a foundation of stones, in which case a couple of lengths of scraw would suffice. But most were built entirely of scraws, placed earth to earth, and perhaps secured by hammering in pegs. These stools would need to be repaired each year. The top turf, at least, was usually renewed, having weathered and crumbled away; but some stools might require rebuilding 'fae the very ground'. Cattle were liable to tear at them with their horns and knock them down. A wool-bag could be thrown across the stool to absorb dampness and to prevent the soiling of the fleece.

Wood replaced turf, and clipping-stools began to be made by joiners. The making of stools was a part of the work of Argyll Estate joiners. Some shepherds, however, made their own. Finlay Clark would get a tree growing with suitable forks, cut the parts he wanted, and 'jeest [leave] them tae the win' for a year, an' then ye jeest, in the wintertime, put the legs on them, four legs, an' ye jeest put a plain wee plate-board running across that, an' the sheep wid lay in there'.

Clipping days were among the busiest in the shepherd's year. Clipping of the *hoggs* (yearlings) and the *yeld* (barren) ewes would be done in early June, if the weather suited, and would be followed, about a month later, by the main clipping, of the 'milk' ewes, that is those that had lambed. A clipping rotation operated within the Argyll Estate farms in Kintyre, until the arrival, in 1937, of a new manager, Willie Muir. By that system, all the Estate shepherds clipped from farm to farm as a shifting squad until the work was completed. The clipping began at Ballygroggan; Largybaan and Glenadale were done the following day; then Strone and Balnamoil/ Glemanuill were clipped by split squads; then Scavach/Kerran and Dalbuie; then Auchenhoan; then Corrylach, Stramollach and Bordadubh on the last day.

That system worked well enough as long as the weather held; but in wet weather sheep cannot be clipped, so the squad would be idle. Those who were within reasonable distance of home would return there for the night; others stayed with friends or relations nearby; the rest would sleep where they were. Willie Muir maintained that the system was thus unsatisfactory, and also that it involved excessive travelling. Thereafter, Estate farms joined their labour in smaller units. For example, Ballygroggan, Largybaan and Glenadale clipped their own stocks as a unit, assisted by

A nineteenth-century shepherd, presumed to be a Reid of Southend. He wears the standard shepherds' plaid: his overcoat, haversack, and occasionally his blanket. He holds a clay pipe in the hand that also holds his *cromag*, which is, however, too short for working use. Courtesy of Mrs. Barbara Wilkie.

any neighbours who were willing to participate. Auchenhoan, being isolated, brought in the Feochaig, Glenahervie and Kildalloig shepherds, and reciprocated at the clippings on these farms. Retired shepherds could be hired for the duration of a clipping where labour was scarce.

Prior to that revision, Argyll Estate clippings might involve as many as thirty men, fully twenty of them clipping. The rest would be 'drawing' the

A twentieth-century shepherd, Robert McInnes, with his red-haired collie 'Glen', both of them just back from the hill. Dalbuie, 1950. Courtesy of Mr R. McInnes.

sheep from the fank or rolling the wool, with one man packing it into bags. Finlay Clark, as a boy, saw fourteen men clipping and two 'crogging' in Barr Glen. His job was to open and close the fank gate for the 'croggers'. 'Crogging' — from Gaelic *cròg*, to clutch — was identical with 'drawing'. Boys who were unable to use shears expertly enough were usually put to the work of crogging. The left ear and horn of the sheep would be caught together in one hand (to avoid wrenching off the horn), and, with the other hand, the wool between the forelegs would be seized. The animal would then be drawn to a clipper, who would catch the opposite horn and ear. The crogger then caught the hind legs of the sheep and heaved it on to the stool.

A clipping in the 1920s, probably at Gartavaigh. The clippers are ranged along the middleground of the picture. At the left, a man is handing a fleece to the packer, who is standing inside a wool-bag suspended from the trams of the cart. In the foreground lies a filled bag, and, behind it, a pile of fleeces. Courtesy of Mrs May Barbour.

At Stramollach, a big clipping, there would be some 1500 ewes managed on the day. Robert McInnes reckoned that a good clipper could handle more than a dozen sheep in an hour, or about a hundred in eight hours. In 1895, at Putechan, Peter MacNab in Corlach and John MacDiarmid in Killocraw between them clipped 220 sheep. They started work at 10.10 a.m. and finished at 3.45 p.m., with a break of forty minutes for dinner. That was judged to be a remarkable performance, and was duly reported in the *Campbeltown Courier*, with the comment that 'keen competitions have lately taken place in the district'.

But a steady clipping rate was only possible when the wool was clean. If the fleece was gritty — on a sheep that had been rubbing its back under a 'sandy broo' (brow) — then, as Duncan MacKeith put it, 'two or three bites, an' yer shears were blunt'. Obviously, the less frequently shears required sharpening, the quicker the work proceeded. Density of fleece varied from place to place, and that too affected the speed of the operation. The heaviest fleeces that Robert McInnes ever clipped were on Stramollach sheep. 'Ye'd tae use the full strength o' yer han' tae close the shears', he said. At the Moil, the sheep were much lighter in the fleece. The difference was in the quality of grazing — Stramollach was 'deep land', whereas the Moil was shallow and rocky. Robert summarised thus: 'It's the land that makes the wool'.

Until about the turn of the century, Argyll Estate shepherds received the annual perquisite of a stone of wool, which was sent off to a manufacturing firm. A portion of the processed wool was kept by the firm as payment, and with what was returned the women knitted stockings and other clothing.

On the Argyll Estate, the legs of sheep were invariably tied with a buckled strap before clipping, as a safety measure to prevent the shears being kicked out of the clipper's hand and sent flying. But that precaution was by no means general in Kintyre.

Prior to clipping, and until the reform of 1937, a fat sheep would be killed on each farm to feed the squad. Broth and mutton were served, but not until the work was completed. The squad was sustained on baskets of sandwiches and large kettles of tea brought out during lulls in the clipping, usually when one batch of sheep had been finished and the herd stationed outside the fank was ready to drive in another batch. Food was provided by the women of the place, assisted by the wives of neighbouring shepherds.

Droving

Nowadays, sheep are never shifted far on main roads, which is hardly surprising considering how lethal modern traffic can be; but, until the early 1930s, when motor lorries were introduced for the transportation of livestock, flocks of sheep were a common enough sight on Kintyre roads. Even beyond the 1930s, there was some movement of sheep on main roads — when hoggs would be driven to the wintering farms — but the progressive upgrading of roads with tarmacadam and stone chips proved injurious to the feet of sheep and dogs alike over long distances.

None of the shepherds born around the turn of the century experienced the long-distance droves, but their fathers did. Donald MacCallum's father, John, drove wedders from Fort William to the Moil to be fattened for the following year's market. In certain years, favourable weather would allow the shipping of the stock from Corpach to Cairnbaan — whence they would be driven by road to the Moil — or to Campbeltown itself, if the Mull of Kintyre could be rounded safely. These hardy shepherds, if unable to find accommodation at the droving stances, would simply occupy some corner in the open and 'draw their coat over their head'.

In the accounts of Largie Estate for 1876 are preserved the costs of bringing 126 'Highland ewes' from Colintraive to Tarbert, by the steamer *Chevalier*, on 28 October. The freight charge amounted to £3 3s — at 6d a sheep — and was paid to David Hutcheson & Company, Glasgow. The expenses of the shepherd, Alexander Cowan, totalled £1 0s 6d and

A drove of black-faced sheep leaving Campbeltown on the main Glasgow road, c. 1900. Drumore House is at the left, behind the trees. Courtesy of Mr J. D. F. Colville.

comprised: coach — 4s; boats — 3s; harbour dues — 7s; lodgings, etc. — 5s; and allowance on roads — 1s 6d.

Until the introduction of lorries, sheep were conveyed to distant markets — Ayr and Lanark principally — on the regular steamers. The farmers around Barr Glen and Muasdale drove their sheep across the back of Kintyre to Carradale. As Finlay Clark remarked, 'It wiz easier on their feet'. His father would keep one dog and accompany the sheep to market, while Finlay returned home across the hills with the other dogs. If the tide was low at Carradale quay when the steamer berthed, there was usually some difficulty in loading the sheep. Donald Watson in Muasdale sometimes took his sheep to Carradale for shipment, and sometimes to Campbeltown. When crossing to Carradale, the flock would be halted for the night at Garvalt, and joined there by the Barr stock, to complete the journey, as a single body, next day. Willie MacGougan last drove market-bound sheep in 1933, to Carradale.

Wintering

The wintering of hoggs on low-lying farms had two purposes — to separate them from the tups when these were let on the hills (otherwise, immature ewe hoggs might be served), and to give them a chance of thriving on better ground. Robert McInnes: 'If ye don't haiv a good hoag (hogg), ye'll never haiv a good yowe (ewe) — it'll be bad all along the line'. The Laggan and Southend were the main wintering areas of Kintyre. The hoggs were left from 1 October until mid-March in care of the farmers there, for an agreed price. The MacKeiths at Sunadale wintered their hoggs at Machrimore, Southend. They took three days getting there, halting overnight at Whitestone, then Bellfield; but, on the return drove, one day sufficed to reach Whitestone, the sheep being stronger. On any farm with a sufficiency of green fields, sheep would be wintered at home. In July 1876, Charles Moreton MacDonald of Largie paid to Robert MacKinnon, tenant of Gortinane on Largie Estate, £50 for the wintering of an unspecified number of hoggs there.

Wintering charges, about that time, ranged from 4s to 8s per animal, but, as Duncan Clerk remarked in 1878, '. . . it is better to submit to such high rates than lose a great proportion of the young and weaker part of the stock'. Such was the complaint of John MacMillan MacNeill Esq. of Carskey, 'tacksman' of Coirranmore, Glecknahavil and Lecknacroive. In the severe winter and spring of 1836 and — in particular — 1837, he lost twenty-nine sheep on Coirranmore and sixty-seven sheep and nine head of black cattle on Glecknahavil and Lecknacroive, which loss he estimated at £150 (or in excess of a year's rent of these latter possessions, jointly let).

The wintering of sheep beyond Kintyre was prevalent in the nineteenth century. In 1866, nearly 30,000 sheep from Argyll as a whole wintered in other counties, principally Perthshire, Stirlingshire, Ayrshire, Dunbartonshire, and Renfrewshire. In 1883, with foot-and-mouth disease affecting parts of central Scotland, restrictions were imposed on the movements of sheep and cattle into Kintyre. The records of particular cases considered by the Kintyre committee responsible for the enforcement of the Contagious Diseases (Animals) Act of 1869 provide some indication of the density and range of sheep movements to and from Kintyre.

In April 1883, John MacNicol, in Courshelloch on Largie Estate, contravened the regulations by shipping on the steamer *Inveraray Castle* eighty-five black-faced hoggs from Bute to Tarbert, without a permit. He was prosecuted. Earlier, in February, a hundred sheep which had wintered in Stirlingshire were shipped to Campbeltown on the *Kinloch*, but, having come from a 'cattle plague' district, were prevented from landing. On 1 May, an application was received from a representative of the Carradale Estate for permission to ship from Wemyss Bay a flock of hoggs which had wintered near Kilmacolm, Renfrewshire. On 30 May 1884, John

Sommerville, tenant of High Lossit, asked for — and was granted — a special licence to ship 130 black-faced hoggs from Larne to Campbeltown. These sheep had wintered on another farm of his, Drumnadonough in County Antrim.

In 1856, John Lorne Stewart, Kintyre chamberlain of the Argyll Estate and an independent farmer — having High and Low Knockrioch, Tomaig, and Glenahervie — sent three hundred ewes to Ayrshire for wintering. From that stock he selected three *gimmers* (two-year-olds) for exhibition at the Paris Show of that year. He also sent three three-year-old ewes, two two-year-old *tups* (rams), and a three-year-old tup. These formed part of a representation of 172 cattle and 182 sheep organised by the Highland Society. Stewart himself was unable to attend the show, being occupied with the purchase of the Island of Coll, but his overseer John Baxter and head shepherd David Norris accompanied the sheep to Paris and received two awards — a second, with silver medal and £16, in the tups section, and a third, with bronze medal and £8, in the ewes section.

A Disappearing Breed

Most shepherds and their families had to cope with isolation. That factor was not inherent in the places themselves, most of which were indeed remote enough, but in the depopulation of the hill farms. In places which had supported several families, farming in joint-tenancy, only one family came to live. Gleneadardacrock — which is surrounded by hills and out of sight of any other habitation — was said to be the 'loneliest' shepherds' cottage in Kintyre. The winters were passed in reading, making music — many shepherds had fiddles — and carving crooks.

There are now few shepherds in Kintyre who work exclusively with sheep, and still fewer who regularly walk the hills to tend their flocks: 'hill bikes' have removed that necessity. In any case, manning levels on most hill farms do not allow for full-time shepherds; and the unremitting spread of coniferous afforestation has ruined many a good sheep hill. A century and more ago, there were those who looked — with bitterness or nostalgia — at land which had once grown crops and was turned over to sheep. Now, elderly shepherds look at land which had, in their time, yielded crops of fine lambs, and see only the devastation of the forestry ploughs or a heartbreaking vista of alien trees.

CHAPTER 6

Peat-Cutting

The progressive stages in the working of peat may be summarised thus: the paring of the bank to expose the soft peat below; cutting; spreading; turning and 'fitting' the drying peats; finally, the removal of the dried peats for stacking at the house. Beneath that superficially uncomplicated system, however, lay a mass of divergent practices and beliefs. There was — and is — no entirely standard method of working peat.

Many of the variations in method were slight, and in a more general account would scarcely merit notice, but at peat-working, as at any other traditional country industry, individualistic minds exercised their influence on the management of the job. There was pride in personal skill and an awareness of how and why a particular technical variation had evolved. Shepherds banded on the hills, at the wide-ranging sheep gatherings, enjoyed scrutinising any peat-banks they came across, and would discuss the style of the cutting and the condition of the bank. Uniformity of the spade scars along the face of the bank particularly pleased them.

The basis of this account comes from Robert McInnes, with comparative detail incorporated from other sources. I have worked at peats with Robert McInnes for several successive years on the hill farm of Lochorodale, and so have gained a practical understanding of his methods. He has been involved in peat-cutting since childhood. The labour is no longer truly one of necessity. He continues to cut peats because he wants to, and because he belongs to that tradition. He was born in 1917 at High Glenadale — now deserted — in the hills above Glen Breackerie. His father, also Robert, shepherded there from 1911 until 1935. Robert began helping his father at the age of twelve, replacing his elder brother when he went elsewhere to work as a shepherd. The peats were cut beyond the head of the glen, close to the Largybaan march. As his father cut and laid the peats on the bank, Robert spread them with a fork.

Making a Start

The time to begin peat-cutting was a matter of individual judgement. Adverse weather was the main delaying factor, but in most years cutting

83

D

would commence in late April or early May. The schoolmaster at Rhunahaorine noted on 6 May 1864, in his logbook, that 'the parents being engaged in peat-cutting, several of the children have been absent today'. In the following year, on 12 May, he again complained: 'The attendance is not satisfactory — the elder boys assisting at peat-cutting'.

Hard frost was the peat-cutters' greatest anxiety, and the main deterrent to cutting in early April. Experienced cutters agree on the damaging effects of frost. John MacKay: 'If ye get frost, the peats don't dry right through tae the hert (heart). There a kinna *scam* (withering) comes on them. They're more or less ruined. They're naw the sem (same). Tae putt them on a fire, there nae heat or strength off them.'

The Beatties in Largybaan often cut peats early in April. They reasoned that, if they had protracted trouble with lambing, the season might be rather far advanced before they would get a chance to start cutting. But they did have a method of protecting the peats from frost. They would build a double line of peats on the edge of the bank, and lay a single row along the middle of the wall, to cover the seam and to consolidate the mass. Having time later, they would scatter out these peats and then, perhaps, cut and spread another batch. Most shepherds would wait until mid or late May, by which time the bulk of the lambs had come, and gather the remaining unlambed ewes into a field. They were thus freed, for parts of their days, to get peats cut.

Robert McInnes judged peat to be ready for cutting when the warmth of the sun had filled it with 'an element of life'. That 'life', he said, could be seen and felt on the peat — the dense, black stuff especially — as an oil or grease. Calum Bannatyne heard that theory — 'Ye darna (daren't) cut peats till the sun comes tae rise the oil up oot the ground' — but was never inclined to try it. The black peat was a better product if it dried slowly. Too much sun too quickly forms a hard skin on peats, which effectively retards the drying process, and cracks and warps them. A 'canny err' (gentle, steady air) will dry them perfectly. An occasional shower of rain does no harm to peat early in its drying. Robert McInnes: 'They're dryin a wee bit more gradually, wi' the result that they're dry through an' through'.

Having tested and approved an unworked piece of ground — by cutting a turf and trying the peat below it: if 'greasy', suitable; if 'soily', unsuitable — the main consideration was to open the bank (locally 'bink') at its lowest point, to be certain of unrestricted drainage. 'If ye hae'na got it that the watter's gettin aweh (away), you're in a mess; ye're in among the watter tae cut peats, an' ye can't cut peats among watter.' An open drain would then be cut to carry away whatever water might accumulate. On hilly ground, the natural slope eliminates flooding, but when cutting on hollowed moorland — such as on the peat ground at Lochorodale — drainage is a continual concern.

The length of bank to be opened is marked out using a pinned line. That length is then cut using a rutting-spade, inserted to the depth reckoned necessary to get below the tough upper turf. The breadth of the bank can then be measured in boot lengths — perhaps three or four — and the opposite edge lined off and rutted. Two or three parallel cuts between the margins, afterwards 'cross-rutted', subdivides the turf into squarish scraws.

These scraws can then be sliced off the bank with the rutting-spade and tumbled to the side. A second worker, easing up the scraws with a *draining-hawk* (a fork with the three prongs set at right angles to the short shaft) and tossing them clear, greatly relieves the pressure needed on the spade. A tidy peat-worker will always fit these scraws along the bottom of the bank, so restoring the natural moor covering and ensuring dry and level ground as he progressively, year by year, cuts the bank away.

These procedures were conditional to all farm leases granted by the Argyll Estate: '... The peats to be cut regularly with hags in straight lines so as the water may run off and there may be no standing pools, and the parings laid regularly grass side uppermost'. That these methods were generally disregarded is plain from John Smith's comments in 1795: 'The injudicious and irregular mode of cutting peats which almost universally prevails is, in many respects, a very serious evil. The moss, by cutting it in pits and holes, is soon rendered a perfect bog or quagmire, unfit for giving any supply of fuel; it is made dangerous, and often fatal to cattle; and almost incapable of being brought, if wished for, into a state of cultivation'.

Cutting

The peat-cutter's main tool is the peat 'knife' or 'spade', in Gaelic *fàl-mhòine*. The iron head is narrow, with the cutting 'wing' projecting from one side of it, and socketed for the insertion of the shaft. In Islay, the handle of the peat-spade is customarily a cow's horn, but in Kintyre the handle is of wood, identical to an ordinary spade handle, and of a piece with the shaft. The knives were made to individual specifications by local blacksmiths, and invariably outlasted several shafts. In June 1847, McNair the blacksmith in Campbeltown (p. 121) charged Alexander Wilson two shillings for a 'peat sped' and a shilling for the shaft. There are now no smiths in Kintyre, and anyone wishing to start cutting peats has usually to acquire a secondhand tool. In 1983 the late Archie McMillan in

,

The peat-spade that Archie McMillan made, propped against an abandoned peat-bogie at Lochorodale. The bogie, which has an iron frame and iron wheels, must have been pulled by a horse or pony. Photograph by the author, 1987.

Campbeltown made a peat-spade which was traditional in design, but fashioned entirely of welded steel. He gave it to Robert McInnes to try, and, though heavy to handle, it proved very serviceable, particularly with tough, rooty peat.

A man alone can cut peats efficiently enough, but a much greater bulk of peats will be gained in a day if he is assisted. Working alone, he stands on the pared bank and lifts each cut peat on the end of the spade and lays it on the edge of the bank, or throws it wide if the peat is tough and can take such treatment without breaking (broken peats increase subsequent handling). If he has a helper, that person stands below the cutting level and lets him cut one peat, then another, and closes a hand on each peat so that the two can be lifted and laid on the bank in a single motion. This, in Kintyre, is called *tapping*, and the assistant is a *tapper*.

When I am at Lochorodale with Robert McInnes, I generally do the tapping. When we have an easy rhythm going between us, we try to maintain it for as long as possible without interruption, and that means getting as great a bulk of peats as we can stacked on the upper bank. The extractable depth at Lochorodale is two long peats (say, about 15 inches, wet), and as we work along the bank I will build these peats into a wall

John MacDonald 'tapping' to Robert McInnes on the Lochorodale peat ground, spring 1986. Photograph by the author.

sufficiently far back from the bank edge so that, when we take out the second depth, these additional peats can be built at the edge. We are thus able to cut an entire face of peat without having to break off and barrow accumulated peats out to the drying ground, to make space for uncut peats. When a second helper is present, the bulk of the peats can be barrowed out as the cutting proceeds. If two barrows can be manned, then the tapper can load these alternately with peats straight from the knife.

Drying

A peat-cutter must have room to dry his peats. If the ground allows him to work a long bank, taking his peats from a continuous face, then they can be

John MacDonald forking peat on to a barrow from the bank edge.
Lochorodale, 1986. Photograph by the author.

forked into a narrow spread along the bank. But if the bank is a short one, necessitating the cutting of two or three faces, then the first batch of peats will have to be carried well out, usually on barrows. If the ground close to the bank is poor for drying, having boggy patches about it, then the peats will have to be taken to drier knowes even farther out.

If the drying ground was so far from the peat-bank that the use of barrows was impracticable, then *slipes* — drawn by horse or pony — would be used. Slipes were generally home-made, so that no one description could entirely represent all slipes. The design was simple enough, and this description — from Willie MacGougan — will be adequate. The slipe was

'Fitting' peats in the Mull of Kintyre area, c. 1920. Courtesy of Mrs May Barbour.

about 4ft long by 2½ft broad, a slatted wooden framework mounted on wooden runners. At both front and back of the frame, three stout pegs were fitted, to contain the load. A horseshoe was attached to the front, on to which the horse's drag-chain could be hooked, and a handle on one side of the slipe — for tipping out the load — completed the construction.

At Stramollach, the peat ground lay in a hollow, and the drying ground lay beyond the ridge of the hollow. Slipes were necessary there, and Duncan MacNicol had several big ones, and a *garron* (small, sturdy horse) to pull them. The slipes were loaded and emptied alternately, one man continually leading the horse between the bank and the spreading ground.

The drying of peats is entirely dependent on weather, and between the spreading of peats and their removal might lie weeks, or even months, of tedious attendance and frustration. If time allows, the individual peats can be turned where they lie, to let the damp underside dry off. When sufficiently dry to stand on end without buckling — which destroys their shape and renders stack-building difficult — the peats can then be 'fitted' (footed) into pyramidal clumps of six or eight, with one laid horizontally on top. As the drying process advances, several 'fittings' can be combined to form small stacks. In damp weather, when peats are not drying sufficiently to be stood on end, they can be fitted criss-cross, three high.

As soon as peats were dry enough, they would be carted off the hill. The MacPhails in Skernish kept lightly built carts for no other purpose than carrying peats. Two of these 'peat carts' would be continually employed for a week, transporting peat from Garvalt. The Watsons in North Muasdale would cut about a hundred cartloads of peat from Cnoc na Seilg, a hill overlooking High Clachaig.

An exceptionally wet summer might render impassable the tracks which led to the peat-banks, and the entire year's provision might have to lie on the hill throughout winter. The summer of 1985 brought just such conditions, and peats which were cut late in the season failed to dry sufficiently to be removed. By the side of the Mull road, tons of peat lay in fittings into the next year, gradually wasting under the hard rains and frost. Robert McInnes was fortunate enough to get his peats home, albeit inadequately dried.

One summer in Stramollach brought constant rain, and the hill was boggy. Robert McInnes was forced to stack the peats on the hill, but he had a cartload of draining tiles brought to him, and, as he built the stack, he inserted a tile here and there in place of a peat, and thatched the whole. The peats, tile-ventilated, dried gradually under the thatch, and could be carted away in the spring. He had known peats abandoned on hills and allowed to be scattered — 'Nob'dy wid attend an' putt them in a lump o' any kind'. By spring, they had dried entirely, but the substance had gone out of them. 'It wid be lik' hay that wiz too long bein' made — the value would be gone.'

The building of a peat-stack is skilful work, if the stack (*cruach*) is to be stable and watertight. The neat and regular appearance of the stack is, however, all on the outside. Inside, the 'heart' is a mass of peats, thrown anyhow. The external work is what matters. The outer peats are systematically built, from the very base, interlocking and with a slope to shed rain. As the stack rises, its walls are gradually tapered, keeping the heart always packed tight. At the head of the stack, the two rows of peats almost meet, and the gap between can be filled with the *stoor* (dust) of peat. After a final row of 'rigging peats' has been laid on the very head of the stack, it can be thatched with rushes or (more usually nowadays) covered with a tarpaulin or suchlike. The stack might be ventilated by inbuilt birch or hazel branches along the middle, or by incorporating a series of draining tiles, spaced 3ft apart and some 4ft from the base.

The Laggan Moss

The greatest concentration of extractable peat lay in the Laggan — or Moss — of south Kintyre. It is now an area of prime farmland and military installations — R.A.F. and N.A.T.O. bases occupy an extensive westerly portion of it — but Dugald MacIntyre, the Kintyre gamekeeper and naturalist, remembered, in 1931, the Moss '. . . as a great haunt of grouse and wild fowl', and that '. . . a thousand brace of grouse [had] been bagged on it in a season'. To the centuries of peat-cutting, by which the bogs were gradually drained and levelled, MacIntyre attributed the spread of agriculture there. But that was not the whole truth. In 1810, James Malcolm complained that the tenant of Durry was cutting peat for sale, as well as for his own use, and that the Moss would '. . . be reduced so much below the level of the circumjacent waters, as to draw them thither, and render not only the present convertible surface useless, but be the means of producing a Stagnant Lake'. Besides, drainage schemes, independent of peat interests, were implemented during the late eighteenth and nineteenth centuries. The tenants of Durry and North and South Backs, for instance, were offered a premium in 1827 of £4 for every acre of 'the Moss Land' brought into cultivation.

The extent of peat-cutting on the Moss may be deduced from a petition sent in 1788 to the Duke of Argyll by the tenant of Aros, Lachlan MacNeill. His lease was about to expire and he wished to renew it, but was unwilling to pay extra rent. He reminded the Duke that when the rent of the farm had last been set, many people from Campbeltown had been cutting peats on Aros ground, 'which enabled [MacNeill] the better to pay his rents'. Since then, however, 'the Tacksman of the Coalworks of Drumleman has erected a Fire Engine and Executed a Canal halfway to Campbeltown [and] the Inhabitants thereof are now so well supplied with Coals that there is no demand for peats'. MacNeill's complaint, basically, was that the cutting of the 'Coal Canal' — started about 1783 and completed about 1791 — was allowing more coal at cheaper prices to reach Campbeltown from Charles McDowall's coalmine at Drumlemble. He was granted an award of 'damages' because, by the old lease, Aros was 'subjected to a Servitude of Peats and Turff' to the Duke's tenants in Campbeltown and neighbouring farmers.

MacNeill's case was almost certainly exaggerated. In 1807, the Campbeltown Coal Company, in a reversal of roles, was complaining bitterly to the Duke about the amounts of peat being cut without permission and sold in Campbeltown by farmers and others. The company wanted limitations on peat-cutting, 'to increase the sale of their Coal'. By 1794, about forty cartloads — or some thirteen tons — of canal-borne coal were being burned daily in Campbeltown, although 'poorer folk' continued with peats.

Peat from the Moss was certainly sold in Campbeltown from the eighteenth century until the early twentieth century, and gave full-time employment throughout that period to small numbers of men known as 'cadgers'. Charles Mactaggart, in his valuable little book, *Life in Campbeltown in the 18th Century*, remarks that these cadgers 'gave the Town Council more trouble than any other class of workmen, being given to carrying short weight and to refusing to work for customers who were not prepared to pay them more than the authorised scale laid down'. In the early part of the eighteenth century, prior to the introduction of carts, peats — and all other goods — were carried by pack horses or ponies. The standard peat-sack was huge, measuring four yards long by almost a yard wide. An account survives, for the period April 1843 to April 1844, of the quantity of peats driven to Campbeltown from the Duke of Argyll's lands — 4820 cartloads. The bulk of it must have come from the Moss.

John MacKay, a Cutter and Carter of Peats

One of the last, if not the last, of the peat-cutters and carters of the Moss is still alive (1987) in Campbeltown. His name is John MacKay and he was born in 1898 at Darlochan, the son of a ploughman. He was 'amang' peats from the age of seven. His commitment was quite different from that of, say, a shepherd who wanted only enough peats to feed his own fires. Peat-cutting for John MacKay was a part of his livelihood, and his main customers were the Campbeltown distilleries, principally Benmore, Glengyle, and Lochhead, though most of the others, when short of peat, took supplies from him in various years. It is from peat, by which malted barley is dried, that malt whisky takes much of its essential flavour.

The peats cut on Aros Moss were hefty — about 2ft long and 7in broad, with a depth of about 3in, or roughly twice the size and weight of hill peats. They were cut horizontally from the bank, and no 'tapper' was employed. The cutter loaded them directly on to a barrow. Seven peats were heavy enough to manage, and these were wheeled out and tipped. There was a 'knack' to tipping the barrow so that none of the peats broke. The peats were not spread to dry, as on moorland, because the great quantities that were cut could not have been accommodated on the drying ground. Instead, one peat was laid longways, and three more were propped against it. This was called *skyling*, which means 'spreading' (the peats were in a sense spread, but not in the usual sense). These peats were cut with one end thicker than the other — perhaps a difference of half-an-inch — and that thicker end, which required greater exposure to the air, would be placed uppermost. When these peats had dried enough to stand, each lot of four would be 'fitted' together. Finally, the dried peats would be barrowed off the drying ground and heaped ready for carting or for building into stacks.

Neil Kelly, Lochside, with a load of Moss peats for a Campbeltown distillery, c. 1925. Courtesy of Mrs Catherine Brodie.

On the Moss, all scraws removed in the stripping of banks were replaced with the growth downwards, a practice opposed to that of hill peat-cutters. There thus formed, behind the advance of the extraction, a black, bare platform which, the Moss workers maintained, gave a better drying ground than vegetation.

John MacKay and his workmate would be occupied a month or more — from early May until June — cutting the peats. They started at 8 a.m. and stopped at 6 p.m. They had a basket of food with them, and carried water to the Moss, which held no drinkable water. A fire was lit with withered heather and old strewn peats, and tea — '... the best o' the lot, tea that ye boilt in the open ...' — would be brewed in a kettle.

The carting of peats to Benmore Distillery in Campbeltown occupied John MacKay and his partner for a fortnight in the summer. Each would drive three 'recks' (loads) daily. They began work at 4 a.m. and would be at the distillery at 6, waiting for the gate to be opened. Later, Glengyle would be supplied, but two loads per cart would be as much as daylight would allow by then. During winter, when the whisky was being made, other distilleries might order peats if their stocks were dwindling.

Irish peat was shipped to Campbeltown in various years, to supplement local supplies. On a single day in November 1886, four schooners arrived with cargoes, the largest importation ever recorded. Some, at least, of that peat was brought from County Donegal, for in December 1899 a Campbeltown smack was wrecked on passage to Lough Swilly to load peats. The Irish peat John MacKay dismissed as mere 'turf'.

The shipment, in 1913, of two cargoes of Kintyre peat was considered, at the time, to be 'probably unprecedented'. That winter, abnormally high barley prices had curtailed whisky production in Campbeltown, and the cutters, having a lot of peat left unsold, struck a deal with the Ardrishaig distillery.

John MacKay would cut about 200 tons — or 400 cartloads, roughly — in a season. The peats would be stacked on the Moss, working from the cart itself, which was backed into the face of the stack. The stacks were big — about 60ft long by 12ft wide, and 12ft high — compared with domestic stacks, their scale representing the extent of the digging.

The stacks were not thatched in any way, yet 'winna take the renn (rain)'. That imperviousness John MacKay attributed to the nature of the peat. Moss peats, he said, could be stacked damp in September — after a wet season — yet would be dry when removed in March. In his estimation, they were superior to hill peats.

When he was a young man, 4s 6d was the price of a cartload of peats. During the First World War, or shortly afterwards, the price was increased to 25s, but the carts were then bigger — 'really two carts o' the other size'. Of that sum, the peat-cutters received £1, and the Argyll Estate — to which the Moss belonged — 5s. Transactions were handled by an agent of the Duke's (latterly, however, the business was managed directly from the Estate office in Campbeltown). If, for example, thirty cartloads had been delivered to a distillery, the cutters would receive a 'line' from the agent for that number of loads. That line was taken to the distillery and endorsed there. The agent then collected the money from the distillery, deducted the Duke's share, and only then would the cutters be paid. 'The Duke had the best o' it,' John MacKay reckoned. 'He had nothing tae do. We had tae do the toilin. Aye.'

When Peter Kelly was farming Gortan he cut peats there. He, too, sold to distilleries — Springbank regularly, and Glen Scotia occasionally — but not on the scale of the Moss cutters. Thirty or forty cartloads might go to distilleries in a year, but the income from peat was not material to the economy of the farm. He often took on an Irishman — usually an unemployed drainer — to help with peat-cutting. In some years, when the work of the farm was very heavy, the Irishman would 'do the lot', and lived on the farm until the cutting was done.

Few sheep-farms in Kintyre were without accessible peat deposits on their own ground (Auchenhoan being a notable exception). Low-lying and coastal farms without peat had to be supplied elsewhere or do without, but until the present century, few farmers were willing to buy coal when there was access to peat ground and the labour to extract it. Most of the farms in the Glenbarr/Muasdale district got peats from Garvalt. When Finlay Clark was fee-ed in Rosehill, a four-mile journey by horse and cart was necessary each day before a stroke of work could be done. A greater distance — some six miles — was travelled by farmers from the Macharioch district of Southend, who cut their peats at Glenrea. An old peat-road struck into the hills at Keprigan. They started off from Macharioch at 4 a.m. and got a depth of one good peat at Glenrea.

Kilirvan was a traditional peat-cutting ground for Argyll Estate tenants in Southend. The tenants of the farm were accustomed, from 'time immemorial', to 'raising moss-mail' (peat rent) from every person who cut on that farm. The charge was 6d for every 'darke' — *darg*, day's work — until 1775, when the lease was granted to George Campbell and Neil Fleeming. They complained of 'trespass upon their grass' by the peat-cutters' horses, and got the moss-mail increased to 10d. Subsequently, however, the farm was divided between Fleeming and George Campbell's son, Archibald, and the 'common moss' lay in Campbell's portion. Also, the right of moss-mail had been withdrawn, and Campbell resented the loss of that income and wanted his neighbour to bear half of the loss. But the Duke's chamberlain, Dugald Campbell, having interviewed both parties at Campbeltown on 17 April 1787, rejected Archibald Campbell's claim.

Moss-Blocks

Peat was not the only fuel that could be dug from the bogs. Wood lay in some peat seams, and at times bedevilled the cutting operation. Generally, only twigs and branches occur, complete with bark, but peats that contain wood fragments are liable to disintegrate when handled. Entire trunks of trees were occasionally discovered, and these would generally be dug around and left embedded. But if the trunks were small enough, they could be removed from the bank and left to dry. These would later be carted home with the peats and sawn into 'moss-blocks' which burned admirably.

'Utter and Intolerable Drudgery'

The cost, in time and labour, of working peats was for long an argument against the operation, particularly when it conflicted with the demands of managing a farm. I cannot think of many farmers in Kintyre who still cut peats other than as a commercial investment. The work is no longer considered worthwhile. The few individuals who cut peats do so because they enjoy the work and have adequate time to devote to it. Peat-cutting is a pleasure now; in the past it was a grim necessity. The following account was written in 1933 by 'an octogenarian', and expressed forcefully the feelings which must have embittered many an unwilling labourer at peats:

> The present-day farmer, who has coal tipped down at his door, when and in whatever quantities he desires, can hardly realise the time and labour that had to be expended, summer after summer, in cutting, drying, carting and stacking peats for winter use; often, too, at a time when other urgent things were clamouring for attention. The labour both of men and women, young and old, had to be enlisted, and weary, dirty, long-drawn out work it was: the very recollection of it bringing not so much an ache to my bones, though that is vivid enough, as a sense of utter and intolerable drudgery. What a boon coal was to the farmer, in liberating all this labour to other and more profitable ends, cannot be too strongly emphasised.

The author of the Old Statistical Account for Saddell and Skipness, the Rev. George MacLeish, had similar criticisms of the dependence on peat:

> ... The inhabitants have long been subjected to many inconveniences as to their fuel. Turf or peats were their only fuel: they are found in the hills; but the cutting, with the whole expensive process of drying and carrying them home, used to occupy the farmer and his whole family for a great part of the summer season; and in a wet season, he ran the dreadful risk of wanting fire to dress his victuals, or warm him during the inclemency of winter. This was the deplorable situation of the people here, and over all the Highlands, two years ago, and is in a great measure so, even this season (1793).

The sentiments of the Rev. Alexander Campbell in Kilcalmonell and Kilberry, and the Rev. Dr. John Smith in Campbeltown were substantially the same. 'At present,' Smith wrote, 'two or three months of the best season of the year are spent by the farmers, and other inhabitants, in preparing a miserable and precarious kind of fuel.' The Rev. Alexander Stuart in Killean and Kilchenzie merely noted '... the scarcity of fuel in many farms, on which the peat mosses are now exhausted'.

The tax on coal transported by sea was also strongly complained of, but its abolition was secured — in 1794 — even before some of the accounts were published. By 1843, there was little evidence that coal was much relied upon in country districts of Kintyre. On Gigha, turf had become so scarce that coal was being shipped from Ayrshire. In the 1790s, Gigha peat was so depleted that it could not be cut with spades. The islanders, John Smith recorded, 'work the moss with their feet, and bake and shape it into peats with their hands. This operation makes the peats dear, but they are very lasting'. Despite the mining of coal around Drumlemble, the local resource was not much utilised beyond that district and Campbeltown, partly because of its inferior quality and partly because it was cheaper to ship coal from Ayrshire than to cart it long distances from the Campbeltown area.

Coal

By the end of the nineteenth century, the arrival of a coal smack or 'puffer' was an annual sight at bays and beaches around the coasts of Kintyre. Where possible — particularly on the sheltered east coast, in bays from Skipness south to Peninver — the boat would be beached and unloaded directly into carts at ebb water. But along the west coast — much of it open Atlantic — the coal-boat skippers would not risk beaching. At Muasdale, flat-bottomed rowing-boats, with flush-planked floors, were kept at the shore exclusively for coal ferrying. Each of these boats could carry about two tons of coal, which was loaded from the anchored vessel and ferried to the beach to be shovelled into waiting carts. Loads for villagers and nearby farmers would be delivered immediately, but those for outlying farms were heaped in a field adjacent to the old post office for later collection.

The boys of the village would converge to 'dook' for fallen coals, wearing aprons and wading out to where the carts were taking on the coal. Sometimes, William Watson recalled, an 'odd lump' would be 'slipped into the sea' for them. Some cart-horses feared the water. They would tremble and, finally, collapse in the sea, and might have to be unhitched and replaced. In all communities, the business of ordering coal was left to one person, who might be a farmer, a shopkeeper or a tradesman. The coal was usually shipped, from Ayrshire, in July or August.

CHAPTER 7

Illicit Whisky

Whisky is not quite the traditional drink it is commonly supposed to be. Distilled liquors were evidently unknown — or, at least, uncommon — in Kintyre until the late sixteenth century. In September 1591, the 'pursmaister' (treasurer) to Alexander Campbell, laird of Cawdor — journeying from Kintyre to Stirling — accounted for a delivery of 'aquavytie' at 'Taylone'; but the place of origin of the spirit cannot be inferred. The rent in 1636 for the farm of Crosshill — jointly tenanted by the burgesses of Campbeltown — was six quarts of aquavitae, the herbally flavoured spirit from which whisky derived.

The traditional drink was ale, home-brewed from oat and bear malt, which were substantial elements in the produce rents of the seventeenth century. That ale was also flavoured with local herbs, and with imported flavourings such as ginger and liquorice. It was made on many farms, but there were professional brewers such as Donald Morrison in Machrimor, who appears in Malcolm MacNeill of Carskey's estate journal on 13 April 1722 as having received five bolls of malt. About 1770, two breweries were established in Campbeltown, one at Dalaruan and the other at Bolgam Street. In 1791, only the former seems to have been operational, and must have brewed the 400 bolls (some 25 tons) of grain which was made into ale that year in Campbeltown.

Distilling evidently became established in the eighteenth century, though as late as 1772 in Kintyre Thomas Pennant described whisky as 'a modern liquor', spirits having traditionally been prepared with 'thyme, mint, anise, and other fragrant herbs'. The wars in which Britain became involved during the late eighteenth century pushed up taxes on exciseable liquors, and in the Highlands whisky began to be made commercially in the small stills permitted only for household use. In 1797, the licence duty was raised to £9 per gallon of still content in the Middle District of Excise, which included Kintyre, and the result, according to Duncan Colville, was that legal distilleries went out of business in Campbeltown for the ensuing two decades, 1797 to 1817. Illicit distillation, at the same time, increased proportionately to take up the market. Further legislation failed to stimulate licensed distillation on a large scale, until 1822–3 when the laws were wholly revised and an annual licence fee of £10, coupled with a modest duty on spirits, brought the industry back into the open. The emergence of the modern industry — in Campbeltown, at least twenty-seven licensed distilleries were established between 1823 and 1827, many of them by former 'outlaws' — eclipsed the illicit trade, which continued, however, beyond the mid-nineteenth century. Malt (p.   ) as well as whisky was dutiable. The malt tax — which was both fiercely resented and opposed — was extended from England to Scotland in 1713, following the Act of Union in 1707, and remained in force until the mid-1850s.

A government report on the distilleries of Scotland, prepared in 1798-9, alleged that Kintyre landowners actually encouraged illicit distillation because they wanted rents paid. John Smith, writing in 1795, remarked on their partiality: 'When acting as justices of the peace they are seldom inclined to inflict due penalty on those who follow these occupations without a licence'. These lairds, according to Smith, maintained that '. . . distilling should be encouraged, as it will bring the tenant a good price for his bear'. He cited a moralistic tale to refute that argument:

> A landlord in Kintyre, a few years ago, allowed a miller on his estate, and in his neighbourhood, to keep a dram-house, as smiths and millers too often do, to the great prejudice of tenants and all around them . . . As it was a place of little resort, almost all the liquor must have been drunk by the gentleman's own workmen and tenants. He saw his work neglected, and his workmen in rags; and, at the end of the year, put a stop to a practice which would have soon beggared half the neighbourhood. All landlords would follow the same course, if they would duly consider their own interest, and the evil consequences of these shops of poison.

There is no doubt that illicit whisky was of incalculable economic importance in Kintyre, and in the Highlands as a whole, for as long as the trade was able to flourish. Distilling, in the main, was no pastime, dabbled in for a little pocket-money. It was both heavily invested in and highly organised, right from the cultivation of the bear to the distribution of the end-product. It required a degree of commitment that sanctioned violence and even murder. A passage from the Excise Supervisors' Instructions of 1778 states the matter plainly: 'When you are on the round with the Collector, you are to ride armed with pistols'.

On the night of 31 October, 1814, George Arthur, supervisor of Excise at Campbeltown, was killed on the road near Killocraw. He and an Excise officer, Charles MacArthur, had attempted to stop a cart which was suspected of carrying smuggled goods. Two women and two men — James MacKinlay and John MacMillan — were with the cart, and 'an affray ensued, during which Arthur was so severely wounded in the head that he died in consequence next day'. Both MacKinlay and MacMillan were accused of murder and stood trial on 15 March 1815. Although 'no person was near the deceased except MacMillan . . . it did not clearly appear from the evidence how his death was occasioned'. The case against MacMillan was found not proven, and MacKinlay was found not guilty.

Close to the head of Drumore Burn, which enters the sea a little north of Bellochantuy, an exciseman named Doig is supposed to be buried. The spot is well enough known as Doig's Grave, but I have been unable to verify the tradition, which was recorded in *Memories of a Highland Gamekeeper* by Dugald Macintyre (who is disconcertingly unreliable as an historian). Doig was supposed to have pursued smugglers, alone, into that 'lonely glen' and been murdered there. 'With a stone from the mountainside at his head, and a smaller one at his feet, "Doeg the Imprudent" rests there from age to age.'

Bradley claimed that, in the 'palmy days of smuggling', before 1821, 'a majority of cottagers and day-labourers in Cantire supported large families by the profits of smuggled whisky'. A *smuggler* (as illicit distillers were locally known) 'could clear ten shillings a week after all his expenses were paid, and this sum enabled him to keep a horse and a cow'. He added: 'A wife was an indispensable portion of his stock in trade, and early marriages were very frequent'.

The Argyll Estate was consistent in its opposition to the illicit industry. Pennant noted that 'the Duke of Argyll . . . obliges all his tenants to enter into articles, to forfeit five pounds and the still, in case they are detected'. Yet that penalty was no deterrent — 'the trade is so profitable that many persist in it'. These 'articles' were, in fact, incorporated in leases; but not, for whatever reasons, in all leases. The clause ran: 'The said Tacksman obliges himself and his foresaids not to distill any grain into spirits or retail spirituous liquors any manner of way without a special licence from the Duke or his Chamberlain in these bounds under the penalty of forfeiting the sum of £5 Sterling . . . for each trespass together with the still or stills used by them . . .' Its last appearance was in 1777, in the lease of Balimontgomery. The Duke himself wanted no part of the proceeds — the fines went 'for the use of the poor', and the money raised from the sale of confiscated stills was given to informers.

There was certainly money to be made from informing. Campbeltown Town Council, in 1799, offered a reward of two guineas 'to any person that will inform against the Town Miller or Multurer or their Servants that shall be guilty of grinding malt in the Town Mill without licence'. That was one of several measures taken to stop illegal distilling in the district. Only malt for the 'Ale Brewers' was to be ground, and that only by licence. In the following year, 1800, food scarcity prompted the council to organise a force of men to '. . . scour the country in order to seize and secure the stills, thereby to prevent the abuse or consumption of grain by distillation, and to induce the tenants to bring their grain to market'.

No fewer than twenty-two of the Duke of Argyll's tenants in Kintyre were convicted of malting or distilling illegally in the period 24 October 1800 to 2 April 1801 (Appendix 1). Owing to bad harvests and consequent grain shortage, distilling had been completely banned in 1801 and 1802 (and again from 1809 to 1811, and in 1813).

Equipment and process

The illicit distillers' basic equipment is shown in Fig. 33. The still itself is mounted on a crude fireplace built of stones. Peats would have been used as fuel, and the creel in which these were carried is upended beside the still. From the 'head' of the still projects the 'arm', carrying the vapourised 'wash' — fermented malt — down through the coiled copper pipe, or 'worm', which is unseen within the water-filled 'worm-tub'. That cool water caused the vapour to condense into a liquid known as 'low wines'. A second — and occasionally third — distillation produced whisky that was ready for sale. At the base of the worm-tub can be seen a funnel connected with the worm outlet, or 'feadan' (p. 105), and a container into which the spirit dripped. That container has been embedded in the ground at a suitable level, for which purpose the spade — at right, its shaft alone clearly visible — was no doubt used. The man on the right is pouring a sample of whisky into a small container. The equipment of illicit distillers in Kintyre, and elsewhere in the Highlands, was kept to the very necessities, owing to limited capital and risk of seizure. The worm was usually very short, the abundance of running water rendering a longer one unnecessary.

Such was the final stage of whisky-making; but, before that process could begin, a great deal of troublesome and time-consuming preparation was required. The bear had first to be steeped, which in illegal distillation usually meant putting it in pools and puddles. It was then spread to germinate, often in secluded bothies or caves. The next stage was to dry the grain, and that was usually done in the kilns attached to corn-mills, with or without the sanction of the miller, who might well be subject to intimidation. (Often, however, malt was bought directly from legal maltsters in Campbeltown — p. 105). The resulting malt was then ground at a mill, and extracted with boiling water to produce 'wort', which, when fermented, became 'wash'. At that stage, distillation began. The whole process, from steeping to the final distillation, could take a month, during which time the raw materials, in their various states of preparation, were

The MacAllisters distilling illicit whisky. Courtesy of the Scottish Ethnological Archive, National Museums of Scotland. These 'smugglers' have been identified, with reasonable certainty, as Archibald MacAllister — 'Baldy Ruadh', or Red Baldy, at right — and his sons James — 'Big Jamie' — and Archibald, who is kneeling. They were of County Antrim origin, and operated there and in Islay and Kintyre, as circumstances dictated. The photograph — the original of which was given to the late Father James Webb, parish priest in Campbeltown, by a descendant of theirs in Campbeltown, Archibald Wilson (d. 1957) — was evidently taken in County Sligo, Ireland.

vulnerable to detection, as the extracts from the Excise correspondence book show (p. 113).

Sites

Whisky could be made almost anywhere. The romantic image is of a still concealed in some glen, deep in mountainous country. Most sites certainly were in the remotest of places, but many were not, and these would offer all the more convenience to the business. More than forty per cent of the stills made between 1811 and 1817 by Robert Armour, coppersmith and plumber in Campbeltown (p. 104), were for townsfolk. Not all of these distillers would have operated in town, but many certainly did.

When, in 1885, structural alterations were being done to the shop —

then owned by Archibald Blair — at the corner of Main Street and Shore Street, Campbeltown, workmen found 'a still vat buried pretty far in the ground', and a secret vent leading up into the main chimney in the gable. 'It is supposed,' remarked the *Campbeltown Courier* reporter, 'that at one time the ground beneath the flooring of the shop has been a vault, where secret distilling operations were carried on.'

By a similar means the tenant of one of the divisions of Glenahervie was able to distil whisky in secret. Behind the dresser in the kitchen of the house a recess had been formed, in which a 'sma' still' was installed, with a flue leading off into the chimney. Also in the Southend district, some stills were operated in holes gouged by Conieglen Water between Machrimore and Waterfoot, before the course of the river was straightened about 1817, and the land levelled and cultivated. Others were operated in caves by the sea. Duncan Colville, in 'The Origin and Romance of the Distilling Industry in Campbeltown' (1923), mentions two sites in Glen Breackerie. One, at the junction of two small burns above Carrine steading, was revealed to him by an old woman who remembered how, as a schoolgirl, 'the sight of the excise officer ... with his cutlass by his side, struck terror into the minds of the children at Colinlongart School'. In a plan of Amod farm, surveyed in 1857, a 'smuggling bothy in ruins' is marked up Glenadale Water.

Sometimes a small bothy, or hut — roofed with branches, turf, and rough thatch of some kind — would be built to weatherproof the still, but frequently it was simply set up in the open, under a bank or rock beside a stream. On the seashore, distillers were able to keep a watch for Revenue boats. Experienced excisemen, according to John McCulloch in *Highlands and Western Islands of Scotland* (1824), could trace illicit stills by examining mountain streams for effluent, but stills were usually detected by the smoke. Calum Bannatyne was told that distillers in the coastal glens often went to work when the wind was blowing strongly onshore and gusting the waterfalls up into a fine spray, which concealed the smoke from the sight of Revenue cuttersmen watching far at sea. Jimmy and Maggie MacKinnon at Muasdale Inn heard that when an exciseman was about, one of the smugglers 'wid appear wi' his jacket turned outside-in'.

The sites which can be identified with reasonable certainty are those which were excavated from the banks of streams and consolidated with stone. These are dispersed throughout Kintyre, but are difficult to find for the simple reason that they were situated with just that idea in mind. No survey of illicit still sites has been done in Kintyre, and probably never will be done. There is now a lack of the traditional knowledge that could have eased the problems of identification. Angus Graham, in his 'Survey of the

Ancient Monuments of Skipness' (1919), mentioned merely four sites, and avoided treatment of 'the whole subject in full'. The example on which he concentrated was at Allt an Uinsinn, about 200 yds north-west of the Pier House at Skipness. The site was re-surveyed in 1968 by the Royal Commission on the Ancient and Historical Monuments of Scotland, whose revised findings I follow. The stream had been dammed to form a small pool, below which a platform was made, measuring 15 ft by 6 ft. The side of the platform adjacent to the burn is roughly faced with stones, while the inner end is bounded by a rock face.

The other sites to which Graham referred were, one in Allt a Chreamha, one in Gleann Airidh Mhicheil, and the other, in the bed of a burn, north-east of the abandoned farm of Lagan Ròaig. That was undoubtedly the 'wee squerr (square) bit, levelled oot', which Hugh MacFarlane of Tarbert discovered when, as a young fisherman, he wandered along the burn to pass a summer's afternoon. The skiff fishermen of Tarbert moored their boats by day in bays all along that coast, and no doubt in earlier times bought the Lagan Ròaig whisky. Indeed, Graham mentions — albeit rather vaguely — that 'the people who used to live in Laggan were famous as distillers of whisky'. A mile-and-a-half north of Lagan Ròaig, in Camus na Ban-tighearna, stood an ash which was called Mrs Black's Tree, after a Tarbert woman who carried illicit whisky there, concealed in skins beneath her skirts, and sold it to the herring fishermen.

Women were involved in all stages of the whisky business. Dr I. A. Glen, in her 'A Maker of Illicit Stills', remarked on the large numbers of women involved in whisky-making — of two hundred consecutive purchases of equipment detailed in the Armour account books, no fewer than fifty-eight involved women, either singly or — more usually — in partnership. (A hundred transactions involved men only, and the remaining forty-two involved mixed groups.) Certainly, in 1772, Pennant stated that women made whisky while their husbands were 'in the field' (p. 126). Some farmers apparently gave the job to maid servants and other 'inferior persons', thus protecting themselves from prosecution.

The 'Still Books' of Robert Armour are extant for the period May 1811 to September 1817, and preserve a record of the sales of stills and other distilling equipment. The complete still consisted of the pot, head, arm and worm, and could be bought for less than £5. Stills were usually made of copper, but tin and 'cast metal' products were among confiscations in south Argyll in the final years of the eighteenth century. Armour himself occasionally made a tin still, but the head and worm would be of copper. Tin was much cheaper, but corroded quicker. From 30 to 40 lbs of metal went into a copper still, giving the pot a cubic capacity of 10 gallons or more. There were evidently two sizes of pot, one with about 12 lbs of copper to it, and the other with about 20 lbs. Armour also repaired equipment, both at his workshop and at the houses of his customers. Worms were mended, stills 'bottomed', and 'feadans' fitted (the *feadan*, which is Gaelic, was the spout or valve attached to the discharge end of the worm). Armour's stills were in use over the greater part of Kintyre, and also found customers in Gigha and south-west Arran.

Many illicit distillers bought malt directly from maltsters in Campbel-town, thus sparing themselves the trouble of converting bear (p. 101). Four of the account books of one of these maltsters, John Colville, are preserved in the Argyll and Bute District Council archive at Lochgilphead.

Transactions with illicit distillers constitute two of these books. One covers the period 1814 to 1819, and the other 1823 to 1826. In the first book, 127 customers appear. Of these, the majority — sixty-eight — were women, probably because women, and especially elderly women, would have been less capable of making malt in remote and difficult places. In the second book, seventy-six customers appear, nineteen of them carried over from the first. Forty-six of these were male, against thirty females.

Many of these distillers were regular customers, buying all the year round. In 1824, for example, Flory MacTaggart of Knockhanty purchased malt on thirty-four occasions. Her usual requirement was nine pecks — priced from £1 3s to £1 11s 6d at various times, with £1 7s the norm — but on six occasions she doubled the quantity to a boll and two pecks. Some of her whisky she sold to Colville — in quantities ranging from a pint to three-and-a-quarter pints — as did many of his other customers among the illicit distillers.

Most of Colville's customers appear by name only, but seventy-one of them — spread across both books — are also identified by locality, and these comprise Appendix 2. John Colville died in the cholera epidemic of 1832.

It has been recorded, by C. F. Gordon Cumming — *In the Hebrides* (1883) — that smugglers from the Western Isles travelled overland from Rhunahaorine to Skipness in armed bands, their 'rough shelties' laden with creels containing whisky destined for Glasgow. The Ayrshire coast was a popular landfall of Kintyre smugglers, and John Lamb, in *Annals of an Ayrshire Parish* (1896), refers to an old West Kilbride woman who, in the middle of the century, 'remembered the Highlandmen having their casks of whisky from Skipness hidden amongst the whins, whilst they lay all night at the back of the dykes, waiting for carts to take them inland'. John Campbell has a long tale about smuggling from Grogport to Ayrshire. The smugglers were met on the shore by a native with horse and cart, and the kegs of whisky were quickly concealed under bags of corn. But one of the smugglers had an unnerving 'premonition' in which he saw 'a tall man walking'. He and his companions were soon afterwards surprised by five or six *gaugers* (excisemen), and their whisky seized.

From the mid-eighteenth century until the early nineteenth century, smuggling was rife. The islands of Sanda and Rathlin were the main haunts of the smugglers. Their vessels, built for speed, brought cargoes of spirits — principally rum and brandy — tobacco, tea, salt and other contraband to the islands. The goods were cached there until they could be carried to the mainland and distributed by vessels ostensibly engaged in fishing and legitimate coastal trading. That much of the overseas contraband was successfully delivered is certain — in 1789 a Customs record in Campbeltown referred to 'the quantity of foreign spirits poured in upon us of late from the Island of Sanda'. But there were many captures. On 16 February of the previous year, for example, 250 casks of spirits and thirty chests of tea were among the seizures from a vessel discharging a cargo in Carskey Bay.

Incidents at Muasdale

In 1829, the exciseman stationed at Drumore na Bodach was Alexander Anderson. On 15 April, Alexander MacPherson and Angus MacDonald — described as 'sheriff officers and constables in Campbeltown' — called on Anderson for assistance in arresting two men convicted for breach of the Revenue laws.

They set off north, but, on reaching Clachaig Mill, about seven o'clock in the evening, they were distracted by two men hurrying away with several loaded horses. Suspecting that the men had illegal malt, they entered the mill to see whether any of it remained there. The miller, Malcolm Blue, appeared and they asked him to whom the eight bags in the mill belonged. He replied that he did not know.

Five of the bags contained ground malt, one unground malt, and the other two undried malt. Anderson asked the miller if he had a certificate for the malt. Blue replied that he had not and that he did not know if the owners had a certificate. Anderson then told him that he presumed the malt to be smuggled, and that he had to remove it to the Excise store at Barr.

Anderson left MacPherson and MacDonald guarding the malt, and approached John MacMillan, farmer in Clachaig, for the use of two carts and horses. MacMillan and his farm-hand, Peter MacFarlane, accompanied

Anderson to the mill, and the bags were loaded into the carts. About a mile from the mill Anderson advised the constables to go on, promising that he would follow as soon as the malt had been secured.

On the main road, heading south to Barr, Anderson noticed three men running along the high ground towards Ballachagoichan. Fearing an ambush in the pass — which was 'very steep and difficult for horses to get up' — he decided to turn; but the unknown men also turned, and began pursuit. When they drew close he saw that their faces had been blackened.

The manse of Killean and Kilchenzie was near, and Anderson ordered MacMillan and his farm-hand to head the horses through the gate. Just as the horses halted at the manse, two of the smugglers leapt the wall and seized the head of the leading horse, while the third smuggler took hold of the other horse and tried to turn it round. Anderson ordered him to let go, but the smuggler swore at him and began to force the horse. Anderson struck the smuggler on the head with a stick, but the smuggler, calling for help, began to stone Anderson. One of his accomplices joined him and, together, they pelted the exciseman, who fled around a corner of the house and shouted to John MacMillan to assist him. But MacMillan thought the better of it, and his servant also stood by and watched. One of the horses was driven off, but Anderson was able to secure the other.

The Rev. Donald MacDonald was not at home, but his wife agreed to the remaining malt's being locked in the manse barn. Anderson then set off after the constables. Returning later that evening, he was met at the manse gate by a boy who told him that Mrs MacDonald wished to speak to him. She informed him that he had been gone only an hour when the malt was carried off by the smugglers.

Christian MacKeich, aged twenty-six, a servant with the Rev. MacDonald, said that an hour after Anderson left, the minister's seven-year-old son had come into the kitchen and told her that 'the bags left by the gauger were carried away'. She went outside and saw a loaded boat being rowed northwards by two men.

The Clachaig miller, Malcolm Blue, aged forty, maintained that it was the practice 'with people who bring malt to be ground to leave it frequently at the Mill in the middle of the night and when [he] finds it there in the morning he grinds it and gives it to those who afterwards call and claim it'. He explained that he retained a 'multure' (p. 123) from all malt ground by him, and that he never accepted money instead. He claimed again not to know to whom the malt belonged, but, being examined on oath, declared that 'he heard different people say that [it] was the property of John MacGeachy'. The nature of the oath being explained to him by the Rev. MacDonald, he was once again interrogated, and incriminated Archibald

MacLachlan and Malcolm Milloy too. He had also heard that James and Duncan MacIlchattan had removed the malt from the minister's barn, and that MacLachlan and Milloy had rowed it away.

John MacMillan, aged forty-two, farmer in Laigh Clachaig, admitted that, during Anderson's clash with the smugglers, he 'was afraid of his own life if he interfered'. The horse which the smugglers Gilbert Reid and John MacGeachy had driven off returned that night with harness, and the abandoned cart was later recovered near Beachmore. He had since seen Reid and MacGeachy, but remained 'afraid to challenge them'.

His young farm-servant, Peter MacFarlane, recalled that a man, whose face was blackened, had jumped the manse wall and whipped the halter out of his hand. The smuggler kept his face behind the horse's head, but MacFarlane had recognised him as John MacGeachy.

Catherine MacFarlane, aged fifty-two, the wife of John MacQuilkan — beadle of the parish church of Clate — stated that after Anderson had left, Archibald MacLachlan, Malcolm Milloy and James MacIlchattan entered the barn and were looking at the malt. She was splitting seed potatoes at the time, and heard a voice outside remark: 'It would be a good opportunity to carry off Kate *and* the malt'. When summoned to breakfast, she locked the barn door but left the key in it because she 'had no suspicion any person would touch the malt in that place'. Re-examined under oath, however, she admitted that the minister's servant, Margaret MacEachran, had without explanation asked her to leave the key in the door. When she asked the girl to lock the door, her answer was: 'Never mind it — there is no fears'.

Twenty-five-year-old James MacIlchattan, son of Robert MacIlchattan, cottar at Auchnacloich, claimed that he had merely shifted the bags of malt from one part of the barn to another, at the request of Catherine MacQuilkan. He had gone to the shore to get work shipping potatoes, but there was no work and he returned home. His elder brother, Duncan, recalled evasively that he had been stowing potatoes in the hold of a vessel, and that when he went on deck he saw a rowing-boat, but he 'did not know any of the men, nor did he know at the time what was on board of the boat'.

John MacGeachy, Crubastle; Gilbert Reid, High Clachaig; Archibald MacLachlan Sr., Gaigan; and Malcolm Milloy Jr., Gaigan — all described as 'smugglers and sometimes labourers' — were subsequently charged with theft. All except MacLachlan fled and were declared fugitives. (Reid certainly returned, because in the minute books of Killean and Kilchenzie Parochial Board the following entry occurs on 18 September 1863: 'Gilbert Reid, pauper at Clachaig, appeared praying the Board to make payment in his behalf of a pair of shoes obtained from Mr Neil Paterson, shoemaker, Barr. The Board agreed . . .'.)

In his declaration, dated 2 June 1830, MacLachlan — through a Gaelic interpreter — said that he now lived at Cregan, having removed (or been removed, perhaps) after seven years as a cottar to John Beaton, farmer at Gaigan. His age was fifty-seven and he was married, with three daughters and a son. He claimed to have been 'confined to bed' at the time the malt was seized, but his plea was rejected and, at Inveraray on 3 September, he was sentenced to six months' imprisonment.

An assault at Clachan

The reluctance to get involved in action against smugglers — as seen in the previous account — no doubt occasionally stemmed from sympathy with or actual involvement in the illegal business; but its origins were often in the fear of vengeance. The beating given to a middle-aged Clachan waulk-miller (a fuller of cloth) in 1831 shows smugglers at their most vindictive.

Dugald MacAlpine had the misfortune of having a relative, John MacIsaac, who was boatswain on the Revenue cutter *Chichester*. On 20 December, MacIsaac and four other seamen were on duty at Clachan. He invited MacAlpine to take a dram with him and his crew at Stewartfield Inn. After a drink, all but one of the seamen left MacAlpine and went to Clachan Mill to search for smuggled malt. They discovered a boll of malt in the kiln, destroyed it, and returned to the inn.

When MacIsaac and his crew left the inn, MacAlpine accompanied them to the door. As he stood there, someone told him that he was wanted in an upstairs room. He went to the room and found a company of drinkers: Angus Livingstone, miller at Shenikill Mill, Clachan; Lachlan Black, tenant in Laragnafiach; Neil MacCallum, crofter at Priestfield; Charles MacAlister in Clachan; Alexander MacAlister, son of Donald MacAlister, crofter at Monebeg; and Dugald Walker, the landlord.

Livingstone, to get matters moving, removed his neckcloth, thumped the table, and boasted that he could knock out every man in the room. Lachlan Black disagreed, and wagered a half-pint of whisky on the issue. MacAlpine, taken in by their play-acting, advised Black to go home, but Black turned his head away and laughed. Suddenly, the candles were snuffed out and MacAlpine was knocked to the floor and beaten unconscious. When he recovered, he found himself in another room. His persecutors refused to let him go, but while they were ail in conversation, he escaped.

Some eighty yards from the inn he was overtaken by Charles MacAlister, who caught him by the neckcloth and struck him on the face

and body. The beating was suspended when twenty-year-old Alexander
MacKillop appeared and remonstrated with MacAlister; but he would not
free his victim. He forced him back towards the inn, and at the bridge there
began to beat him again. When another young man, Charles MacMurchy,
appeared, the two men were lying on the bridge. MacMurchy immediately
pulled MacAlister off, with the reproach: 'It's a shame to see you beating
such an old grey-headed man'. He raised MacAlpine to his feet and then
held MacAlister. 'It was God sent you my way or they would have my life',
MacAlpine assured him.

MacAlpine was baffled at his treatment, at the time, but next day he was
told that the destroyed malt had belonged to Dugald Walker and that
MacAlpine had been condemned as an informer. Of the incident, Angus
MacAlister of Balnakill, a local landowner, wrote (to Daniel Mactaggart,
procurator fiscal in Campbeltown): 'I ... request your immediate
attention to this shameful and disgraceful case'. But Charles MacAlister
did not stay around to answer the charge of assault.

An encounter with smugglers

The following account, from 1815, describes smugglers proper, that is,
men who by their own evidence were concerned only with the running of
whisky from Kintyre to an undisclosed destination, probably Ayrshire or
one of the Clyde ports. There were five of them, of whom only one —
Donald MacMillan, a Dalintober fisherman — had any obvious seagoing
experience. Some of the others probably had a reasonable practical
knowledge of small boats, and could have taken an oar and worked with
sails; but their main function was undoubtedly to lend the expedition
muscle. One man can manage a small boat great distances, but one man
could not have defended a valuable cargo.

From the smugglers' own evidence, they took their boat along the east
coast of Kintyre and loaded, probably from a succession of places, about
twenty casks, 'some more than an anchor (anker — about eight gallons),
and some less'. Their destination was 'the Low Country', or Lowlands of
Scotland, suitably vague information from the mouths of smugglers.
Fatigued by a night's rowing, they sought the inlet of Port a' Chruidh to
rest and conceal themselves, by day, from the Revenue cutters.

On 6 April, a boat was launched, with four men under the command of
William Mason, gunner and boatswain, from the *Earl of Moira* Revenue
cutter off the Cock of Arran. That evening was passed at anchor in Loch
Ranza, where a shore search yielded 'some implements for distillation'.

Next morning, Mason and his crew headed for the Kintyre coast, reaching Skipness about noon. In a small sandy bay near Skipness Point they saw, by telescope, some sacks lying on the shore. They landed and found that the sacks contained barley. Seeing a smoking house in the distance, Mason despatched two of his men, with a pistol and a cutlass, and instructed them to signal any discoveries by firing a shot.

Mason and the others continued northwards along the coast and soon saw, rising over the rocks at Port a' Chruidh, a boat's sail. The suspicious boat was quickly got under way, and Mason gave chase. To bring her to, he fired about twenty shots from a musket — at first directing them high and distant from the vessel, then progressively shooting closer and closer to her, until he was sending shots among the oars. Her crew, no doubt beginning to feel uncomfortable, headed for the shore and grounded in a wooded bay — possibly Camus an Tobair — where people were at work cutting timber.

Mason followed the boat in and drew alongside. One man — an Irishman, John Barber — lifted one of the casks in the boat and ran with it into the wood, hastened no doubt by a shot which Mason sent his way. But the remainder of the crew remained defiantly with the cargo. Mason recognised all of them: James MacLean, tailor at Dalaruan; Donald MacMillan, fisherman at Dalintober; John MacIsaac, formerly farm-hand to Donald MacMillan in Smerby; and Peter MacViccar, son of the Smerby miller.

Mason immediately demanded the boat and cargo, 'as a seizure in the King's name', but the smugglers were having none of that talk. Mason, with one of his seamen, John MacMillan, moved to board the smugglers' boat, but, before they could complete the move, John MacIsaac jumped into the Revenue boat, threw MacMillan down, and wrested the cutlass from him, cutting his own fingers in the struggle. Mason raised his cutlass to intervene, but he too was grabbed and thrown down, by James MacLean and Donald MacMillan, who half-strangled him with his neckcloth. All the weapons that the smugglers could find in the boat were taken, and a musket and a pistol dipped into the sea to render them useless.

Mason then tried to remove a part of the smugglers' cargo to lighten the boat and tow her off, but Donald MacMillan raised a cutlass and 'said he would split [Mason's] head in two with it'. After half-an-hour, MacMillan, according to Mason, tried to break the deadlock with a deal. He would surrender half of the cargo if allowed to keep the other half; but Mason refused the deal, insisting that he would have 'the whole or none'. (MacMillan cited a precedent for the compromise, but Mason refused to believe him, and George Eade, one of the cuttersmen, later maintained that he had been present on the occasion, and that the whole cargo of sixteen ankers had been seized, at Toward, and that 'the only thing left with the smugglers ... was their boat to carry them home a distance of near forty miles and which was not worth twenty shillings'.)

Mason decided to send his crew to recover three casks of whisky which the smugglers had jettisoned during the chase, and which were floating in sight. He then went into the smugglers' boat, but they would not have him and insisted that he sit on a rock. Donald MacMillan and James MacLean joined him on the rock, and called for whisky. By the time his boat returned with the casks, he had seen, approaching a quarter of a mile away, the two cuttersmen landed at Skipness.

His crew restored to full strength, and firearms again available, Mason decided to force the issue. His plan was to tow the smugglers' boat out to sea, clear of a noisy crowd of woodcutters who had gathered, armed with stones and sticks, to encourage the smugglers with such advice as, 'Put the bougars to death!' The smugglers by then had been handed long branches from the wood, with which they thwarted the cuttersmen's attempts to tie a rope to the stern of their boat.

Becoming desperate, Mason 'ordered the colours to be hoisted', warned the smugglers that if their resistance continued he would fire at them, and lifted a gun and loaded it in their sight, demanding that they throw the branches overboard. But MacMillan and MacLean maintained their hostile stance, saying that 'they might as well go home dead bodies as lose their whiskey as it was all they had in the world'. They pushed their chests out towards him with dramatic recklessness, daring him: 'Shoot away! We'd as soon part with our blood as our cargo'.

Having but one cartridge left, and aware of the increasing hostility of the woodcutters, Mason decided to withdraw, and pursued another 'suspicious boat' which had appeared. That boat also proved to be engaged in smuggling, but carried only empty casks, which were seized and landed at Tarbert. The cuttersmen put to sea again that night and searched as far as the Kyles of Bute, but saw no more of Donald MacMillan and his crew.

The smugglers' account of events corresponded closely enough to that of the cuttersmen, but in fundamentals only. They admitted boarding the cutter's boat and disarming and assaulting her crew — the basis of the charge of deforcement laid against them — but their version of many of the peripheral incidents was quite at variance with the evidence of their adversaries. That is hardly remarkable, and the truth no doubt lies in the dark, inpenetrable gap between the two versions.

Routine investigations

These three cases have some dramatic impact, but the everyday lives of smugglers and gaugers alike were not so exciting. The correspondence book kept by the Excise at Campbeltown, from 1847 to 1854, discloses a rather more mundane state of affairs. A selection from the many investigations will fairly represent the excisemen's ordinary scale of operations.

On 3 August 1848, at a fair held on 'Tanloan Ferry green', four persons were found selling spirits, without licence, from tents. Four-and-a-half gallons were seized from Hugh Gillis, spirit retailer of Ballochroy. He was described as 'a respectable man and in moderately good circumstances'. He pleaded ignorance of the law. Janet MacInnes, Ballochroy Glen, had a half-gallon 'exposed for sale', but no proof of sale was obtained. She was about to serve exciseman Abberly, but learned what he was and refused. She gave her excuse as 'poverty'. Duncan Currie of Baycarr (Beacharr) lost an identical quantity of spirits. He was in 'poor circumstances' and denied having sold whisky. Margaret MacCallum, Tayintruan, lost two-and-a-half gallons. She made the mistake of serving Duncan Cook, cuttersman, with a gill of whisky, which cost him 3d.

In October 1848 a bag containing six bushels of malt was discovered among seaweed at Cleate, distant from any house. By December, the malt remained unclaimed, which is hardly surprising. It was advertised for auction, but failed to realise the amount of duty payable on it and was withdrawn.

At the mill of Barr in December 1848, three men were discovered grinding illicit malt. Two escaped, but Duncan Currie was caught and subsequently jailed for three months at Campbeltown. The malt had just been removed from the adjoining kiln. The miller, John Thomson, could himself have been penalised, but he claimed that 'when he gives the key to parties to dry grain they hand it about from one to another and . . . may dry malt without his knowledge'. He did not argue that he could not prevent smugglers drying malt, but only that he was not responsible.

Three tuns, containing about 200 gallons of 'wash', were discovered in a garden at Auchafarrick in January 1850. The garden was in Robert MacSporran's farm and was overlooked by the house of his brother John, also a farmer. They were the suspects, but there were six other houses, occupied by servants and cottars, on the boundary between the two MacSporran farms. The brothers denied any knowledge of the wash. Both were prosecuted on 6 March for allowing illicit distillation on their premises, but the case was dismissed.

Thirty bushels of malt — 'in operation' — were found in a cave at Crubesdale in January 1850. The malt was destroyed, the excisemen 'having no means of removing the seizure'.

An informer and two witnesses were all paid 2s for their parts in the conviction of Angus Bell, who, on 28 May 1850, was fined £25 for 'allowing illicit distillation to be carried on in his garden'.

Exciseman William Rumford on 4 September 1850 bought half-a-pint of whisky in the house of Donald MacLean at Westport. MacLean was in 'poor circumstances' and had no licence to sell spirits.

In the kiln at Tangee, leased by James Clark, remains of malt were found on 13 February 1852. Clark claimed that the malt had been dried there without his knowledge by Adam MacCorkindale, Clenegart, which his 'kilnsman' Bernard MacKillop confirmed. MacCorkindale, a cottar, did not deny the offence. His excuse was that he had 'made but a small quantity purposely to make beer for a delicate female'. He was subsequently fined £50, reduced to 10s.

John Thomson, miller at Barr, had frequently been in bother since his first appearance in these records, and was finally, on 28 May 1851, convicted of having allowed malt to be dried illegally in his kiln. He was fined £25, mitigated to £3. On 11 March 1852 he was again in trouble for the same offence. He implicated John MacMillan, a cottar at Clachaig, but MacMillan denied that the malt had been his.

On the farm of Driumayeon, Gigha, on 8 April 1852, ten tuns containing thirty gallons of 'low wines' and 120 gallons of 'wash' were discovered and destroyed. The farm was occupied by John Galbraith, John Smith Sr. and Jr., Archibald MacKay, John MacNeill, and Neil Smith, described as 'crofters in poor circumstances'. Four of them testified that the distillery belonged to Dugald Blue and John Gillies of Ballochroy on the mainland. Blue had been prosecuted on 16 December 1851, and fined £50, which remained unpaid. Gillies was 'a young man having no visible means of subsistence'.

Barr Glen was productive of many discoveries of illicit malt: for example, on 10 February 1851, twenty bushels 'in operation' were destroyed at a 'vault' on the summit of a hill; on 28 February 1852, fifteen bushels were destroyed on a hill 'remote from any human habitation'; and on 15 April 1852, four tuns and sixty gallons of wash were destroyed at the head of a glen 'between two and three miles from any habitation'.

Oral tradition

A great body of illicit whisky tales survived with that generation which has largely died out in the past decade. These tales were common in most parts of Kintyre, and demonstrate how extensive and inveterate was the industry.

When Donald MacCallum's father, John, was a boy in Gleneadardacrock, he attended Glen Breackerie school, and would pass Glenahanty farmhouse on his way there and back. The Mathiesons in Glenahanty made plenty of whisky, and would occasionally induce John and his brothers to take a drink of it on their way home. One evening, the whisky 'took the heid' of one of the brothers. He had complained, 'It's burning my throat', but was told: 'Drink it up — it's good'. He fell into the burn and was sick when he reached home, and had to be put to bed. His father — 'a very cross man' — had persistently warned the boys against overeating in the houses they stopped at, and, oblivious to his son's true condition, he beat him with a stick where he lay, reminding him fiercely: 'I told you no' tae be eatin too much!' (That story may be dated to about 1866. In the census of 1861, Donald MacCallum, shepherd, was in Glenedardcrock with his wife, Christina, five young sons, and a daughter.)

Archibald Campbell, who farmed Dalsmeran, further down Glen Breackerie from Glenahanty, kept a picture of eight stacks of barley grown in Glenahanty; but the Mathiesons' barley was evidently never sold — it went entirely to their 'moonshine'.

In a couple of stories, women figure as smugglers, taking whisky to Campbeltown for sale. The first, from Calum Bannatyne, involved a MacNeill woman of Amod. She had a jar of whisky and was stopped by an exciseman on Knocknaha brae. 'I'll take that', he said. She bent to the road, pretending that a bootlace was undone, and, surreptitiously taking up a 'big knappy stone, let go at the jar o' whisky'. The exciseman's evidence was destroyed, and he had to let her go.

In the second story, from Mrs A. Wylie, a Knockhanty woman was smuggling whisky, secreted in bottles under her skirts. A gauger apprehended her at Witchburn, and she pleaded to be allowed one mouthful of the stuff before surrendering it. He relented, and she spat it into his face and disappeared into a close at Big Kiln.

Several accounts of the thwarting of excisemen feature fictitious disease scares. In one story, from Adam MacPhail, two brothers at High Clachaig had taken a cask of their whisky into the house just before New Year, to have a supply ready for customers. One happened to glance at the window, and saw a pair of excisemen approaching through the mist. He cried, 'We're caught now right', but his sister was made of stronger stuff. She put one of the brothers out into the barn to conceal himself, and with a knife cut a wrist of the other and speckled her skin with his blood. She sent him

E

upstairs to bed and then sat on the cask and spread her skirts over it. When the excisemen knocked, she called them in. 'Any o' the men about?' — 'Oh,' she said, 'John's away tae the hill, an' Donal's in bed — he's got the measels, an' A'm jeest covered wi' them'. They looked, put their hats back on their heads, and withdrew.

To the concerted action of some Drumlemble women was attributed the recovery of a still confiscated at Knockhanty. A 'runner' had carried news of the seizure to Drumlemble, and when the excisemen's cart reached the village, on its way back to Campbeltown, a gang of women were waiting with their aprons full of stones. The excisemen had to flee, and the precious still was returned to Knockhanty.

In a story told by both Willie MacGougan and Donald Watson, a cask of illicit whisky, distilled by a man named MacKinlay, was seized at Upper Barr. The excisemen carried it to the 'hotel' in Glenbarr — now the village store — and then found a farmer who agreed to cart the whisky to Campbeltown. The farmer, however, let MacKinlay know of the arrangement: 'I'm goin away wi' your whisky at three o' clock tomorrow mornin to Campbeltown. An' when we leave Barr I'll catch the rope on the horse as far in front as I can get, an' I'll tell them aboot the witchcraft that's round here, an' if they're no' feart I'll leave them feart. An' you be in Killegruar Plantin, an' see if anythin can be done'. MacKinlay was waiting in the wood at the given time, and the cart and company passed. Along Patchen shore, the farmer proposed to the excisemen: 'I think we'll go into the cart for a sail'. They climbed into the cart, and the whisky was gone.

Neil Thomson had an enigmatic fragment of a tale, in which the most interesting feature is perhaps the reference to a smuggler who is also known from legal records. That smuggler, Gilbert Reid (p. 108), was being pursued, in the hills above Muasdale, by a gauger who was close enough to recognise him. 'Stop, Gilbert — stop!' the gauger was shouting, but Gilbert stopped only long enough to shout back: 'It's not the time!'

There were stories that Barr Glen whisky was sometimes buried in bogs until it could be smuggled away by boat from Carradale. Occasionally, peat-cutters would expose the remains of little barrels which were popularly supposed to have been abandoned or lost by smugglers. An old man was fond of telling Adam MacPhail in Skernish that there was a barrel of whisky buried across the burn from that farm. He maintained that the whisky would still be 'quite good', but of course it was never found.

Duncan MacKeith's father, also Duncan, tasted the last whisky made around Sunadale, about 1860. A 'lump o' a boy', he was sent to the hill that day and happened to see two old men in the act of dismantling a still. They called him down to the site and gave him a mouthful of whisky so that he could say 'that he tasted the last that wiz brewed in the place'.

The last illicit distiller in Kintyre was supposed to have operated finally about 1880 in the glen which forms the march between North Lagalgarve and Killocraw. That man, who lived in a cottage nearby, frequently carted peats, and would conceal his jar of whisky under a load. He was even known to carry it openly at times, suspended from the axle of his cart.

CHAPTER 8

Crafts and Industries

Until the seventeenth century, tradesmen were relatively few in Kintyre. The people themselves did whatever work they wanted done: house-building, shoemaking, thatching, spinning and tailoring, basketweaving, and many another job. Blacksmiths were always a specialist class, and, in any case, an equipped workshop was needed to carry on that skill. Weavers, too, were specialists.

The improvements that overtook agriculture in particular, and rural society in general, from the mid-eighteenth century on, boosted many trades and created others. As agricultural implements were modernised, the skills of the blacksmith were increasingly required, and as the standards of house-building were raised, more masons and joiners were needed, and slaters appeared on the scene. The agricultural improvements themselves created work for drainers and dyke-builders, for instance.

The range of occupations found in a country parish in Kintyre at the end of the eighteenth century can be illustrated by a list compiled in Killean and Kilchenzie: weavers — 38; tailors — 19; shoemakers — 17; day-labourers — 14; blacksmiths — 10; innkeepers — 7; millers — 6; wheelwrights — 5; house-carpenters — 5; schoolmasters — 4; shopkeepers — 4; masons, distillers, fiddlers — 3; pipers, sewing mistresses, boatbuilders — 2; and a gardener, ferryman, clergyman, and tuck-miller and dyer.

Farmworkers

One of the most striking characteristics of post-war farming is the scarcity of people on the land. The upsurge of mechanisation has meant that work is done quicker and with minimal hands. Most farms are now worked entirely by the families that have them. The thinning of the work force on the land has been going on for a century and more, but it is hard to imagine that it could go much further. The census of 1779 (p. 3) gives some indication of the density of labour on the land then, but it is merely an indication: only Argyll Estate farms were included, and female and seasonal workers not at all. A single example from the nineteenth century will perhaps make the point more effectively. In 1841 the small Leerside farm of Corphin — now deserted (p. 11) — had eighteen people attached to it. In addition to the farmer, Lachlan MacIsaac, and his brother Donald, there were three male 'agricultural labourers' and a young 'female servant'.

Hired farmworkers were, indeed, the backbone of the rural economy, and they worked long and hard. In the final quarter of the nineteenth century, the men started at 5 or 5.30 a.m., 'sorting up' the stables and the horses. About 6 they had breakfast, and an hour later were expected to take the horses out. They worked in the fields until 6 p. m. — with an hour at midday for dinner — and later still during harvest. After attending to the horses, they left the stables in a body about 7. During the winter months the starting times and meal breaks were much the same, but they finished about 5 p. m. On some farms, however, they were expected to return to the stables about 7.30 to clean the horses, feed them their oats, and bed them. Thrashing was done before breakfast, a custom which survived until the end of the century. On Sundays, all the men had to turn out and tend the horses in the morning, but at midday and evening one man was enough, and they took 'turn about' at it.

Female workers started in the dairy at 5 a.m. and began milking half-an-hour later. They finished milking about 7, and had breakfast. After mucking out the byre, they worked in the fields until 5.30, having the same midday break as the men. After tea and porridge in the evening, they milked again for an hour-and-a-half. In winter, the times were similar, but there was little milking to do and they often had spare hours to themselves.

In 1935, south Kintyre farmworkers were called out on strike by the Scottish Transport and General Workers' Union, and work immediately stopped on most farms. Owing to picketing, farmers' attempts to 'recruit labour from the ranks of the unemployed ... ended in failure', and quay labourers refused to load sheep and pigs on to the steamer *Dalriada*. But the 'crushing blow' to the farmers was delivered when Campbeltown Creamery workers were brought out on strike. 'When the victory became known,' the *Courier* reported, 'scenes of great rejoicing were witnessed at Drumlemble. The workers danced with joy to bagpipe music played by an itinerant musician.'

The strike was largely the result of the National Farmers' Union's refusal to acknowledge the STGWU as a union for farmworkers. The farmers were prepared to negotiate only with the Farm Servants' Union, but the workers rejected its organiser, Joseph Duncan, as their leader. At a workers' meeting on 20 August — three days after the strike began — Duncan was recognised in the audience and attacked. He had to be rescued by a dozen policemen, and a 'hostile crowd' — numbering almost a thousand — pursued the escort to Campbeltown Police Station, stoning Duncan.

The terms of settlement included: 'complete recognition of the Scottish Transport and General Workers' Union'; the reinstatement of all workers, without victimisation; all workers to be paid overtime at a rate of 1s an hour after 6.15 p. m. and, on Saturdays, after 12.15 p. m.; on the recognised Saturdays off — which were to be increased by four in the year — girls would be free to go immediately after breakfast; all girls engaged by the half-year to be paid £5 more annually; all milkers to be paid a minimum weekly wage of 10s. The capitulation was signed by Samuel Mitchell, secretary of the Campbeltown branch of the National Farmers' Union, at the Royal Hotel, Campbeltown, on 21 August — just four days after the action began. In his diary entry for 25 August, Archibald McEachran in Kilblaan remarked that the strike had 'occasioned much ill-feeling between masters and servants'. That was the first organised action by Kintyre farmworkers to improve their conditions, and such measures were never again resorted to.

The extent to which children worked — and were obliged to work — on farms must seem remarkable now. Their seasonal tasks can be charted from school logbooks. The book kept at Rhunahaorine from 1864 to 1876 reveals that scarcely a month of the school year was unaffected by thinning of class attendances. Potatoes were shipped in January, February or March, depending on markets; 'spring labour' extended over March and April (on 24 April 1874, the pupil-teacher was given leave to 'assist his parents in potato-planting'); in June, 'weeding' drew children away from school, and in July turnips were singled; in August and September 'shearing' was the excuse, and in October and November potato-lifting was going on (the attendance on 24 October 1865 was only eight pupils, out of a roll of about eighty). Holidays for 'feeing markets' — notably Lammas — and for the annual ploughing matches were given.

Blacksmiths

The pre-eminent craftsman in all agricultural communities was the blacksmith. His traditional role had been the making of armour and weapons, and he was favoured by his chief with rent-free land and perquisites. When the warring temperament of the Gael was suppressed in the eighteenth century — or turned to the furtherance of the British Empire — the smith's skills were turned increasingly to the service of the settled farming communities. Roads were being made, so horses had to be shod; implements of agriculture were being introduced in metal, or with metal parts, and these had to be made and repaired.

At the end of the eighteenth century, the smith was still receiving such perquisites as the head of a *mart* (fat cow), a cheese, or some corn. In Killean and Kilchenzie Parish in the 1790s it was noted that 'blacksmiths are paid with so much corn, a practice troublesome to them and the tenants both, and which ought to be laid aside, and money substituted in its place'. He still had his plot of land — usually an acre, and referred to as 'the Smith's Acre' — but paid for it. In 1794, the tenant of Bealochantuy, John MacIlreavy, was obliged to give the smith there 'two cows' grass and the planting of four barrels of potatoes' at an annual rent of £1 4s. The smith at Kildavie, in 1807, was allowed a cow's grass and 'the small garden up the waterside', in addition to his house and smithy, at a rent fixed by the Duke's chamberlain and payable to the tenant-farmers. Some farms were bound to particular smithies, but that obligation was evidently unusual. The tenants of Kilmichael East and South obliged themselves, in 1806, to 'carry their ironwork to the smiddy appointed'.

In the ledgers of A. McNair, farrier and blacksmith in Campbeltown, the full extent of smiths' work is represented. Many farmers around Campbeltown did business with McNair, but one example will suffice, that of John MacIsaac in Corfine (p. 11). Between 25 March 1845 and 8 May 1847, he took work to McNair on eighty-five days. November was evidently a slack month on the farm — in November 1845 MacIsaac had only one small job for the smith, and in November 1846 none at all. By far the greater part of the work was done in connection with the repair and renewal of plough parts. During that twenty-five-month period, four new socks were fitted; on thirty-three occasions a sock was 'laid' or 'steeled' (re-tempered); twenty-three 'feathers' — the projecting wing of the sock — were made and fitted; on twelve occasions the coulter was re-steeled; a 'reist' (mouldboard) was made; two soles were made. Sixty-four horseshoes were made or renewed, at times with MacIsaac's own iron, at times with the smith's. Graips (forks) were repaired, an axle made, a wheel shod with new iron, unspecified hooks and rings were made or repaired ... and other work besides (a small part of it unintelligible or indecipherable in the ledgers).

A few farmers contracted McNair to do specific work over a fixed period and at a fixed rate. Robert Templeton in Drumgarve, for example, paid McNair £2 to 'shoe the horses and lay the plough irons' from 22 November 1844 until 22 November 1845.

Every village had its smiddy, and there were smiddies, here and there, remote from concentrated populations (for instance, in 1890, at Smerby

Dugald MacCallum working at the east forge of Machrimore Smiddy, in 1962. From *Monuments of Industry*, and courtesy of the Royal Commission on Ancient Monuments, Scotland.

and Carrine). Five MacCallums successively worked the smiddy at Machrimore. The third, Duncan, a native of Largieside, died in 1903. He was gifted with a great understanding of horses and cattle — as many smiths were — and would be summoned 'when illness came upon animals'. (Incidentally, the distinguished veterinary surgeon, Dr Duncan McEachran — p. 62 — was the son of a Campbeltown blacksmith.) Archibald, the fourth MacCallum, was also a native of Largieside, and worked at Saddell and Tangy before moving to Southend. He died in 1937 and was succeeded by his eldest son, Dugald, who retired in the late 1960s. The earthen-floored smiddy at Machrimore — which is featured in *Monuments of Industry* (1986) — was equipped with two forges. One of its distinctive features was a horse-frame, or 'trave', for confining awkward animals while they were being shod.

Five generations of Bannatynes, in direct line, were blacksmiths in Glenbarr. That line ended with Hector, who, working to the last, died in 1939 at the age of seventy-seven. The last working smith in Kintyre was Hector MacMurchy of Kilchenzie, who died in 1981.

Mills

Querns (p. 38) and water mills co-existed in Kintyre, probably for centuries, despite repeated restrictions on hand-milling. As early as 1284, an Act of the Scottish parliament was passed to prohibit hand-milling except through stress of weather or in the absence of mills. Forfeiture of the quern was the penalty.

The earliest type of water mill in Kintyre was probably the 'clack' or horizontal mill, so called because the water wheel, or *tirl*, revolved horizontally underneath it. The wheel was directly connected to the top stone of the mill by an iron shaft, with no intermediate gearing, so that millstone and wheel turned at exactly the same speed. It was, as Alexander Fenton put it, 'a simple adaptation of the hand mill to water power'.

The site of a horizontal mill has been identified at Balmacvicar, and in the archaeological survey of Kintyre (p. 15) is described alongside a reconstruction drawing. The mill was housed in a small single-storeyed building at the burnside, but millstones and machinery have disappeared. The lower chamber, or 'under house', is quite well preserved, and at the inner end can be seen an opening through which water poured from a lade and dam, traces of which remain. It is unlikely that Balmacvicar was, in any real sense, a public mill. In any case, it is remote and inconvenient for any but a few of the scattered settlements on that coast; but its situation was ideal for horizontal milling, which required a small stream running off steep terrain.

The earliest records of Kintyre mills appear in the seventeenth century, but there were no doubt mills in operation earlier still: Kilkenzie (1633); Saddell (1634); Kileonan, Kinloch (Campbeltown), Machrimore (all 1636); Carskey (1651), and Kilellan (1659). In the valuation rolls for Argyll in 1751, the following Kintyre mills appear: Loup, Barneugh (possibly between Tarbert and Whitehouse), Skipness, Ballochgarren, Achaleskan (both Killean Parish), Laigh Barr, Tengie, Saddell, Raonadil, Campbeltown (more than one), Kylipol, Smerby, Kilchrist, Machrimore, Lossit and Pennyland.

Mills were built by the landlords, who recovered their costs by the *multure*, or milling charges. These were levied either through their own millers or — more frequently — by leasing the mills, just as farms were leased. Every tenant-farmer was bound — or *thirled* — to a particular mill, and into every lease was written the following clause, or similar (this from the lease of Corphin and Blarferne in 1776): 'They shall bring all their grindable corns that shall grow upon the said lands, seed and horse corn excepted, to the miln to which they are or shall be thirled or astricted and to pay the accustomed multures therefore and to perform the other services for upholding the miln and miln dam and bringing home milnstones according to use and wont'.

The multure ('mooter', locally) was paid in meal, usually a peck in every boll, which was a sixteenth part. The miller's servant, if he had one, was also entitled to a share, which was a 'maum' — from Gaelic, *màm* — or *guppin* (what could be lifted in the cup of the hands) out of every sack of the *melder* (the quantity of corn taken to the mill to be ground at one time). At Knocknahaw Mill — also called Killeonan Mill — the multure in the eighteenth century was one peck in every twenty-one pecks. The deviousness of millers was often complained of. Archibald Cameron of Southend heard the following little story. A miller in Kintyre asked his son: 'Did ye mooter that?' — 'I don't remember', said the boy. 'Well, away an' mooter it again', was the miller's answer.

In a legal dispute over thirlage between George Macneal of Ugadale — owner of Knocknahaw Mill — and Charles Rowatt of Kilkivan, in 1819, the evidence included an account taken down from 82-year-old James Raeside at Kilkivan. He had four acres of land there, and took his corn to Knocknahaw to be milled. In his youth, it was 'a black miln covered with thatch', and the meal was 'often spoiled with the rain and mice'. The mill was later rebuilt with lime and stone, and roofed with slates or tiles. Farmers were occasionally unable to get their corn milled there through 'want of water' to turn the wheel, and relied on the miller's advancing them a little of his own meal until the work could be done. Raeside once took his corn elsewhere to be milled when there was no water at Knocknahaw, but his own miller challenged him, and Raeside agreed to allow him additional multure out of the next melder.

All tenants were bound to help maintain the mill dam and lade, and to bring home millstones. Raeside described the fetching of a stone to Knocknahaw: 'Upon these occasions there was a great deal of work in pitching upon the best horses and preparing the strongest ropes for bringing home the stone, and as in his young days the horses were dressed with ribbons and a piper playing before them, great crowds of spectators used to gather ... to enjoy the fun'.

Andrew McKerral, in an unpublished manuscript, has left an account of the bringing of a stone to Machrimore Mill, Southend. After the stone had been finished, the miller got the tenants assembled to fetch it. Through the hole in the middle of the stone, a long pole — or *wan* — was inserted, to which horses were yoked. The ends of the wan were 'held and steered by some of the men', and in that way the stone was 'trundled along the shore, across the Conieglen Water, and finally to the main road and the mill'.

A rare — perhaps unique — picture of Knocknaha Mill, taken from a postcard of about 1900. According to the late Robert Russell in Knocknaha, a 'big flood in 1918 took aweh (away) the watter fae it, an they never sorted it'. It is now entirely ruinous, but the derelict mill-house still stands. Courtesy of Mr Murdo MacDonald.

These stones were quarried, in one piece, of local stone. Sites have been found at Ugadale (near Bruce's Stone), Rhonadale, and Skipness. Several millstones have been preserved, most noticeably a part of one at the entrance to Smerby Farm, and not far from the mill which operated there. In Southend, stones were hewn out of the rough conglomerate found along Brunerican shore, where, McKerral noted in 1945, a specimen — either unfinished or rejected — 'could be seen a few years ago'.

When, in 1817, the lease of Machrimore Mill became due for renewal, there were four applicants, including the tenant Hugh MacCallum. The highest offer, from Robert Colville, was accepted, and he paid 70 bolls of meal and £90 against 55 bolls and £60 paid by his predecessor. The rent paid by the tenant of that mill in 1636 was 15 bolls of meal, 1 boll of malt, 4 dozen of poultry, 6 geese, and £11 12s.

The nineteenth century mills at Machrimore and Tangy survive in good repair, and the latter is now a holiday home owned by the Landmark Trust.

Flax

Flax, as mentioned in Chapter 3, was grown on many farms. Pennant, in 1772, remarked that before illicit whisky-making became rife, 'the women were accustomed to spin a great deal of yarn (for much flax is raised in these parts) but at present they employ themselves in distilling while their husbands are in the field'.

Such flax as was exported — almost £2000 annually from Campbeltown in the 1790s — was in the form of yarn; yet fifty weavers in and around Campbeltown were employed working cotton yarn from Glasgow. At that time there was a lintmill in Kintyre, but most people would not take their crop there because of the high cost of having it processed — 2s 6d a stone, or about a quarter of the value of the stuff. The mill itself was built in 1792, and an associated bleachfield, for the bleaching and drying of the cloth, was established two years later with the 'encouragement and aid' of the Duke of Argyll. His commitment to the project was manifest in the exceptionally long lease — thirty-eight years — which he granted. That field was originally a part of the farm of Strathbeg, and was detached at an annual rent of £9; but Strathbeg no longer exists in name, and the whole farm is called Bleachfield. The industry was founded by George Langlands, land-surveyor, to employ his eldest son Ralph. In 1797 Ralph complained to the Duke that his house was built over the mill and that 'when the whole machinery is at work the noise is so very great that those in the dwelling-house can scarcely hear each other speak'. He asked for help to build another house. The mill itself was converted to wool-production (p. 129) some time before 1814.

John Smith favoured the expansion of flax-cultivation, and proposed that tilled land be 'let to the poor' to give them 'employment . . . in every stage of its manufacture'. He estimated that an acre of flax, when converted into bleached cloth, would be worth more than £100. Flax was sown in April or May, laboriously hand-weeded, and harvested by pulling it from the ground. The crop was then steeped in ponds to loosen the stems, and spread to dry before 'scutching' it (beating the fibres free). A wooden 'scutcher', along with a bunch of Kintyre flax, is displayed in Campbeltown museum.

Malcolm MacNeill of Carskey, in 1737, received from Archibald MacNeill in Muilbuij (Mulbuy, in Glenadale) nine pounds of lint, for which he paid 6d per pound. In the 1780s, eight farms on Skipness Estate paid lint — from one to two pounds in weight — as part of their rents. In 1816, Robert Wallace, tenant in Kilmory, described himself — in a petition to the Duke of Argyll — as earning his living as a 'flax-dresser'. The cottar class also had an interest in flax. For instance, Catherine Muir or MacIntyre at Grianan was leased 'a cot house, cow's grass [and] potato and lint land', from which she and her daughter were evicted in 1838, having failed to pay rent.

Ms Elizabeth Cuninghame with chemise made from Glenlussa lint. Photograph taken by the author at Bayvoyach, Machrihanish, 1987.

Flax-growing at Whitestone is commemorated in the place-name Creagan Lìn (Flax Rock), which is on the west side of the main road and a little north of the farm buildings. Midway between that rock face and the road are two circular depressions, once connected by a channel, in which flax was steeped. Further towards the farm are two smaller hollows. The crop, according to Graham MacKinlay, was processed at Lintmill.

Ms Elizabeth Cuninghame, retired in Machrihanish, has a chemise — minutely embroidered 'ET', for Elizabeth Templeton, at the collar — made from lint grown at Drumgarve in Glenlussa in the early nineteenth century. Her great-grandmother was Agnes Templeton, a sister of Elizabeth's.

Spinning

The production of wool and cloth, and the making of clothing, were almost entirely local industries, and little was exported. Both flax and wool were spun by the women. Prior to the introduction of the spinning-wheel, spinning was a slow job involving spindle and distaff, which had, however, the merit of being portable. Women could spin as they herded cattle or went on journeys.

The spindle was known as the *dealgan* or *fearsaid*, and was variously designed. Some were conical, others were made from a straight stick with a whorl — a circular stone, or a section of bone, with a hole through it — fitted over them. Whatever its design, the spindle had to be weighted sufficiently to twirl when set in motion by the thumb and forefinger of the spinner. As the dangling spindle spun, it twisted into thread the mass of fibres wrapped around the distaff — *cuigeal* — which was a wooden rod tucked in the crook of an arm. The finished thread or wool was wound on to a reel.

These appliances had become rare in Kintyre by the 1870s; but the spinning-wheel, which was introduced in the eighteenth century, was also going out of use then. Most spinning was done during the winter when the days were short and there was little to do but feed and tend the beasts. 'Nothing could be more cheery,' wrote Peter MacIntosh in 1857, 'than the whizzing of three or four spinning-wheels around a blazing peat fire ... during a winter night, and the beautiful young girls, with their sweet voices, chanting a Gaelic song ...' A romantic description, but no doubt faithful to the tenor of his memory. Children were usually given the work of teasing and carding the wool before it was spun.

Wool

MacIntosh remarked that 'the women were in the habit of assisting their neighbours with *luathadh*, or waulking woollen cloth'. Waulking was the shrinking of the cloth in readiness for the tailor. The cloth was first soaked in heated stale urine — collected in a tub at the door — to soften it and set the colour, and then the women, in unison, kneaded and pushed the cloth round and round a long table, singing song after song to suit the rhythm of the work. Water-mills for the waulking — or 'tucking' — of cloth were established in Kintyre from at least the early eighteenth century. The mill at Smerby was in existence by 1720. Dyeing was also carried on at these mills, and perhaps weaving too. Some weavers worked both wool and flax, others wool only.

The woven cloth passed into the hands of the tailor. Many tailors — commonly, and curiously, known as 'whip-the-cats' — were itinerant, and went from farm to farm, living with the families until the work was done.

At work, they could be found sitting cross-legged on the kitchen table. They took with them on their rounds not only needles and scissors, but also 'the news and gossip of the glens', and they were popular wherever they went. Many were musical, and enlivened ceilidhs with their fiddles. Tenpence a day, 'with victuals', was a tailor's wage in the 1790s. Women's clothes were generally sewn at home by the women themselves or by a local seamstress.

Wool was increasingly, in the nineteenth century, factory-processed. Some farmers in Kintyre sent their wool to mills in the Borders (in 1889 Archibald Armour in Broad Street, Campbeltown, was agent for Clark Brothers, tweed-manufacturers at Galashiels). Other farmers had the work done locally.

The first woollen mill in Kintyre — established at Lintmill (p. 126) — was also the last. It went out of production about 1910. Thereafter, the village that had grown around it — with a public-house and grocery store — declined and was finally demolished to allow improvement of the Campbeltown-Machrihanish road. The mill was powered by water from Chiskan burn, collected by a dam. It lay disused for some years after Samuel Mitchell in Dalivaddy gave it up, but in 1886 it was reopened by David Greig Jr. in Chiskan, who fitted it out with new machinery. The equipment included teasing and carding machines, an automatic spinning-machine — or 'mule' — with 260 spindles, and three handlooms. The mill was converted soon after to steam power, 'in consequence of the uncertainty of the water supply'. A model of the engine is displayed in Campbeltown museum. In 1905 the mill was taken over by Duncan Ramsay and once again entirely refitted, but its days were numbered.

In 1819 a mill was started at Auchaleek, under the name of the Auchaleek Woollen Company. The lease was granted on condition that the company produced 1200 yards of cloth, or an equivalent in yarn or cloth and yarn together, each year. The business was plagued by financial troubles and changes of partnership. In 1824 the company complained that the water supply was insufficient to turn the machinery for even six months of the year. The business was abandoned in 1844, and the tenant, Henry Paul, was allowed to sublet the premises to a company interested in farina-making.

In 1875, James Wyllie was advertising the carding, spinning, dyeing and weaving of wool at Muasdale Weaving Mill. In 1881, the business was still going.

Farina

The production of flour from potatoes — 'farina' — seems to have begun in the mid-1840s, which suggests that its purpose may have been to salvage blighted crops.

The few accounts surviving from the records of the Muasdale Farina Company include receipts for both 'good' and 'deaseased' potatoes (and, in 1865, the Strath Farina Works was advertising for 'damaged potatoes'). The Muasdale company was working in 1846, and its surviving records continue until 1856.

The mill of the Largie Farina Work was situated at Tayinloan and operated from 1846 until at least 1855. Its records show shipments of flour to Glasgow — for example, on 7 December 1853, 160 bags (20 tons) to Duncan McCorkindale, 49 West Nile Street. Both the Muasdale and Largie works were popularly known as 'starch mills', and appear as such in the earliest Ordnance Survey maps.

In 1845, John Lorne Stewart (p. 82) and Charles Munro in Campbeltown applied to the Duke of Argyll for a piece of ground opposite Machrimore meal-mill to erect a farina factory, but the outcome of the application is unknown.

The Auchaleek farina venture in 1844 was undertaken by three Campbeltown merchants, John Colville Jr., David Colville Jr., and John Galbraith. It was an 'entire failure' and was abandoned after a year.

In the late 1850s and 1860s, Samuel Mitchell operated a farina works at Strath. He may have taken over from John Greenlees, who, in the census of 1851, was described as a 'farina manufacturer' at Lintmill, employing five men.

Tile Works

Too little is known about the making of draining and roofing tiles in Kintyre. There was, in the 1840s, a 'brickfield' and tileworks at Drumore, Campbeltown. In June 1842, the 'largest kiln' was reported as 'not yet built'; but the tiles already made had been of good quality and had sold well. An undated trade-card survives of the 'Kintyre House and Drain Tile Work' at Drumlemble, but no more is known of it.

'Wrights' were usually carpenters of some description, sometimes specialising in wheel- or cart-making, and most communities had one or more of these craftsmen. In 1832, when the contents of the house of Alexander MacMurchy in Clachan were sequestered to meet his arrears of rent, in a small room off the kitchen a 'wright's bench' was found, with six chisels, four 'plains', two saws and a 'machine for turning'.

Thatchers — another group of craftsmen, indispensable until the late nineteenth century — are discussed on page 150. Shoemakers were often itinerant. In the 1790s they earned 8d for a pair of shoes, and got their food and lodging.

The Kelp Industry

Seaweed that is washed ashore on Kintyre rots in banks, thousands of tons of it, year after year. Except for gardeners with traditional ideas, nobody wants it. Yet, well into the present century, there was lively competition among farmers to get a share of wrack for spreading on their fields. Further back, seaweed was burnt to produce kelp, and contributed inestimably to the survival of many poor families on the coast.

Kelp-making began, in Scotland, in the early eighteenth century, and by the end of that century had become essential to the economy of most estates in the West Highlands and Islands. Kelp was used in the manufacture of glass and soap, and its great profitability followed the disruption of the Spanish barilla trade to Britain during the Napoleonic War. In the early 1820s, the drastic reduction of import duties on barilla (a seaside plant), the other main source of industrial alkali, compounded by the reduction — and final repeal, in 1825 — of the Salt Tax, virtually ruined the kelp industry. (Chemical manufacture of alkali from salt had been perfected by then.) Kelp-making continued, however, into the present century. In Kintyre, it persisted along the west coast — particularly around Muasdale — and evidently ended about 1910.

There seem to be no (available) records of the state of the kelp industry in Kintyre during its peak years nationally, but no doubt it was extensive and lucrative there as elsewhere in the Highlands and Islands where seaweed was abundant and labour cheap.

The first — and only — published description of kelp-making in Kintyre was written in 1859 by Edward Bradley ('Cuthbert Bede'). The location is a little bay below Glencreggan, and women — 'dressed in their oldest clothes tucked up to the knees' — are pulling wrack from the tidal rocks where it grows:

> When they have gathered a lapful, [they] carry it to the shore, or lay it in heaps upon the rocks, whence it will be transferred to the cart. The kelp-cart is made to perform many journeys backwards and forwards from the half-sunken rocks to the shore; and the horse plunges through the breakers and up the loose shingle,

Kelp-making near Glencreggan, Kintyre, drawn in 1859 by Edward Bradley and published in the *Glencreggan* (1861).

> scattering the bright wave-drops from him at every plunge, while his driver freely uses the whip and screams at him in Gaelic horse talk. Two other men attend to the fires, turning over the heaps of smouldering kelp, and keeping them in a blaze within their circles of stones, or in shallow pits, while the columns of smoke go up like beacon fires and are answered by hundreds of others along the coast ...

Bradley remarked that, although kelp-making had 'somewhat declined', the industry remained essential to the livelihood of many families. The season lasted from June until September. The main market for Kintyre kelp was in Glasgow, and during the season of 1859 the average price was £6 a ton. About a sixth of the value was paid over to the laird for permission to cut and gather the seaweed. Some twenty-four tons of wrack went into the production of a ton of kelp. Bradley rightly judged the money to be hard-earned. The women he drew at kelp-gathering (Fig 38) assured him that the job was a 'very sorry subsistence', and that they 'often got back home too tired to change their wet and dripping clothes'.

The documentary evidence on kelp-making is curiously meagre. The Argyll Estate might have been expected, in its leases, to have conserved that resource rigorously in its own interest, but there are relatively few specific examples of any such interest. In 1798, two blocks of sheep-farms — Inengoich, Inenbea and Inencocalich, and Borgadilmore, Borgadilbeg and Glemanuilt — were leased with the clause: 'Reserving to the said Duke all mines, metals, minerals, coals, planting woods, fishings of all kinds in and upon the said lands and the power of making kelp upon the shores

Kelp-gatherers drawn near Glencreggan by Edward Bradley in 1859.

thereof . . .' But the lease of Inenmore and Inenbeg, of the following year, has no such reference to kelp. In 1817, two farms on the east coast of Kintyre — Mid Peninver and Gartnacorrach — were subject to the following (more precise) restriction: 'Reserving also the sea ware or wreck growing, or that may happen to grow, or be driven on the shore of the said lands fit for making of kelp, and to build such houses and to occupy such grounds as may be required for the operations before mentioned'.

When, in 1856, the grazing of Davaar Island was leased at an annual rent of £40 to Angus MacDonald, 'flesher' in Campbeltown, Lady Charlotte Campbell of Kildalloig had this condition inserted: 'The tenant to have no right to the wreck or seaware along the shore except for spreading on the pasture, and the proprietor, or others having proper authority, to be at liberty to gather and burn seaware for kelp'. There is a kelp-kiln still plainly visible on the grassy foreshore at the ruined cottage on Davaar Island. Two years later, the same lady went to law to prevent Robert MacKenzie, farmer in Low Glenramskill, and Duncan Drain and his family in New Orleans smallholding, from 'trespassing' on that part of her land across which the track from New Orleans to the main road passed, and still passes. The action was contested, and, in the evidence prepared in defence of the right-of-way, it was mentioned that the first subtenant in New Orleans, John Ryburn, paid a rent of £14 in the 1820s, besides £4 'for the kelp made thereon'.

In the valuation rolls for 1876–77, the 'seaware shores' of Killean and Kilchenzie Parish — belonging to the Duke of Argyll and Keith Macalister of Glenbarr — were declared 'unlet'. That certainly did not mean that no kelp was being made on these shores; simply, that the industry was no longer lucrative and organised. Indeed, in the *Argyllshire Herald*, a notice — dated 12 June 1876 — appeared with the warning that '... no person has authority to sub-let the Duke of Argyll's shores for the present season, and any parties who shall make, or sell kelp made on the shores, without authority from the Chamberlain's Office, will be prosecuted'. In August 1873 45½ tons of kelp were shipped from Campbeltown.

A few kelp-makers appear in the census of 1861: John Cameron (43), on Sanda Island; Mary Armour (55), at Bulloch, near Rosehill; and Catherine MacLauchlin (60), at Muasdale village. There were undoubtedly many more people who worked at kelp from year to year in its season, but these three individuals chose to describe themselves as 'kelp-makers'. During evidence taken in Kintyre, in 1892, the Royal Commission on Labour heard that 'a few of the ploughmen's wives along the west shore added to their husband's income by making kelp'.

Calum Bannatyne's parents worked at kelp on Rosehill shore. He was born at Rosehill in 1900, and remembered nothing of the work, though he heard plenty about it. 'I wiz lyin in a crib o' some description, sleepin; an' the longer I wid sleep, the better for them. Whenever I wiz needin a feed, she jeest came along, had a seat — which she well deserved tae hae — an' gave me a sook, ye see, an' my father worked on.' His father had a horse and cart, and would load the cart with wrack (*barr-dearg*) and 'cope' it on 'the green', where Calum's mother would spread it. Once spread, she would 'turn it the wey ye turn hey, wi' a rake'. Other kelp-workers would borrow that rake when it was not needed, for not all had a rake, and worked instead with a long stick. The kiln would be kindled with grass or straw, and, once burning, would be fed with the dried wrack. Calum believed that his father cemented the base of his kiln, for easier removal of the solids, but I was unable to find any trace of such a construction on that shore. The kelp, when formed, would be removed and covered with a tarpaulin, or stored in caves, to keep it dry until there was enough to cart to the buyer at Muasdale. 'They'd be aafu' (awful) lucky,' Calum said, 'if they made six poun' any summer.'

He referred to the practice of 'cheatin the buyers' by mixing stones with the kelp. 'As long as they could keep the kelp in big lumps it wiz all right, as long as they dinna overdo it.' Consequently, according to the account Calum had from his mother, the buyers wanted a ton-and-a-half of kelp for every ton paid for. That may well have been so. In 1792, the Duke of Argyll was complaining that 'much discredit has fallen of late upon the Highland kelp from the quality being debased', and in Mull and Morvern 'a proclamation [was] made at all parish churches that if any person was detected in mixing stones with the kelp they would be prosecuted with the utmost rigour'.

There were, in the 1970s, some old people living about Glenbarr and Muasdale who, in their youth, saw kelp being made; and there may yet be a few who have such memories. Margaret Littleson, who was born at Dalkeith in 1881, remembered kelp-making on the shores of her father's farm until a few years beyond 1900. She did not recall women being directly involved in the work, but 'they'd be down with their men's tea'. The wrack was spread on rocks with a graip and then burned. Her father, Donald Black, carted the kelp to Muasdale Inn, where it was weighed and stored until there was sufficient to ship away. 'If they had any other job,' she said, 'they winna be at it, ye know. It wiz a long tiresome day for them, always standin over, feedin the kiln, keepin it burnin. We winna be goin near them very much, because they wir always busy.' Returning home on the road by Bellochantuy, she would see the smoke of the kelp fires burning late into a summer evening, as the men raked their kilns.

Bradley — earlier quoted — described kelp-kilns as 'circles of stones or . . . shallow pits'. The surviving examples which I have been able to locate are rectangular and narrow.

One, on grassy foreshore north of Dalkeith Farm, measured 10 feet long by 16 inches broad in the depression of the overgrown stone surround.

A better-preserved example, on the island off Port nam Faochag, Gigha, measured 8 feet long by 20 inches broad in the depression. It is largely constructed of upended slab-like rocks formed around a natural rock outcrop. In both of these examples, one end of the structure is open.

On the foreshore at the northern end of the Second Waters bay, there are two large well-preserved kilns. One is 27 feet long with a pit nearly 3 feet broad and about a foot deep. The foot-wide walls are neatly and evenly

The kelp-kiln (*làrach-feamanach*) on the island off Port nam Faochag, Gigha. The island is connected to mainland Gigha at high tide by a causeway. Other kelp-kilns can be found farther north, along the Croft Shore. Photograph by the author, 1987.

built of lime-mortared stone. North of that kiln, and perhaps originally connected to it, is a smaller one: 23½ feet long, and with — at 6 inches — a much narrower pit. These kilns are exceptionally well-made, and are the only examples of mortaring which I have seen.

CHAPTER 9

Building the Houses

To describe the early country buildings of Kintyre as 'natural' might not be inappropriate. The description would hold, for most houses, well into the nineteenth century, which, even in the scale of human history and prehistory in Kintyre, is not so long ago. By 'natural' I mean not only that the building materials were direct products of nature, but also that these materials were taken from the very environment. The stone for the walls, the mud or limestone that mortared the walls — if mortar was used at all — the thatch for the roof ... all came from the land. That explains why the ruins of houses out in the hills seem so much a part of the landscape. There is nothing unsightly about them. They return naturally to the land just as the corpse of an animal does.

This was more so with the houses that preceded stone-building. These could be built of turf, turf-and-stone, wattle (interwoven rods and twigs), wattle-and-turf, wattle-and-clay, or cob (clay and stone mixed), none of which structures would survive more than a few years' disuse. Small stone-built houses probably began to appear on farms in the first quarter of the eighteenth century. Even towards the end of that century — in 1787 — tenants on the Argyll Estate had to agree not to 'have any creel or wattled houses on their lands except shielings', and as late as 1824 the walls of one of the dwelling-houses on Kileonan Farm were built of mud and were 'only kept standing by being proped (*sic*) up with very strong supports'.

John Smith, in 1794, when he wrote the Statistical Account of Campbeltown, remarked: 'The country, at present, is infested with rats, mice, and other vermin, which when they have once taken possession, can never be dislodged from mud walls and thatched roofs. The introduction of buildings, impervious to such intruders, would be of considerable advantage to the farmer, by saving a great deal of his grain from depredation'.

A thatched and clay-mortared steading at that period consisted of kitchen, room, byre, stable, barn, and sheep-house. An estimate for building such a 'tennament' at Glen—le (name ink-blotted) in 1770 amounted to £24 0s 9d. These were the costings for erecting the barn, which was to be 20 feet long, 14 feet broad, and 6 feet high.

	s	d
side walls	18	
two gavels (gables)	18	8
raising and leading (carting) the stones	8	
leading and working the clay	8	
timber and speicks (sticks) and binding of two couples	12	
twenty-one speicks for rib and roof at 8d per piece	14	
laying on the timber and wattles	5	
fail divots (turves) and rigging (ridging — p. 149)	6	6
fore door with crooks (hooks for hanging it) and band (fastening for crooks)	5	6
back door	2	6
six turse (trusses) straw for thatching	6	
divoting, rigging and thatching	8	
£5	12	2

Tenants were lease-bound to leave the houses 'in a sufficient condition' at the end of tenancy; but usually the buildings needed to be repaired, for which purpose the incoming tenant was given a sum of money which he had to refund when the lease ended. Repairs were costed by 'sworn appraisers in every parish'. At Ballinabrade in 1770, 3s was the estimate for repairing 'ane cupple in the old Byer that is broken — taking it out, binding it again ... and making up the walls'. At Little Glenramskill, in that same year, wattles for a repair were costed at 2s, and a new couple for the sheep-house at 3s. In 1777, 2s 2d was the estimated cost of repairs to doors and a window in the kitchen of Altnabouduie.

In 1775, Captain Alexander Campbell, the Duke of Argyll's chamberlain in Kintyre, warned that outgoing tenants would not be allowed to '... robb houses of fixed furniture, nor glass or shutters of windows, nor door leaves, or by any means to pull down or take away the timber of biggings once built on a farm'.

Building

Generally, the people built their own houses by collective effort. They could start with nothing but what the ground provided, or they could use the stone of existing buildings. That instruction was often written into Argyll Estate leases in Kintyre, as with the 'mid shore division' of Crubistill in 1791. The tenant there, Peter MacIlchallum, was to 'pull down so far as not already done the old houses of the said farm and to erect a sufficient new tenement'.

Co-operative effort was quite often written into leases as an obligation. Thus, Neil MacNaughtane Jr., in North Carrine, was committed to building 'one half of the new steading of houses' on his father's holding, Mid Carrine, in 1794. In the following year, John and Robert Greenlees in South Putechantuy had to build fourteen couples of a tenement proposed for the North farm, but were allowed 'any stones that remain of the old houses after building the new'. In 1806, Neil MacCualisky in North Cattadil was bound to assist William Brown in South Cattadil with the building of his 'new tenement'.

Not until early in the nineteenth century are actual costs acknowledged in leases. In 1824, David Andrew in North, and James Cordiner in South Glenamuckloch bound themselves to share equally the 'whole expence' of building a new steading on the South farm and of repairing the houses on the North farm. In the following year, Alexander Maconochie in North Machrimore received an allowance of £24 towards the removal of the old houses, and their rebuilding on another site.

Time limits were seldom specified, but in 1795 John MacKendrick in the 'north high farm' of Killocraw — one of four divisions — was allowed one year, from the start of his lease, to construct 'houses, barn, byre, stable and other offices suitable to the farm'.

To most people now, such a commitment would be frightening. To these people it was simply work that had to be done, and which, for most of them, was well within their capabilities. There were some tenants who shirked even repairs, and many who built badly, but there is nothing remarkable in these failings. It is inherent in human nature that there will be those who are lazy, who are content with poor standards, or who simply resent obligations of any kind. It is also true that the system of short-term leasing — nineteen years was the norm — did not inspire all tenants with a commitment to improvement.

Allt Dorie House

Calum Bannatyne had a story about the building of a house called Allt Dorie somewhere at the head of Glenadale. I cannot be more specific because I have so far failed to locate the ruin, and no one of whom I have enquired has any knowledge of it. Certainly, Allt Dorie — the name does exist, belonging to a stream — was never a documented farm, and therefore never a farm; but it is quite possible that there was a smallholding of that name.

A man by the name of Lightbody was in love with a MacNeill woman in High Glenadale (Malcolm MacNeill was tenant there from 1829 till 1867, and a Matthew Lightbody, of Auchrobert, Lesmahagow, entered the tenancy of Ballebrenan in 1836 — but these notes prove nothing.) They decided to marry, but had no house to go to — scarcely an uncommon predicament — so Lightbody's father, who was 'kinna religious', prayed for divine assistance:

> An' it came a stormy night the night o' the marriage, an' on the glenside there wir a grett (great) landslide, wi' earth, an' it berred (bared) the rock, pure berr rock. Aa' (all) the earth slid intae the burn an' the burn carried aweh (away) the earth an' left nothin but the rock. An' the next night there wir a grett fall o' rock off o' this face, an' supplied all the stones they needed for tae build, aye, two houses. An' they aal (all) got about it an' carried thir (these) stones on hand-barrows up this steep hill an' up tae wherr (where) they wir goin' tae build the house, an' the house wiz built in that summer an' it wiz ready for them tae occupy when they wir fed up wi' thir fether an' mother.

Calum described the house as he remembered it — a ruin — and as it had been described to him by old folk. It had, he said, 'nae foundation; they jeest started on the top o' the ground an' built fae there'. It was constructed of stone and clay, with a division for animals in 'the high end'. There was no chimney to it, and the roof was thatched with rushes. Some fifty yards distant from the house, a circular enclosure was built.

The lack of foundation to the house is noteworthy. An accurate observation or not, the practice was general, according to James Malcolm in 1810:

> As the walls, whether dry or bedded in mortar or clay, are never sunk into the ground to form a more secure foundation, but always laid on the surface, it is not surprising that they should so soon and invariably spread out, owing generally to the great weight of roofs disjointing the timbers, bringing on a premature decay and making them at all times extremely dangerous.

In general, any building of substance would be founded on subsoil firm enough to support it, the top soil having been cleared away. For farm buildings generally, from the late eighteenth century on, as construction methods improved, better foundations increasingly came into use. But in unimproved areas, and for small buildings, this happened much later.

The earliest stone-built steadings in Kintyre would have been raised without mortar, that is using the drystone method. That class of building has largely disappeared, either through rebuilding or collapse. Later, a simple mortar — mud or clay — was used to bind the stones and to block out draughts. Later still, lime came into use.

Mortar

There were, of course, no definite and demonstrable transitional periods between the abandonment of one method and the adoption of another.

Remote hut — one of two on the site — at Earadale, on the coast south of Craigaig. The NW corner has been converted into a 'twinning-pen' — for confining lambs with reluctant foster-mothers — but the building's earlier function is unknown. The interior measures 15 feet by 9 feet, and to judge by the skimpiness of the structure it is unlikely to have been a permanent dwelling. The other hut, some thirty paces to the SW, is oval-shaped and measures 12 feet by 7 feet. These are unlikely to be shieling-huts, because a good supply of water was essential for cheese- and butter-making, and the only water nearby is a miserable surface flow some 90 paces to the N. Photograph by the author, 1986.

Lime mortar came into use for Lowland farm buildings in the seventeenth century, but seems not to have appeared in Kintyre farm buildings until the nineteenth century. Even then, it was slow to gain acceptance. John Smith, in 1795, mentions only clay and mud as the prevailing mortars, and lime merely as a recommendation.

In 1810 James Malcolm complained of the tenant in Largybeg, who was then rebuilding his steading: 'The walls to his new buildings are composed of stone and mud instead of lime, when at the same time there appears to be abundance of limestone in every part of the farm'. The steading of Laigh Gartvain had, however, been 'newly built on a very superior plan', using limestone from Ireland. The tenant, Hugh MacMillan, had promised as much in a petition, dated 18 August 1807, to the Duke. He and his father-in-law, George MacVicar, had, he argued, always kept the farm in good order, but the houses were 'long and narrow' and he wanted to build a new 'tenement of greater dimensions, to be removed a little further south, to consist of stone and lime walls, the present being built only with clay mortar'.

The lime mortaring of walls undoubtedly meant a great deal of extra work — in itself a deterrent — and was costly in fuel. Its use was, like so much to do with buildings, linked to the social and economic status of its users. Limestone was quarried and then burnt in a kiln. The resulting white lumps — quicklime, or calcium oxide — were slaked (mixed with water) to produce building lime. Pure slaked lime, from high-quality stone, could be used for interior plastering. Lesser-quality stuff when mixed with sand — the proportions varied from three of sand to one of lime, to six of sand to one of lime — provided mortar. Donald MacIntyre in Kilkeddan, petitioning the Duke in 1836 about the costs of rebuilding the steading there, pointedly remarked that these costs were independent of his own 'work of men and horses in driving stone and lime, and manufacturing lime'.

Wood

The one material which was denied tenants, unless they applied for it directly to their lairds, was wood. Tenants of the Argyll Estate were bound to 'take care of the woods and planting presently growing', and also, frequently, to plant trees around the gardens and barnyards of the farms, or, as directed by the chamberlain, on any other part of the farm. A hundred saplings were supplied by the Estate for planting. Once planted, the trees were the responsibility of the tenant, who had to fence the plantations from cattle and 'train up and take care of the trees'. These clauses were common to all Argyll Estate leases in the late eighteenth and early nineteenth centuries, but specific instructions were occasionally inserted. Hugh MacLiver in Laigh Remuil, when he signed his lease in 1795, obliged himself to plant an unspecified number of trees in 'several glens' which were 'adapted for planting by being well sheltered'. When, in

1791, Dugald Stewart took on the lease of Craigmore — then a valuably wooded property, apparently — he accepted that, at any time, three inspectors could be sent to the woods, and that if the trees had been 'hurt by cattle to the extent of £5' during the preceding six months, 'then this present tack is to cease and be at an end'.

No doubt these measures were, by most tenant-farmers, resented as a waste of time. No doubt, too, many disregarded the regulations and took wood when they wanted it, if they could get it. There is record, in 1774, of the fining of twenty-seven men for illegal wood-cutting in Kintyre, but these offences were probably connected with the making of tan from the bark of trees.

There were few 'environmentalists' then, in either camp. The motivation of estate owners, in their plantation policies, was one of profit. Timber was scarce, therefore it ought to be grown rather than imported. In the late eighteenth century, boatbuilders were having to import timber from Norway and Wales, sometimes at a cost greater than the value of the timber itself; and wood for farmers in Kintyre had to be transported '... sometimes fifty, sometimes a hundred miles'.

Shipwrecks were a frequent — if unpredictable — source of plunder, and much timber for roofing and for furniture was lifted from the shore. In 1815, the brothers Hector, Archibald, Robert, Peter and John Kelly in Mid Darlochan were implicated in theft from the brigantine *Saltcoats* which stranded on 15 December in Machrihanish Bay. The cargo having been salvaged, her hull was sold to the Coalwork Company of Campbeltown; but a few days later 'she was broke in pieces by a violent storm, and a great quantity of the timbers and planks belonging to her were drove on shore'. The company employed men to gather the wreckage, but others were gathering for themselves, and a heap of wood was discovered at Darlochan. When a warrant was issued for the arrest of John Kelly, farmer there, he incriminated his sons.

Couples and rafters for the roofing of houses were supplied by the Argyll Estate directly to tenants. Occasionally, however, the 'comprysed value' of necessary timber would be paid out at Campbeltown if a tenant found, or was asked to find, his own supply. Existing roofing timbers would, as far as practicable, be re-used, and this economy the Estate naturally encouraged. The clause frequently recurs in leases: '... His Grace the said Duke furnishing the necessary timber for the couples and rafters so far as the timber in the old houses shall be found insufficient for that purpose'.

Wood supplied for roofing was not always put to that use. In 1810, Peter MacMurchy in West Darlochan was threatened with forfeiture of his lease for having misused much of the timber granted to him, three years before,

Balinatunie, a fairly typical Kintyre steading of the early nineteenth century. The farthest compartment was probably the byre. The middle compartment was the kitchen/living-room, where most of the beds would have been. Fireplace and chimney are intact, and there are two large windows facing eastward, and a smaller one in the opposite wall. That compartment has been modified into a sheep-pen by the blocking of the windows and the rebuilding, in drystone, of the near partition. The remainder of the building — which was lime-mortared — was probably the 'room', a parlour of sorts (now entirely ruinous) which was sometimes fitted with boxbeds. To the south of the steading, on the other side of the track in the foreground, was another line of buildings, evidently unmortared, and now completely tumbled. A stackyard adjoins these. Balinatunie's desertion predated 1861 (p. 11). The rush-invaded rigs beyond the steading are visible. Auchenhoan houses are at the top right of the photograph, which was taken by the author in 1986.

for the rebuilding of his steading on another site. Instead of rebuilding, he had set about 'patching up the premises as well as he could'.

Some tenants went on with rebuilding at their own expense. Edward Armour in Glenramskill erected a barn and a stable using materials which he himself paid for, 'altho' it was agreed that His Grace was to find him rough timber'. In 1810, he was proposing to renew the roof of his house and to build a 'potatoe house', and he solicited timber for these projects.

Roof timbers

Until the nineteenth century, the usual roof support was the cruck-frame, which developed because of walling — turf and turf-and-stone — that was

The shepherds' house at Killypole (Lossit Estate), which dates from the late nineteenth or early twentieth century, abutted by the ruinous earlier steading. Killypole was deserted about 1955. Photograph by the author, 1986.

too weak to carry an A-frame. Cruck-frames rested not on the wall-head but at floor level or a little above floor level. The remains of two in a ruined dwelling-house at High Kilkivan were lodged three feet above floor level, in wall recesses. Each frame was in two parts, scarf-jointed a little below the wall-head. John Smith, writing in 1795, mentioned that the 'couple-side' — that is, one arm of the arch — could be formed of a single timber, with a natural bend, or, as above, of two pieces pegged together at the eaves. Already in Kintyre, he noted, that method had begun to be replaced by the method — 'less troublesome and expensive' — of resting the couples on the wall-head.

The value of wood, relative to other building materials, is plainly shown in an estimate of John Smith's — published in *The Agriculture of Argyll* — for a dwelling-house 30 feet by 16 feet, with walls 10 feet high. Even discounting the wood necessary for the doors and windows, which are not specifically costed, timber is the single most expensive article, accounting for £13 5s of the total £30, or 44 per cent. The cost of stone — the basic structural material — is trivial by comparison, and would not have even figured in the reckoning of a tenant who himself proposed to undertake the work, assisted by his labourers.

More detailed, but uncosted, are the timber requirements for two steadings, submitted in 1810 by Major Malcolm MacNeill of Carskey to James Malcolm. MacNeill had a complaint. While the sheep-farms neighbouring Ballimontgomery — leased to him by the Argyll Estate — had obtained timber from the Estate, he had not: '... I am altogether unable to discover upon what principle it has been withheld from me, as I cannot see the slightest shade of difference in the circumstances attending these divisions of the Moil of Kintyre; indeed, if there are any to strengthen the claim of one above another it is in favour of Ballimontgomery, as on the other divisions there were some kind of houses, whereas there was neither house nor hut in Ballimontgomery at my entry'.

He submitted an estimate of wood requirements there, and another for the construction of houses at Achinsavill, the lease of which he had recently renewed. Not only do these documents detail the amounts of timber needed for building steadings at that time, they also list the buildings of which a typical sheep-farm and a typical arable farm would consist. The steading of the sheep-farm, Ballimontgomery, was the smaller, designed to accommodate a shepherd and his family, with perhaps a servant or two. Achinsavill was to be built on a bigger scale, and dwelling-house, barn and stable would all require more materials. In both, the house consisted merely of a kitchen (which was the main room) and 'room':

Ballimontgomery

	couples	'rib and roof sticks'
kitchen	2	21
room	2	21
byre	4	35
barn	4	35
stable	2	21
sheep-house	4	35
storehouse	2	21
	20	189

Achinsavill

kitchen	4	35
room	4	35
byre	6	49
barn	5	42
stable	2	21
storehouse	2	21
carthouse	1	14
	24	217

Actual measurements of roofing timber are included in a petition, also of

1810, from Hugh MacMillan in Gartvain to the Duke's chamberlain, Duncan Stewart. MacMillan's implicit offer was that he would 'build stone and lime walls', but only if he got the timber he requested: 18 balks, 10 feet long; 20 'couple feet', 5 feet long, and 41 ribs, 7 feet long.

Thatch

When the roof had been secured and covered with turf, the thatch could be laid on. According to Smith's account of 1795, dealing with Argyll as a whole, the main thatching materials were straw and rushes, laid on loosely and tied down with ropes of the same materials.

Smith argued the superiority of heather for the thatching of farmhouses, maintaining that it would, if 'well put on ... last 100 years, if the timber will last so long'. Edward Bradley's references to thatch in *Glencreggan* (published in 1861) suggest the preponderance of heather. Describing the interior of a farmhouse, he wrote: 'The side walls of the room are not so high as a grenadier, and the timbers of the pitched roof rest upon them, and are all laid open to view, together with the heather that forms the thatch.' And describing a cottage: 'The roof is composed of heather-thatch, laid over turf upon larch poles.' But Bob Smith, formerly curator of Auchindrain Country Life Museum and himself a skilled thatcher, remarks: 'A roof covering entirely of heather is very expensive indeed, taking a long time to gather and prepare, especially in the West where heather is generally of inferior quality.' An underlay of heather thatch, however, did not require the same careful preparation as a full thatch, and was very common. A 'run-off layer', usually of rushes, would be laid on top and replaced at two to four-year intervals, while the underlying heather would last for decades. William Anderson Smith ('Gowrie'), writing of the Tarbert district in the mid-1860s, described the cottagers 'collecting ferns from the most precipitous places, and thatching their houses with them, in preparation for the winter'. John Smith considered 'fern' the best substitute for heather. A 'good coat, if well put on' could be expected to last from ten to eighteen years, an estimate which Bob Smith dismisses as excessive. 'Fern', as used here, is bracken — the common fern is useless as thatch. Bracken was pulled at its peak of growth — June/July — and stripped of its branches, by hand, leaving the central stalk as the thatching material. That was women's work, and was slow, hard and tedious.

The renewal of thatch was often neglected, as James Malcolm reported in his survey of 1810. For example, he found at Dalrioch '... the byres, stables etc. wretched indeed, requiring thatch and everything else'. At

F

A small decrepit thatched house in Kirk Street, Campbeltown. It was demolished c. 1900, and the site added to the adjoining Old Lowland Church (at right), which was rebuilt as a church hall in 1904. Strathaird Place is at the left. The 'needles' and ropes which fastened the thatch to the roof can be seen. Courtesy of Mr J. D. F. Colville.

North Putechantuy, he condemned the use of oat-straw for thatching — being a soft material, it has a very short life: two years at most — and the tenants' system of thatching itself: 'Performing part this and part the next season in a long range of buildings, prevents the proper junction of the new and old thatch and runs away with a large portion of an article which is of but very short duration, and would be better employed in the farm-yard'. In that same year, Robert Colville complained of the condition of the roofs on the farm buildings at Glenmanuilt. He stressed the '... impossibility of keeping the houses waterfast with thatch all owing to the low glen and constant rains, which rotts (*sic*) the thatch before the same is in use 6 months'.

The weight of rain-sodden thatch occasionally collapsed a roof. That was the experience of William MacGowan, his wife, and four children in December 1874. They occupied a single-storey thatched house in Shore Street, Campbeltown, and, as the *Courier* reported, '... were sitting quietly enjoying their tea, when all of a sudden, without any warning, the

A row of thatched houses at the Roading, Campbeltown, c. 1900. Courtesy of Mr J. D. F. Colville.

roof gave way, sending part of the ruins down among MacGowan and his family. Their state of excitement may be easier imagined than described when they managed to crawl out into the street with comparatively few injuries'.

Most country folk in Kintyre who were born around the turn of the century could remember thatched houses inhabited in their childhood. Indeed, William MacGougan was born in one — at Upper Barr — in 1896. John MacKay, in the Laggan, remembered seeing thatchers at work, securing the straw with rope hitched to 'needles' (sharpened twigs) driven through the turf underlay at two-foot intervals (Fig 43). The rope was further secured on iron pins fixed into the gables, and the 'riggin' (ridging) was formed of scraws laid edge to edge along the peak of the roof.

The brothers Duncan and John MacKeith, born at Sunadale, remembered several thatched houses in that district. Rushes — cut on hills and in some low-lying fields — were the main material. The custom there — as in other parts with a community of cottar-fishermen — was to hold the thatch down with a covering of old herring nets weighted along the bottom edge with stones.

Thatching was generally community work, but there were men who made their living from it and who travelled for employment. Irish thatchers found work in Kintyre until well past the mid-nineteenth century, and one of them, Hector McIlfatrick, composed *The Thatchers of Glenrea* song which is reproduced and discussed in my *Kintyre: The Hidden Past*. A few thatchers — both itinerant and local — appear in census returns. In 1861, for example: Neil MacCallum (55), High Street, Campbeltown, Robert MacLean (55), in Drumlemble, and James Kilpatrick (probably one of the McIlfatrick brothers), an Irishman lodged at South Carrin with the blacksmith there, James MacMillan, for whom presumably he was working.

Scraps of information on thatched houses appear in *Campbeltown Courier* reports throughout the late nineteenth century and into the twentieth century. During a 'hurricane' in November 1881, almost every thatched house in Rhunahaorine village had parts of the roof blown away (and seventeen hens belonging to Mr MacPherson on the Moss of Rhunahaorine were swept to sea on an exceptionally high tide). In Killean Parish, a storm on 21 February 1885 left 'large gaps in the roofs of a number of thatched houses'. In January 1905, a thatched house in Whitehouse was burned down.

The last of the thatched houses were, as might have been expected, occupied mainly by old folk, widows, and paupers. From the records of the Parochial Boards (Parish Councils after 1895) in Kintyre, many of these lingering cottages can be located. In 1890, £3 2s was paid to Malcolm MacCallum for thatching Widow Neil Stalker's house at Rhunahaorine, and an unspecified sum was paid to John MacMillan in Glenecardoch for supplying straw to thatch Christina Galbraith's house at Rosehill. In that same year, the front part of Widow Catherine MacMillan's house at Rhunahaorine needed thatching, and Duncan MacIntosh's house on 'Barlia Shore' was inspected to confirm that thatching was necessary. In 1891, the pauper John MacSporran — described, in the valuation roll of 1885, as a 'house-thatcher' — was granted eight trusses of straw for his house at Tayintruan (which, two years later, again required thatching). In 1895, Catherine Morrison at Lagalgarve received 5s towards the thatching of her house, and in the following year Mary MacConnachy or MacKinven at Rhunahaorine got £1 10s for the same purpose. An account for 15s submitted in 1890 by Donald MacKinnon, Closeburn, for thatching the house of Catherine and Margaret MacPhee at Diargalt (Dearg Allt) was rejected by the Parochial Board of Saddell and Skipness 'on the ground that the work was neither ordered nor sanctioned by the Board'.

Slates and Tiles

There is no record of when slates began to appear on the roofs of Kintyre farm buildings. If James Malcolm, in 1810, saw any slated roofs, then he certainly did not mention them (and it seems likely that he would have remarked favourably on such an innovation). The first reference to slates in Argyll Estate leases appears to have been in 1806, in the lease of Low Ballimenach (Kilchousland Parish) to a Liverpool shipmaster, Joseph Tucker (his mother was a Montgomery of Ballimenach). He committed himself to building 'a good substantial house with a slated roof'. Malcolm visited that farm, but remarked only that the house was 'in good order'.

Four tenants did, however, express to Malcolm an interest in roofing with slates or tiles. The tenant of Kilkerran — whose identity I have been unable to trace — proposed adding a storey to the existing thatched house, and slating or tiling it. He wanted from the Estate only rough timber. Edward Armour in Glenramskill (p.144) wanted to replace the decayed roof of his house and solicited both wood and slates or tiles. The two other tenants were in Southend, at Monroy and North Cristolach.

Slated roofs on farmhouses probably did not become common in Kintyre until the latter half of the nineteenth century. In Southend Parish in 1843, the farmhouses of the 'better class' of tenants were 'excellent and substantial', but the roofs were 'indeed thatched with straw'. By the mid-nineteenth century, the tradition of building with cruck-frames would virtually have ended, replaced by A-frame couples with their ends resting on the wall-heads. Many of the older buildings would, however, have remained in use.

The existence of slate quarries on Easdale and Bute, primarily, meant that slates were obtainable in Argyll at relatively low shipment costs. An estimate for the roofing of a storehouse and granary at Killownan in 1826 included the costing of the slaters' work (the slates, however, were to be brought from Jura). That building, 54ft long by 20ft broad 'over walls', was to be erected for John Breakenridge, who applied to the Argyll Estate for assistance with expenses, '. . . other ways he will be obliged to cover them with thatch'. The estimates, prepared by Peter Stewart and Sons, Campbeltown, are worth quoting in full:

Scantling for a roof at Killownan, 1826

Joiners' work (estimated cost, £33): roofing spars, 12½ft long, 6in broad at bottom, 5in broad at top; a 4½in balk to be fitted in the centre of each couple; all spars to be secured 18in apart, and to rest on a wooden wall-plate 9in broad by 1in thick; the sarking to be ¾in thick, and each board not to exceed 1ft broad.

Slaters' work (£22 10s): the roof to be covered with Jura slates shouldered with

Tile-roofed cottage in Argyll Street, Campbeltown (probably opposite Barochan Place), c. 1900. Courtesy of Mr. J. D. F. Colville.

lime plaster and attached with nails weighing 8lb to the thousand; the ridge to be formed of lead weighing 6lb per foot, at a cost of £4 5s.

Pantiles — a less expensive substitute for thatch — were never as popular as slates, but there was a reasonable demand for them in south Kintyre around the end of the eighteenth century and during the first half of the nineteenth. In 1777, a Campbeltown cooper, Daniel MacIlcheir, agreed to roof his house at Balgam Street with tiles providing these could be purchased 'at or near Campbelton at a price not exceeding two guineas the thousand prime cast'. (In 1810, thirty-three years on, the price per thousand was unchanged.) Campbeltown Town Council, in 1791, advertised a piece of ground at Milnknow, to be built upon according to a plan drawn by one John Maitland. These 'stances' were to be let only on condition that the houses were built with 'Tyled Rooffs'. In Southend district, the inn at Machrimore Mill — built about 1820 and demolished about 1890 — was always described as the 'Red Tile House'. There were also some tiled houses in Southend village, and the farm buildings at Gartloskan were tile-roofed. There is evidence of local tile-making, but it is very scant (p. 130).

Floors

Accounts of social conditions written by visitors to the Highlands require cautious handling. There is a tendency at all times to report on the extremes, which instantly catch the eye of impressionable strangers. The cobbling of floors was easily done, if uncommon; but to the extremes... Bradley: 'There is no quarry, stone, brick or board to tread upon; nothing but the bare earth, worn into irregularities of surface that afford so many channels and little stagnant pools for wet and filth'. Earlier in the century, at East and West Drumlemble, James Malcolm found, on each farm, the floor of the house mostly below ground level, so that even with 'the advantage of a constant fire, sometimes large, in the common sitting apartment, the rooms can scarcely be called free from damp at any season'. To reach the doorway, used in common with their cattle, the occupants 'during many months ... must wade through a sea of water'.

At ten of the steadings Malcolm visited in 1810, he noted the absence of floorboards in the 'bedroom'; and at one — Laigh Gartvain — there were no floorboards in the 'sitting-room'. These, it must be remembered, were not the houses of the poor labourers and cottars, but of the tenant-farmers, many of them individuals of some status in their society. At East Skerroblingorry, Malcolm attributed to the 'cold and damp' clay bedroom floor the illness of the tenant's wife. Previously a 'decent, hearty and healthy young woman', she had been confined to bed for several months after giving birth. In one farmhouse, Mid Machrimore, there was no partition between bedroom and kitchen (and neither floorboards nor ceiling).

'Comfortless and rude within ...'

In most of these steadings, people and livestock sheltered under one roof. The cottages were no different. In 1843, many cottars in Killean and Kilchenzie Parish were without a 'partition in the hut to separate the human from the brute creation'. Frequently, the only access to the human end was through the passage of the byre, which was always 'more or less nasty'.

These conditions lingered until the turn of the century. In 1890, the medical officer of Kilcalmonell and Kilberry Parish, Dr Duncan MacMillan — a grand-uncle of the poet George Campbell Hay — reported that, in Clachan, '... two or three of the houses are hardly fit for human occupation, the cattle and the fowls living under the same roof with the household and only separated from being in actual contact with them by two boxed beds'. His general concern was the insanitary state of the village, in which several cases of diphtheria — one of them fatal — had occurred. The proprietor, Sir William Mackinnon, 'refused to act in this matter'.

Two years later, when Henry Rutherford visited Kintyre to collect evidence for the Royal Commission on Labour, he found 'houses of a very inferior character indeed'. He described one as 'fairly good as to the four walls and roof, but comfortless and rude within'. It was 'divided into a shepherd's cottage and a byre, with but one entrance from the outside. The shepherd on entering turned to the left, and the cow and her family turned to the right'. (Rutherford was told, by an unnamed witness, that the country people were healthy, and that the healthiest 'lived near the cows'.)

In other houses, '. . . the uneven damp clay floor of the only apartment, the absence of ceilings, supplemented by bags hung across on strings and black as ink, the small ill or non-opening windows, the want of elevation above the ground, and decayed thatch on the roof, certainly afforded but too much reason for complaints'.

Rutherford decided to invite statements from the factors of two Kintyre estates on which he found such hovels, so that he might 'know the real explanation of a state of things apparently reflecting so grievously upon some person or persons'. One factor immediately offered the explanation that, when a small farm was absorbed into a larger one, its buildings were often left standing at the request of the farmer, 'to be kept up and used by [him] for his own purposes, wholly at his own expense'. Some of the buildings remained empty, but others were occupied by farm-servants or by subtenants. In other words, the farmers were to blame.

Until about the mid-nineteenth century, the arrangement of most steadings was arbitrary. Farm settlements consisted of clusters of buildings thrown up higgledy-piggledy over the years. Clockeel in 1810 was in four separate farms, but the steadings were 'huddled together . . . like an irregular village, and perhaps some of them very far removed from their respective seats of business'. Malcolm reckoned that the settlement occupied 'nearly or full three acres', and recommended its demolition and the removal of the steadings to an appropriate site on each of the farms. Likewise, the steadings of Largymore East and West were 'so intermixed as to create a vast confusion in the conduct of their respective businesses'. South Putechantuy consisted of 'a number of unconnected and unnecessary buildings, some placed on rising ground, others in holes'. Examples of these types of settlement survive among the upland farms that were deserted. Ballimacvicar and Innean Mòr are good examples.

Other steadings were built in a long continuous line, or in two lines

'... opposite each other, and so close ... as to form a narrow street'. Surviving examples of the former are common enough in hill places — Balinatunie, for one — and of the latter Corphin is a good example, visible from the roadside, though the walls have fallen.

The arrangement of farm-buildings around a central yard — which characterises virtually all Kintyre farms today — began before the middle of the nineteenth century, but the innovation met with resistance, and transformation came slowly.

CHAPTER 10

Hearth, Home, and Diet

In country districts, until the present century, the fuel was mostly peat. The main supply would be stacked close to the house, but if there was a suitable outbuilding — a stable or the end of a byre, or whatever — then a supply of peats would be kept there and continually replenished from the stack. That subsidiary supply, under cover and dry, eliminated recourse to the stack in wet weather. A still smaller supply of peats could be kept indoors. Edward Bradley, describing the interior of a Kintyre cottage in 1859, noticed 'some peat for immediate use ... piled in the right-hand corner', within reach from the fireside (Fig. 48). That was the *cùil na mòine*, or peat corner, which, in improved cottages, was furnished with a 'press', or cupboard, to hold the peats. More recently, the usual container was a large lidded box, placed inconspicuously, but handily.

The word 'focus' is from Latin for 'hearth', and holds, in that primary sense, the full significance of fire in houses. A fire is indeed the focal point of any room, and houses which are 'centrally heated' are poor places for people who have known the pleasures of a living fire. An open fire draws people to it, promising hospitality; it gives out heat, and in a cold damp climate there are days when nothing in the world could seem as vital as a blaze of heat; and, further back, the fire in the hearth was what cooked the food.

The earliest fires burned on the very floor, built on a platform of flat stones or on a single large flagstone. Later, the fire could be held in a rough iron brazier, known as a *grìosach*. That was generally pronounced 'gree-ach', and I have seen it spelled *griag*, which represents a less common pronunciation in Kintyre. In Bradley's description of 'the interior of a Highland hut', the fireplace was bricked up to contain a small grate against the wall of the apartment, but there was no chimney. That construction is, however, hardly typical of the period; indeed, in his previous chapter, he described a farmhouse fireplace as 'a low brick hearth'.

Fires usually burned in the middle of the floor, and the smoke issued from a hole in the thatch. Latterly, no doubt modelled on the chimneys of the more substantial and modern houses, a metal pipe could be fitted into the hole, projecting a foot or more above and below the thatch. But that fitting did little to thin the smoky atmosphere of the houses: 'On calm days

156

the smoke was not unsuccessful in making its way out at this aperture, but on windy days, and especially with certain airts of the wind, it had no escape, and gathered in the room till everything was in a darkness that might almost be felt'. Bradley complained of a 'suffocating smoke' that caught his breath and made his eyes smart. The roofing timbers of these houses would get so blackened by the smoke of years that they would shine. An Ayrshire girl, some time in the nineteenth century, had occasion to visit the farm of Brunerican shortly after arriving in Kintyre. She was so impressed with the appearance of the roof interior that she asked, quite seriously, 'how they managed to get it so nicely coal-tarred as that'.

Chimneys

Chimneys were undoubtedly introduced to farm buildings in Kintyre over a long period, but the innovation is nowhere mentioned in any document that I have seen. Most steadings built or rebuilt from the early decades of the nineteenth century on, probably had a chimney or two, and the idea no doubt took hold first in the more prosperous low-lying districts. Farms which were abandoned to sheep or in the trend of amalgamation in the late eighteenth and early nineteenth centuries lack chimneys. Thus, Balnabraid has a chimney (Fig. 4), but Glenmurril — its smaller neighbour across the glen, deserted earlier — has not. Likewise, the innovation arrived too late to affect the structure of the dwelling-houses between Machrihanish and the Mull. These old chimneys are often — literally — worth looking into, for the hidden craftsmanship in the formation of the vents. In some chimneys may still be found an iron bolt fixed into the stonework and projecting from the outer gable face to the inner (for example, in the east-facing gable of Gleneadardacrock). That bolt, which is concealed within the chimney, supported the pot-chain, or *slabhraidh* (illustrated in Figs. 47 and 48). The height of the pot-hook above the fire could be adjusted — to lessen or increase heat — by raising or lowering it a link on the chain. I. F. Grant, in *Highland Folk Ways*, remarked that the size of the pot-chain 'gave a good idea of the owner's financial position because iron had to be bought and its use was a luxury'. She acquired a 'particularly heavy one' from Kintyre.

Chimneys were cleaned using a brush made from heather clumps lashed tightly together, with a hazel rod to force it up. As the houses were low — one could put a hand on the eaves without stretching — a single rod was usually sufficient, but if extra length was needed, then another rod could be tied on.

A brick-sided fireplace from the latter half of the nineteenth century, of the type which replaced the earliest gable fireplace — simply a lintel-topped recess (as in Fig 4). This example is unusual, however, in that there is no recess, there being no inbuilt gable chimney. It was built as a projecting hearth for the installation — c. 1880 — of a small range, which is now almost buried by debris. This steading — Killypole, opposite Calliburn road-end — almost certainly had an open fire in the middle of the floor when it was built. Photograph by the author, 1987.

Chimneyless houses were occupied, especially in the upland parts of Kintyre, until close to the end of the nineteenth century. Kate MacWilliam's mother, Flora Morrison — born at Bellochantuy in 1876 — remembered being taken as a girl to visit an old shepherd, MacKinlay, and his wife at Savannach (above Lagalgarve), and being fascinated by the fire that burned in the middle of the floor.

In the houses of some of the very poor folk in Southend Parish, a brazier was set against a wall, but, without a vent, 'the smoke nuisance was as great as ever'. That compromise persisted almost to the close of the century. There were, indeed, some people who opposed the innovation. Andrew McKerral heard the argument that the introduction of chimneys — in houses that were still being built to low standards of ventilation — prevented the 'free entry of air' which the hole in the thatch had facilitated, and was the cause of general ill health, and, in particular, tuberculosis.

A farmhouse kitchen, drawn by Edward Bradley in 1859, and published in *Glencreggan*.

Furnishings

Bradley visited and described, in his *Glencreggan*, two houses — one a farmhouse and the other a cottage, both in the Glenbarr district. But some caution is necessary in looking at these accounts, because standards of housing unquestionably varied from one locality to another. In south Kintyre, with its rich farmlands and its progressive Lowland stock, standards would have been higher. Whatever Bradley's deficiencies as an historian — in short, he is unreliable — his eye for the details of the immediate human scene was meticulous.

The farmhouse he dismissed as 'a long shed of bullock-hovels'. Having entered it, he found himself looking into the byre. At the end of an 'earthy passage', he reached the smoky main room, where hens were 'strutting about the floor, scratching in the dirt'. Two small windows, facing each other in the low walls, admitted 'a scanty light ... through their smoked and dirty panes'. An entire wall, except for a small doorway, was taken up by four crudely enclosed box-beds, with bedding heaped on them. Over the peat fire, which had 'moulded into a red-hot cake', hung a massive lidded cauldron. Furniture was elementary: a *kist* (chest), an *ambrie* (wooden cupboard), an old dresser decorated with plates and jugs, and a chair and a three-legged stool at the fireside. At one end of the hearth, a second low stool was occupied by an old woman working a spinning-wheel.

Bradley was afterwards invited into the *spence*, a parlour of sorts reserved for special occasions and visitors. That room was built 'a step higher' than the other room, by the boarding of the floor. It differed from the common room in having a big window which could be opened, a plastered ceiling, and a fireplace 'after the new and improved fashion' (unfortunately not described). Arranged on the mantelpiece were china ornaments of 'Uncle Tom and Eva, Prince Albert, and a dog of doubtful species, together with a shepherdess in a dress of sea shells, and a small basket made of card and ribbon'. Over the mantelpiece hung a mirror, and the furniture — kept polished to a sheen — consisted of a mahogany table, a chest of drawers topped by a writing-desk, chairs, and an enormous four-poster bed, evidently unslept in and covered with 'snowy linen and a smart patchwork counterpane'. He noted the titles of nine books laid on the chest of drawers. A Bible and a copy of *Moore's Almanac* alone would be recognised now. The remainder were now-obscure religious tracts.

The cottage which Bradley visited was one of a row of three. Each had a single door and two facing windows about a foot square, 'not made to open'. He remarked: 'Almost as much light streams from the chimney as through the small dirty windows.' Beds were boxed along one wall. A table, two chairs, a low stool, a dresser holding mugs and crockery, and a spinning-wheel completed the furnishings of the room. The floor was earthen and the 'wattled walls [were] uneven, cracked, and foul with dirt'. Strings of 'smoked herrings' (dried saithe, more likely) hung from the walls, and 'very unpleasant evidences of poultry [were] liberally strewed — together with other abominations — over the floor, and even the beds'.

Inventories of house contents, sequestered for public auction, provide valuable information on the possessions of the ordinary folk. An examination of six such lists, from Clachan in 1832, shows that each house contained: a dresser holding plates — eighteen was the maximum — bowls and cans, in the kitchen; from one to three beds, in kitchen and room, some with chaff mattresses, all with two blankets and a cover; a number of chairs and stools. All but one house contained one or more chests, large and small; two contained a spinning-wheel, and one contained two spinning-wheels; a 'craddle' was found in three houses. One house had both a fir and a mahogany table, and another house a fir table only — the others lacked tables. There were also pots and water-stoups (wooden buckets, usually narrow-mouthed for carrying water from the well). Articles recorded

'Interior of a West Highland Cottage, Cantyre', drawn in 1859 by Edward Bradley, and published in *Glencreggan*.

singly included: candlestick, form, tea-kettle, tea-pot, beef-barrel, *boyne* (tub), wooden pail, mahogany chest of drawers, corner cupboard and *press* (wall cupboard).

In 1838, the goods of Alexander Brolochan, cottar in Arinascavach, were publicly auctioned to settle his arrears of rent — £3 10s for a house and grass. His saleable effects — which fetched £4 10s 11d — were an old bed, two old chairs, an old fir chest, a dresser, an old cart with an iron axletree, and a dun mare.

Much furniture was homemade, usually from driftwood. Sandy Helm's first kitchen-table, after his marriage, was made from driftwood: 'ash boards' formed the top of it. Willie Todd, while shepherding at Auchenhoan, made a straight-backed wooden chair. He had a habit of rocking it on the back legs, and, occasionally, in the passion of a tale, would upset it dramatically. When I visited Donald MacDonald at Ardminish, Gigha, he showed me a bench which his father had made from wood that came ashore, in August 1885, from the wreck of the steamer *Staffa* on Càth Sgeir, west of the island.

Mattresses were usually of straw or chaff. *Battles* (bundles) of straw would be covered with rough homespun cloth, tucked in at the ends and sides, and 'shaken up' daily. 'These,' an old man remembered in 1933, 'far from being uncomfortable or insanitary, were the softest and sweetest beds that ever I lay on. The straw was renewed from time to time, and even at this distance I can recall the fragrance and sense of cleanliness and comfort of the freshly renewed bedding.' Later, chaff was substituted as stuffing and formed a firmer bed. These mattresses were refilled only once a year, at springtime. For a few days after renewal, they would be a 'mighty height', but the chaff gradually subsided under the sleeper's weight.

Lighting

For such as I, reared in a house that was electrically lighted, it is hard to imagine just how gloomy the old houses must have been. A sudden power-cut that occasions fumbling for candles or paraffin-lamps has merely the charm of novelty. Rooms become cosier, and a sense of intimacy and exciting uncertainty bonds even strangers meeting in streets and stairways, but that brief darkness hardly engenders an understanding of how life must have been in the nights of our ancestors. Walking country roads in darkness, it is perhaps easier to understand why superstition burdened their minds, and why an evening of ghost story-telling put fear into listeners and stalled them until others would accompany them on the way home.

Fire in the hearth will radiate light, but not enough to let people function by. The traditional lamp was the *cruisie*, made from iron or tin. It was formed of two small oil-pans, one fitted above the other, into which were laid wicks of rush-pith. Two lengths of pith — got by skinning common rushes — were reckoned sufficient, but on special occasions four would be used, 'and even then the illumination was dismal'. Few of the old people that I spoke with in the 1970s had much to say about cruisies. None had ever seen them in use, and none could tell me what kind of oil was used in them, but it was most likely fish-oil, as was customary farther north, on Lochfyneside, and throughout the islands and coastal settlements of the west. The livers of saithe, pollack and cod — primarily — would be flung into a jar and left. If allowed to rot sufficiently and properly boiled, the oil was surprisingly odourless. Otherwise, the result was little flame, much smoke, and a very bad smell. The paraffin-lamp largely superseded cruisies in Kintyre about 1860.

Homemade tallow candles were well-remembered, not least for the stink they gave off. These were made by boiling and skimming mutton fat — usually cut from sheep found dead with braxy (p. 167) — and pouring it into metal moulds. The wick, which was usually common string, was held in place by tying it to a wooden cross-piece. After the fat had set, the moulds

One of the cruisies on display at Campbeltown Museum. The lower pan measures 6¼in long by 3½in broad. The upper pan has an identical breadth, but is a ¾in shorter. The upright handle — which is 5½in long — has a hooked attachment for hanging the lamp. Photographs by the author, courtesy of Argyll and Bute District Libraries.

were either warmed or dipped in hot water, and the candles would emerge. The moulds could be formed singly, but most combined from two to five containers.

The oldest and handiest outdoor light was simply a burning peat, lifted in tongs, from the fire; but the bearer would sensibly keep well clear of haystacks and the like. A candle inside a glass jar could serve as a lamp, and, as an elaboration of that, lanterns were made from transparent whisky bottles. String would be tied around the bottle, just above the base, and then soaked with paraffin and set alight. After the string had burned a while, the base would separate cleanly with the knock of a hammer (according to theory, anyway). A candle would be stuck into the neck of the bottle, but within the bottle, and the lamp carried around on a string.

Diet

'Diet', as it is now understood — that is, unlimited choice of food, and even virtuous abstinence from certain kinds of food — would have been entirely incomprehensible to most people in any generation born before the middle of this century. Most people had often too little to eat, and many periodically starved.

The matter of diet at the end of the eighteenth century was neatly summarised by John Smith in his *Agriculture of Argyll*:

> Those who have large possessions live well; those who have small ones live poorly. The small farmers, for nine or ten months in the year, make generally two, and sometimes three meals a day of potatoes, with herrings or milk. Such as can afford it salt a cow in winter, and kill a sheep or two in harvest. Oatmeal pottage (porridge) or oatmeal jelly (sowens), make commonly the third meal a day, with milk; and oaten or bear bread, when the potatoes fail, supply their place.

In Kintyre, alone in all Argyll, it was customary to 'take some thin pottage, or a little bread and milk, before they begin work in the morning; and after dinner, should it even be potatoes and herring, or flesh and broth, they have commonly a little bread and milk, by way of dessert or supplement'.

Potatoes

As Smith's account shows, by the end of the eighteenth century potatoes formed the staple diet of the people, and dominated most meals. Often, indeed, a meal would consist of little but potatoes. 'If,' wrote James MacArthur, minister of Kilcalmonell and Kilberry, in 1843, 'the [cottagers] can command a meal or two of potatoes per diem, their ambition goes no higher'. The periodic failures of the potato crop naturally opened the dependent population to great hunger and suffering (nowhere more devastating than in Ireland in the 1840s). In Campbeltown, in 1816, the town council initiated, with £100, a public fund for the relief of the 'poor inhabitants and labourers of the town ... their being in want of potatoes from the scarcity of that article in the country this season'. In 1831, following another crop failure, the council purchased 200 bolls of seed potatoes for distribution to the poor. In Kintyre, by the late nineteenth century, land and manure sufficient to grow about a ton of potatoes were generally granted to farm-servants by their employers.

Meal

The second most important food was oatmeal, relegated from first place some time after the middle of the eighteenth century after the appearance of potatoes. The following account, from 1848, will show what meal meant to the poorest people in the absence of potatoes. It is an extreme example, admittedly, but no less useful for that. Margaret Bruce had the misfortune of being married to an habitual wife-beater, John MacDonald. She lived with him and four of their children at Ballochantuie. He worked at harvesting and also at kelp, but 'to encourage him to work' she had to 'accompany him and work as much as he did'.

On the morning of Monday 17 July, 'there was no food of any kind in the house'. MacDonald gave his wife four shillings, with which she bought two stones of meal and a little tea and sugar. The family got breakfast, dinner and supper out of the meal on that day and on the following day. A woman who had been helping them 'at the peats' also had her meals with them on Tuesday. On Wednesday, Margaret MacDonald gave to a neighbour, Catherine Darroch, a bowlful of meal — perhaps two or three pounds — which had been loaned to her the previous week. On Wednesday night, while she was preparing porridge for supper, her husband 'inspected the meal' and then beat her with a stick and threatened her with a razor 'for spending too much meal'.

'My husband,' she said, 'is not deranged nor is he given to drink, but he grudges every morsel of meal that goes into the mouth of himself and his family and he would rather starve than work.' John MacDonald admitted 'being angry with his wife for spending too much meal', and admitted too that he struck her 'with a small stick'. As a measure of his meanness, a bannock (oatcake) which his wife gave him to eat while he was out fishing in Donald Darroch's boat, remained uneaten until he came ashore. 'With a view to save the meal, I did not eat the bannock for my dinner, but took it home and used it for my supper', he said.

Farmers would have a part of their oat crop milled in the autumn for family consumption. That winter provision would be stored in a big wooden chest, or *girnel*. The *Campbeltown Courier* regretted the eclipse of 'the meal girnel and the flour crock' when, during the blizzards of January 1909, '... the dependence of rural folk on bakers' and merchants' vans for their supplies brought some houses almost to famine rations'. In 1892, at a farmers' meeting convened for the Royal Commission on Labour, one of the farmers complained that the labourers '... parted with good meal for tea and baker's bread. The wives are not so thrifty. Forty years ago, when wages were ever so much less, more was saved'.

Meal Kist Glen — between Arinarach Hill and Ben Gullion — was said to have got its name when the glen was deep with snow and the Arinascavach herd and the High Glenramskill herd hailed each other across the white and silent divide. 'She's full the day!' called the Glenramskill shepherd, and his neighbour called back: 'I wish my meal-kist wiz as full!' It has been suggested — perhaps more credibly — that farmers from the Leerside settlements passed through the glen with their ponies to have corn milled at Knocknaha, and so restock their meal-chests.

Oatmeal could be cooked in several ways, or eaten raw. Dinner at school for some children in the nineteenth century was no more than a fistful of dry meal carried in a pocket. Porridge — *brochan* in Gaelic — was the customary breakfast, and might be supplemented by cheese or eggs. Porridge was also frequently eaten in the evening, for supper. Oatcake, cooked on a girdle and then toasted at the fire, was the other main product of meal. Of oatcake, Bradley complained, perhaps rather too forcefully: 'They are deal boards made easy, and taste like a compressed mixture of bran and chaff. They hurt the teeth, and cause a sensation in the throat similar to what must be felt by anyone who stands open-mouthed before a winnowing-machine when it is in full work'.

Meat

Meat has become, for most Scottish families in the present time, a daily indulgence, but that was not always so. To the poorest folk in Kintyre — the cottars, or 'day labourers', who attached themselves to certain farms — meat, in the mid-nineteenth century, was 'a luxury in which they seldom indulge'. The farmers themselves would slaughter, about Martinmas, a cow or stirk, often purposely fattened. On 26 December 1855, John

Houston, a gardener living at Ballivianan, Southend, bought 43¾ lbs of beef and one stone of salt in Malcolm MacShannon's store at Lephinstrath Bridge.

The meat was preserved by salting and drying, the treatment generally given to all flesh, of beast or fish. It was initially steeped in weak brine for a day or two, then drained and immersed in strong pickle. Finally, it was dried and hung from the ceiling. That practice continued well into the present century. The flesh of pigs and sheep, as well as of cattle, would be preserved as winter food. In the kitchen of Durrie, sixteen hooks — or *cleeks* — were fixed to the ceiling for the hanging of salted meat, but a pig only would be killed and cured each year in John MacKay's time there. At Skernish, the MacPhail family would pickle a pig of their own, and, at Christmas, a bullock would be killed, and half of it sent to another farm. For several days, they would feast on black puddings made from the blood. An 80-year-old man, writing in 1933, had nothing unpleasant to recall about the salted meat to which he became accustomed on the family farm:

> When by chance visitors called on a winter evening . . . one of the dried haunches [would be] taken down, a slice or two cut off, immersed for a few minutes in boiling water, to mitigate the salt, and then fried in a frying-pan over the peat fire: and you and your visitors sat down to one of the tastiest bites ever offered to the human palate.

By the late nineteenth century, the commonest salted meat was mutton, because sheep had become very numerous and could be got freshly dead or dying, so that there was no real loss of stock involved in the filling of crock or barrel. The beast would have been lost anyway. Sheep could also be taken freshly drowned from a drain or bog-hole, and such a carcass was considered 'good clean stuff'. Alastair Beattie: 'If she wiz droont, ye kent there wiz naethin wrang wi' her.' Most sheep that went for salting, however, were casualties of *braxy*, a swift bacterial infection which usually attacks prime animals, and kills overnight. Salted meat, of whatever kind, could be cooked and eaten as it was or else turned into broth.

The practice of bleeding living cattle went on in Kintyre (until the eighteenth century, according to Alex Kerr, but on what authority he does not declare). It was resorted to in times of scarcity. The blood was parboiled with nettles, or any other greens available, and perhaps a sprinkling of oatmeal.

Fresh meat was usually the result of poaching game. Yet, Pennant remarked in 1772 that the Duke of Argyll allowed his tenants to 'destroy with impunity' the crop-predating stags on his estate, 'rather than beasts of chace (*sic*) should waste the bread of the poor'. There would be no such licence given to tenants in the following century.

In the latter half of the nineteenth century, rabbits became prolific in Kintyre, and were both a source of food and of income. There seem to have been two separate introductions of rabbits, the first in the mid-seventeenth century and the second in the mid-nineteenth century. But the earliest reference is inconclusive: the rental of the farm of Machrihanish, in 1669, included '2 duzon' of rabbits annually. But rabbits have been known on Sheep Island since at least the end of the sixteenth century, and Cara was said by Martin Martin, in his *Description of the Western Islands of Scotland*, written about 1695, to 'abound with coneys'. Whatever the truth, the present rabbit stock undoubtedly stems from their introduction to Argyll Estate farms in the 1840s, to increase the interest and value of the shootings.

Many farmers had cause to regret the invasion. In 1868, for example, John Snodgrass in North Clochkeil complained ominously that 'we have suffered so much damage the last three summers with the Rabbits [that] Mother has spoken to our Trustees and they have agreed to meet the Chamberlain and arrange about the farm'.

Rabbit-trapping was a regular winter occupation for many countrymen, some of whom rented tracts of land. Some Southend fishermen began snaring as soon as the lobster season ended. Meat and skin were both marketable. The rabbits were mostly sold to game-dealers and butchers in Campbeltown. In November 1894, William Douglas alone shipped 3786.

Fish

Salted fish formed a substantial part of the winter diet of farmers and of the labourers attached to farms. The MacPhails in Skernish would buy a few ling in Campbeltown, and these would be hung in the kitchen beside the hams. In Largieside, Gigha salt cod was popular, and in Willie MacGougan's time the blacksmith at Tayinloan took orders for the fish and delivered them throughout the district. When supplies of Gigha salt fish arrived at Stewarton Store, a fish would be hung outside to let customers know. Farmers and shepherds and others in the Southend district would go down to the shore to buy salted cod and saithe from the Islay hand-line fishermen who, until 1915, made Glemanuill Port their seasonal base, living there in thatched stone and turf huts. Salt herrings were also bought, in variously sized barrels, as winter food.

Countrymen living close to a rough coast were generally fond of rock fishing. Adam MacPhail cast for *gleshans* (young saithe) along Barlea shore in October. A little rotten, maggot-infested seaweed would be thrown out to gather the fish. He used three flies on his line. The fish would be carried home, gutted, and dried on the bone. *Lythe* (pollack) were occasionally taken. Willie MacGougan fished from the rocks at Glenacardoch Point and Ballochroy in August and September. The season lasted about six weeks, and most of the fish — gleshans — would be eaten fresh, but some were salted for winter. His line was baited with worms, and cast in the evenings. Finlay Clark lured the gleshans with bits of boiled potato. He fished from Glenacardoch Point and the rocks at Ballochantuy. The catch was usually eaten fresh — boiled or fried — but would occasionally be salted.

When Donald MacCallum was a boy in High Glenadale, his father would go down to the fishing rocks at Port na h-Olainn and might return with *stenlock* (full-grown saithe) and lythe, 'as much as he could carry'. Calum Bannatyne, when he was shepherding on the Moil, fished for gleshans using flies. He would take with him enough small hen-feathers to keep him going. He fished in summer evenings, using the customary long rod with fixed line. The fish would be gathered using chopped limpets, or 'sollach' (probably Gaelic *solladh*). The old men, he said, chewed the limpets and spat them into the water. He would stay on the rocks beyond sunset — when the fish began to take more urgently — and on a good evening could return home with a score of fish. Some were eaten fresh, some were salted and dried. The density of the pickle was tested by placing an egg in it — if the egg floated, then the solution was strong enough. (When preparing pickle for a pig, a severed trotter could be dropped in.) After the fish had been cured, they would be spread on rocks or suspended — tied in twos by the tails — over a string or wire. When dried, they could be taken indoors and hung.

There is a tradition that an old woman who lived in Innean Gaothach (south of Largybaan) would put a pot of potatoes on the fire, and, while the potatoes were boiling, take her rod down to the rocks and have fish home with her in time for dinner. The same story was told of an old woman in Innean Cailleach. In whichever of these high coastal settlements she lived, she must have been phenomenally fit for her years.

Shellfish

Shellfish were eaten in coastal communities and were undoubtedly a valuable support in times of crop failure and famine. Limpets are the only edible shellfish found in collectable quantities along the sea-battered shore between Machrihanish and the Mull, and the middens at some houses on that coast abounded in crumbling shells, which certain shepherds would carry home and throw to their hens.

Limpets are tough eating — the foot is practically indigestible and would usually be discarded — and there is decidedly a knack to dislodging them. If touched or disturbed in the least they will clamp tightly to the rock. Only a sudden blow will succeed. The MacKeiths in Sunadale cut them off the rocks. They maintained that the bigger and tastier 'lempets' were found furthest down the shore, but these could be gathered only at the lowest tides. The limpets would be cooked by boiling, but were never, within living memory, eaten as a meal in themselves.

Winkles — *wilks* in Scots, *faochagan* in Gaelic — were generally cooked as a soup, and served with potatoes. They would be boiled, picked out of their shells, and the tiny meats added to the stock, which could be thickened with a little cornflour. Wilks could also be eaten for breakfast, first boiled and then stewed with oatmeal. They were believed to have a high iron content and would be taken medicinally, in springtime, to 'clean the blood'. When Neil Thomson was a boy in Muasdale, and spring came, one of the adults would say, in Gaelic: 'What about one of ye runnin down an' gettin a few good wilks?' The child might ask: 'Would they be good?' Then the Gaelic proverb would come out: 'When the horse is lean, the wilks are fat'. Neil Thomson remarked on a linguistic distinction which, in Muasdale at least, applied to winkles. A winkle was *faochag*, yet a quantity of winkles gathered for food did not take the plural, *faochagan*, but was termed *maorach* (usually shellfish in general).

Razor-fish — locally *spoot-fish* — were commonly dug out of the shores, with graips or any other handy implement, but were accessible only with the very lowest tides. When these big ebbs occurred, hundreds of 'the poorer classes' would appear around Campbeltown Loch, digging by lantern light if the tide was nocturnal. Two shillings a hundred was the usual price for razor-fish in Campbeltown during the 1880s, and these occasional bonanzas from the outer sandbanks no doubt raised — if fleetingly — the living standards of many poor folk.

Seagull eggs provided food in springtime for those prepared to gather them. There is no evidence that eggs were taken customarily in Kintyre centuries ago, but it would be surprising if such an abundant food source had been neglected. Certain of the shepherds on the Mull shore gathered eggs from the Gulls Den, a rocky creek at the northern end of the cliffs called Aignish. Sandy Helm climbed down into the Den — a risky undertaking — every second or third day while the gulls were laying, and carried out eggs in his lambing-bag; or else went especially to gather, with a bucket or basket. Both he and Calum Bannatyne were accustomed to eating the eggs, but most of them would be fed to calves or broken into dogs' meat.

Liquids

Drinking water would be taken from streams or wells. It had been my reasoned assumption that no settlement would exist where water was not found, but in James Malcolm's report of 1810, two steadings are discussed specifically in terms of their great distance from water. At High Park West and Largymore West, 'every drop of water', consumed in both house and yard, had to be fetched daily by horse and cart, at the expense of a man's time. But these must have been exceptional cases.

In some wells trout were placed to keep the water pure by eating insects. Duncan MacKeith, going to school from Sunadale, would stop to watch the trout in the roadside well at Dearg Allt. Wells had to be cleaned periodically. Alastair Beattie, at Kerranbeg, would scour the well-bottom with a clump of heather.

Milk and buttermilk were the ordinary refreshments until tea became, around the mid-nineteenth century, not only popular, but also cheap enough to put it within the means of most folk. Even so, an 80-year-old man, writing in 1933, admitted that he still occasionally 'turned from it as something foreign and unnatural'. In his youth, tea remained a luxury, and he did not develop a taste for it until 'well on in [his] twenties'.

Peter MacIntosh had a story about an old woman in Glenlussa whose son, a sailor, returned with a gift of a pound of tea. He asked her to have some ready for him when he came back from visiting a neighbour. After he had gone, the old woman put the tea into a pot with water and boiled it on the fire. She then poured the water off, pounded the tea with a potato-beetle as though it were kail, adding milk, meal and butter to it. When her son came back he asked for the tea. She gave it to him, saying: 'I don't think much of your tea; I'd by far prefer *càl plocaidh* (mashed kail)'.

H

CHAPTER 11

Festivities, Customs, and Sports

New Year

New Year — until the mid-nineteenth century celebrated on 12 January*
— was the first and main festival of the year. It was a time of excess, and the
toleration of excess, though toleration was often enough strained. In
Campbeltown, the celebrations centred on the burning of tar-barrels. That
custom was vividly described in an anonymous letter to the *Campbeltown
Courier* in 1913, following the death of the Dalintober 'worthy' Neil
MacLellan, or 'Kipples':

> ... The first time the writer recollects seeing him was on a Hogmanay night away
> back in the sixties of last century. The clock in the old Longrow tower had just struck
> twelve, ushering in the new year. Almost simultaneously there burst upon the
> Longrow a scene which, witnessed as a boy, has remained vividly with me to this
> hour. Down the street came a procession with tar barrels full ablaze, followed by
> hundreds of townspeople, all wending their way to the Cross. The flaming barrels
> were carried on the heads of five picked men, and attendants marched on either side
> battering at the staves with sticks to increase the flame of fire. Continuous cheers
> were shouted from every throat. The windows of the houses along the route were all
> open, with the occupants leaning out to witness the scene ...
> 'Kipples', the hero of the tar barrel brigade, led the van. It was truly a weird and
> heart-stirring sight. As the procession marched onwards, our hero's clothes were
> seen dripping with hot tar. What did he care for risks or danger when the honours of
> the night were his? Arrived at the Cross, the procession marched round it three
> times, and afterwards the barrels were thrown in a heap, while cheers were raised
> again and again till the bonfire had burned itself out.

Several parties might race to the town Cross — or the Quayhead, or
some other 'centre of conflagration' — and it was 'a point of honour' which
would get there first. Sometimes an old boat would be secured, and a barrel
— or barrels — placed in it. Then 'a willing party of supple fellows [would]
line themselves on both sides, and run along dragging the boat on its keel,
the barrels burning in it, until they reached the centre, where their charge

*In 1752, when Britain adopted the Gregorian calendar, dates were moved forward eleven days, so that
the old January 1 became January 12. Many old customs carried on exactly a year ahead, so New Year
was on January 12.

172

Fig. 50 Campbeltown Main Street, c. 1900, showing the late medieval cross, scene of New Year festivities. The cross was taken down for safety during the Second World War, and afterwards re-erected at the head of the Old Quay. From a photograph in the author's possession.

[was] devoted to the general burning'. The Campbeltown ritual, Dr Alan Bruford points out, was identical to that in Lerwick which in 1889 was formalised into the galley-burning of Up-Helly-Aa.

The 'fire-worshippers', as one censorious *Courier* editorial described them, were by no means universally admired. In 1860, a fishing skiff belonging to Dugald Galbraith was burned at the Cross by a 'riotous mob'. Dugald was not amused, and the town council instructed the police to give him the names of the culprits that he might prosecute for damages. In 1880, James Rennie claimed £15 from the council for the loss of a haystack, burned in the wake of the barrel procession; but the council refused to admit liability. The custom ended in that year, and in 1881 the *Courier* remarked with satisfaction: 'No more will we be subjected to the horrors of violent nocturnal bell-ringing, the hoarse "Hooray boys! Hooray!", the horrible smell of burning tar, the lurid glare that made one think of the regions descended by Dante, the oaths and ribaldry, and the persistent attempts to extort backsheesh — all have vanished'.

New Year in the town was also an excuse for stone battles between rival bands of revellers. The men of Campbeltown and Dalintober fought most violently, with raid and counter-raid into one another's territory.

For most folks, however, in town and country, New Year was the occasion for 'first-footing' or for receiving 'first-footers', with handshakes, drams, currant buns and shortbread. First-footers were generally male, and they took with them a bottle of whisky and a lump of coal (which is becoming a rarity as open fires disappear from houses). Good luck was ushered in with the man at the door, especially if he was dark-haired.

Adam MacPhail recalled that in the Glenbarr district, until about 1920, a special glass was passed around the company immediately after midnight. The woman of the house was first to sip from it, and then it was given to all the other women present. The man of the house then received it, and from him it went around all the other men. Every sip taken from it was replaced from the bottle. That ritual was believed to 'keep the luck in the group'.

New Year's Day shinty matches

In most Kintyre communities a game of shinty was played on New Year's Day, and was often followed by such sports as putting the stone, throwing the hammer, tossing the caber, tug of war, and running. There was much drink taken then, as now, and some of the shinty players took to the field in bad temper. If there were scores to settle, then a shinty-stick was as good a weapon as any, and could be used with some pretence at innocence. These violent diversions were not, of course, confined to Kintyre — they were common at New Year shinty and football matches in many parts of Scotland.

Some of these violent incidents — both on and off the field of play — were the subject of criminal investigation, and four such investigations are preserved in the Scottish Record Office. These precognitions are more than just descriptions of violence — they are valuable social records of the times. If nothing else, they demonstrate that drunkenness and violence are far from being recent afflictions of Scottish sport.

Tayinloan, 1818

The earliest case was in 1818, at Tayinloan. Archibald MacMurchy in Lenanboyach struck John Galbreath 'several violent blows upon the head with a shinney or club', breaking his jaw and otherwise injuring him so that on the following day his life was said to be 'just now in danger'. He was unable to speak and could only take food 'through the stroop (spout) of a tea pot'.

The game was played on Dalchennan, a park near the inn kept by Galbreath. It began about midday, but was disrupted from the start by disputes about the practice of lifting the ball and 'giving her a flying stroke out of the hand', which was considered 'contrary to the rule of fair play'. A resolution was adopted by a majority of the players that the ball should be struck only on the ground, and that 'whoever would lift her should be struck with the shinney'.

Galbreath, on 9 March, when he was fit to be interviewed, said that after the teams were chosen he was summoned home. About three-quarters of an hour later he returned to the field and immediately got a stroke at the ball; but Archibald MacMurchy approached him 'in a state of intoxication and very outrageous . . . and damned him for a buggar, saying to him, what right had he to strike the ball'. Galbreath, backed by team-mates, protested that he had been chosen in the opposing side and had a right to play.

Seeing MacMurchy persistently lift the ball, and considering himself well enough acquainted with him to offer some friendly advice, Galbreath put his hands on the man's shoulders and told him that his style was 'contrary to the regulations of all shinney playing' (but not, of course, in these stylish words, which are a transcriber's version of Galbreath's Gaelic, a blunter medium of expression on the playing field, no doubt).

MacMurchy claimed that Galbreath 'threw him down a brae upon his back'. Most witnesses were uncertain as to whether he fell or was pushed. One of the players, Archibald MacPherson — a wright at Gortanafaul — remarked diplomatically that MacMurchy 'appeared to be a little intoxicated when playing at the shinney, and when any person is a little intoxicated and running quick . . . he is more apt to fall, but when two or three persons are after the ball and one happening to fall no notice is taken of it by any person unless it is intentionally done through spleen'. Whatever the truth of the incident, MacMurchy's brother Donald intervened with his shinty-stick raised, and the struggle ensued which ended with Galbreath's being helped home by the brothers Donald and John Sellars in Culfuar.

The New Year shinty game at Carradale Bay was cancelled in 1821 owing to a fight between Duncan Ferguson, labourer at Torrisdale, and Archibald MacKay, farmer at Keranashee. Two years later, in 1823, the match at Crossaig also seems to have been cancelled because of assaults with shinty-sticks before the game had even started. It was to have been played on 13 January, a Monday, possibly because it could not have been played on the Sabbath.

Southend, 1836: the killing of John MacCoag

The last case, from Southend in 1836, was the killing of John MacCoag (MacCaig), and had as little to do with the game of shinty as the two preceding cases. The match was held on Strathmore, the stretch of flat land directly west of Keil Point.

John MacCoag worked as a farm-servant at Gartvain, and his sister Rose visited him there on the afternoon of New Year's Day. He drank a glass of whisky in his house, and together they set off to watch the shinty match. They stopped at the house of John MacKenzie, quarrier at Keil, and MacCoag drank half-a-glass of whisky there. At about three o'clock they left that house and immediately saw 'the shinty players running and crowding together'.

A 'big Irishman named Robert' had interrupted the game to announce that he 'would fight any Scotch or Highland buggar who stood on the strand'. James MacMillan, blacksmith at Drimavulline, both accepted the challenge and advised the Irishman to 'walk off'. He did withdraw, but a man from Mull named MacDonald and another Irishman, MacIsaac, stripped to the waist and decided to have their own fight.

By the time Rose MacCoag appeared, they were 'so covered with blood that she could not recognise them'. Someone ran to the house of Donald MacIlreavie, mason at Keil, and told him there was a 'battle' on the Strath. When MacIlreavie reached the field, MacIsaac was on the ground and being kicked by several of the crowd. He feared that it was a 'murderous-looking business' and called on James MacMillan to help him push the crowd back. MacDonald had one of the Irishman's fingers in his mouth and was trying to 'bite it off'. MacIlreavie went between the men and freed MacIsaac's finger, but the crowd began to press again and he denounced them loudly: 'I have often heard of the inhumanity of the Glenbreakry people, but now I see it when they can stand and witness such barbarous fighting'.

John MacCoag, meantime, had pushed into the 'hubble', removing his neckcloth and shouting that he would 'see fair play to the Irishman'. He and MacIlreavie then broke out of the mob, 'cleeked' — linked by their arms — and pursuing Duncan MacDougall, a farm-servant at Balevianan. MacDougall kept them off with his left hand and swung his stick with the right. MacIlreavie was felled by a crack on the head, and MacCoag followed him and lay 'on his mouth and nose'.

Donald O'May, MacCoag's brother-in-law, caught hold of MacDougall and demanded to know why he had struck MacCoag. MacDougall simply replied that he would not strike O'May, and, as proof of that, handed his stick to a young girl, Mary Campbell. (MacDougall later sent a boy, Archibald MacGeachy, to retrieve the stick. MacGeachy described it as 'old and black-looking, and although not very big, [I] thought when handling it that it was very heavy'.)

Rose MacCoag, too, was knocked to the ground by a shinty-stick. When she recovered, she found her brother 'standing alone on the sand at the shore ... vomiting a little'. When he arrived home he threw off his jacket and lay down. Blood was oozing from his nose and left ear. About four o'clock in the morning, his wife came to Rose's bedside crying, 'Rise, rise, for John is gone'.

MacDougall, along with Duncan MacMillan, farmer in Culinlongart — implicated in the murder, but whose active role no witness could confirm — absconded to Ireland before they could be arrested. There appears to have been more to the killing than principles of sportsmanship. A sister-in-law of MacCoag's had a 'natural child' by Duncan MacDougall, but he refused to acknowledge the child. Her brothers, John and Donald O'May, had not challenged him, but MacCoag and he had 'angry words about it', and MacDougall had threatened vengeance.

Candlemas

Candlemas was celebrated with cock-fighting. The slain birds and those which had refused to fight (and were stoned to death) were the perquisites of the schoolmaster. Each child also brought a small offering of money — originally intended for buying a candle — and the girl who brought most was pronounced 'Queen'. The schoolmaster, in return, dispensed a treat — a bun or an orange, or the like — to each child. A 'less pleasant feature of Candlemastide', as Andrew MacKerral put it, was the exchanging of mock valentines, many of which were of 'a highly vulgar, not to say indecent character'.

May Day

The first of May (*Beltane*) in the Highlands was traditionally marked by bonfires, divination, and bannocks, but none of these customs seems to have been recorded in Kintyre. In the nineteenth and early part of the twentieth centuries, children were given a holiday from school and rambled into the countryside to 'lay blackmail upon the farmers' for the coveted 'cruds' (curds) and cream.

Hallowe'en

Hallowe'en (Gaelic *Samhain*) marks the start of the winter half of the year, and derives from the great winter feast of the pagan Celts. The main festivities were — and still are — held on 31 October, the eve of All Hallows, because in Gaelic usage, as in Jewish, the night belongs to the day after. The spirits of the dead were supposed to be about, and were, in some sense, represented by the *guisers*, who — as the name suggests — disguised themselves in grotesque clothing, their faces masked or blackened. *Guising* is now left mainly to children, who proceed from house to house — some of them with candle lanterns, carved from turnips — entertaining in exchange for fruit and nuts or, increasingly, money. The entertainment value of these visits seems, however, to diminish generation by generation. The offering is now more likely to be a simple joke (often heard on television) than a song or story.

Hallowe'en was formerly a boisterous occasion, when the younger people threw off constraints — rather as the adults did at New Year — and visited mischief on the community. That mischief-making also seems to have represented the activities of the spirits. It usually took the form of battering doors, traditionally with kail-stocks, but latterly with sticks and stones or anything else to hand. In 1882 the *Campbeltown Courier* complained:

> The old customs ... have now become almost obsolete, and the sooner they disappear altogether the better it will be for the peace of the community in general, if what took place in Campbeltown on Tuesday night is a specimen of the proper thing to do on such occasions. A noisy band of youths ran howling and screaming through the quieter streets, smashing every door they came to with sticks and stones, whereby the peaceably disposed inhabitants were very considerably alarmed and disturbed.

A whole set of Hallowe'en customs, which had disappeared in Kintyre by the end of the nineteenth century, involved divination. The main interest was in finding out whom one would marry. At the 'pooin' o' kail-stocks', blindfold boys and girls would be made to take one another by the hand and go into the kail-yard to pull a plant each. If the stock was straight or crooked, or sweet or bitter in its core, so would be the shape and temper of the future spouse; and if the stock was light or heavy with earth about its roots, so would be the purse of the partner. By drawing an oat-stalk from a stack and counting the seeds on it, the girls discovered how many children they would bear, 'not minding if there were a dozen grains'. Pairs of nuts were burned in the embers of a fire to see if married life would be harmonious or not: the nuts might burn peacefully together or shoot apart.

There were various rituals of the magical sort which often unnerved those who risked them. An apple would be eaten before a mirror in dim light, and a piece of it offered over the shoulder to the apparition of the future spouse.

Divination with eggs — dropping the whites into a tumbler of water and interpreting the shapes — might be followed by one of the girls filling her mouth with the water and running around the house to raise a vision. One girl in Glenlussa who tried that was supposed to have encountered a stranger in the uniform of a soldier, who asked her: *Am faca tu Iain?* (Have you seen John?). The girl was terrified, knowing that there was no soldier in Glenlussa at the time, and darted back into the house. The company ran outside to see the soldier, but there was no one there, and the nature of her experience was understood. Next year the girl was at a market in Campbeltown and saw some soldiers — returned from the East Indies — landing from a ship. One of them was the very man whose apparition had come to her at Hallowe'en. His name was John, and he proved to be a friend's cousin. They met, married, and settled in Glenlussa.

One Hallowe'en, two brothers in that glen dipped their nightshirts (normally only a sleeve would be dipped) in the waters of a 'dead-and-living ford' — the part of a stream that had been crossed by a funeral procession. Before they went to bed they left their shirts to dry at a big fire, and watched to see who would come. Eventually, the forms of two girls appeared, went to the fire, turned the shirts and then disappeared. Before the next Hallowe'en arrived, the brothers had married these women.

Hallowe'en of 1855 in the Saddell district was held on 12 November and was referred to, in a set of contemporary accounts, as 'old style'. The evening was spent in ceilidh-houses at Torrisdale and Whitestone, where there was dancing to the pipes of Donald Ferguson and Neil Galbraith. A farm-servant at Whitestone, John Hart, was killed on the road that night in a fight with another servant, John MacPhee.

Fair days

The main fair days in Kintyre were Candlemas (2 February), Whitsun (15 May), Lammas (1 August) and Martinmas (11 November). Of these, the most important were the term days, Whitsun and Martinmas, on which rents were due and farm-servants free to seek new masters. At these 'feeing fairs' farmers hired their servants for the coming term of six months. The busiest fairs were those in Campbeltown, and Main Street, Cross Street, Back Street (now Union Street, more or less) and the head of Longrow would be thronged with labourers and farmers, bargaining on terms of hire. To seal agreement, the farmer would give the servant his 'earls' — *arles*, or 'earnest money' — which was usually a shilling. If the servant wished to reject the offer, he simply handed back the coin.

These were busy days in town, and the atmosphere was festive. 'For weeks previous', a correspondent of Edward Bradley's noted around 1870, 'there was not a tailor or dressmaker within the bounds who was not engaged to make decent clothing for the youngsters . . . The Fair Day finds them always in good spirits, if not in great glee. They rejoice beyond measure at its approach, that they may be disengaged from the trammels that bind them to their sorely-wrought fee . . .'

With the influx of countryfolk came an influx of money, for servants had their wages for the term ended, and settled accounts with the various merchants. There was — at Lammas Fair especially — a host of visiting amusements on which to squander money: boxing saloons, shooting barrows, sweetie stances, gambling boards, haberdashery and crockery stands, whisky tents, photographic booths, 'cheap-johns' (travelling vendors of small wares), and assorted musicians. There was also, occasionally, a major attraction such as a company of actors or a circus.

It was customary for young men to give 'fairings' — presents bought on fair days — to favourite girls. These were invariably sweets, and a popular girl might arrive home with 'enough sweets to stock a confectioner's shop'. There was another unfailing attraction, and in the early 1890s, during fairs, the ladies of Campbeltown district 'attempted to form a place of resort to keep the young men away from the public-houses'. Unquestionably, the virtuous cause was lost.

Candlemas was the annual horse fair in Campbeltown, but at the other fairs, too, horses and other livestock were shown. Dealers from Glasgow, Ayrshire, Arran, and elsewhere attended. At Lammas Fair, harvest workers were engaged. In 1873, wages were 'very high' — £1 1s to £1 6s weekly, with board and lodgings, for men, while 'women to lift' received from 18s to £1. Almost forty years later, in 1914, these wages — at £1 4s to £1 6s — were little improved.

Though street bargaining continued, on a much reduced scale, beyond the First World War, by the 1890s the 'feeing fairs' had begun to lose their usefulness. 'I have not engaged [a servant] in this manner for some years, and hope never [again] to do so,' wrote one Kintyre farmer in the 1870s. 'I wish that this humiliating spectacle of a hiring market could be dispensed with altogether.' Increasingly, the best men and women were being 'earled' in advance of the markets.

By the end of the nineteenth century, the holidays of farm-servants were New Year's Day, the Whitsun and Martinmas fair days (with a day or two extra at each, when changing or renewing employment), and Sacramental fast days. Some servants were also given Lammas.

The Royal Commission on Labour, in 1892, heard the suggestion of a Saturday half-holiday 'universally condemned' by farmers' representatives, who argued that horses 'would suffer from waiting so long in the stable', and that dairy work would be neglected. The workers — and especially young, unmarried men — favoured Saturday half-days, but some older men expressed a preference for increased holidays at the end of each term. At a meeting in Stewarton, servants complained of having to work three hours on the mornings of holidays before they got away, and of having to return in the evening to attend to the horses. They reasoned that not all holiday work was strictly necessary, and should be done on the day before, 'in the master's time'. One witness claimed to have spent two hours at a thrashing-mill on one holiday. It was the general belief that 'the masters would grant them Saturday afternoons, just as they had done the Sabbath day'. A farm-servant in 1914, arguing for a weekly half-day, remarked that 'at present the ploughman has to content himself on market days with the smell of his master's breath'.

The only significant fair in Killean and Kilchenzie Parish was held at Lammas. Even in 1843, 'very little business [was] transacted, except hiring servants for the harvest quarter'. In 1848, the fair was held on 'Tanloan Ferry green', where four whisky-tents were visited by excisemen, with unfortunate consequences (p. 113). By 1876, the fair had become so attenuated that its imminent disappearance was predicted. Labour scarcity was the main factor, and as the fair declined, fewer shows attended it. In that year, the only entertainment was offered, in the barn of the MacDonald Arms Hotel, Tayinloan, by a company of touring actors. A storm blew all day, and the 'sweetie stalls' were not erected, 'much to the annoyance of the young and those who wish to treat their sweethearts on such occasions'.

A storm, many years before, was said to have made ghosts of a crew of Gighamen who crossed to Tayinloan for the fair. They had a drink in the public-house before returning home. Some time after they had gone, the company that remained in the house also left, and met the Gighamen at the door. *Shaoil sinn gun robh sibh air falbh dhachaidh*, 'We thought you'd gone away home,' said one of the company. The Gighamen did not speak, but went on into the public-house. They were all dead. At the shore they had hoisted the sails of the boat, but before they could lift the anchor a squall came in off the sea and capsized the boat.

The origin of Tarbert Fair, which continues to be held — and is therefore the last traditional fair in Kintyre — dates to 1705 when Archibald MacAlister, on whose land the village lay, was authorised by an Act of the Scottish parliament to hold a weekly market on Tuesdays, and four two-day fairs, to begin on 10 May, 16 July, 19 August, and 16 October. Of these, only the July fixture survived, and became *the* Tarbert Fair. J. MacDougall Hay, in his novel of Tarbert, *Gillespie* — book II, chapter 4 — describes a fair day in the mid-nineteenth century.

Marriages

The first stage in formalising a marriage agreement involved the suitor meeting the girl's father and putting his case for the engagement. The proposal having been accepted, a night was decided for the *rèite*, or engagement feast. The wedding arrangements were made there, and the couple's names were afterwards recorded in the church session-book and proclaimed on the Sabbath. Wedding invitations could then be given to relatives, friends and neighbours, who generally responded with gifts for the wedding feast: hens, ducks, meal, butter, cheese, and even fat sheep. The bridegroom supplied a jar of whisky. In Tarbert, the 'women's night' before a wedding is still known as 'the *Cailleachan*'.

On the morning of the wedding day, the bride was washed and dressed in her best clothes for the ceremony. The bride's party assembled in her parents' house — where the celebrations were usually later held — and were met at the church by the groom's party. Pipers played before each procession, and shots were fired as they passed along, a much-condemned custom. As early as 1788, Campbeltown Town Council prohibited the 'dangerous practice [of] firing with pistolls and other fire arms in the streets of the Burgh', and ordered confiscation of all weapons so used. Two masons employed by John Lorne Stewart (p. 82) were badly injured while helping reload a cannon at the marriage celebrations of Stewart's son Duncan in June 1858. When the shot exploded prematurely, Arthur Lydan's left hand was blown off, and William MacCallum lost five fingers and part of a thumb, and had both arms broken.

After the ceremony, the parties joined and proceeded to the wedding-house. A dance, to fiddle and pipe music, began in the barn and continued until the meal was set out. After dinner, the dance was resumed in earnest and was opened to all who chose to come. Young men and women would travel great distances to attend a marriage ball, and were admitted providing they paid a small sum of money 'for the floor'. (That payment suggests a late vestige of the much-reviled 'penny wedding' — prohibited by Campbeltown Town Council in 1705 — which was a pretext 'for holding a profitable festivity, to which members of the public who could pay their footing were freely admitted, and those gatherings were not distinguished for sobriety or moderation'.) The dancing and drinking lasted until dawn. Meanwhile, the bride had been put to bed with great ceremony by her friends, and the bridegroom's party had laid him by her side. The company then gathered round the bed and drank to the health of the couple, who returned the sentiments and were then left to themselves.

Next day the wedding company reassembled and 'made a happy day of it with feasting, walking, dancing, and firing off guns and pistols until the evening, when they dispersed'. On the first Sunday following the marriage, the couple were 'kirked' — escorted to church — 'an ordeal during which they had to endure the stares of all the young men and women of the congregation'.

Christenings

The baptism of infants was a serious matter. There was a belief that an unbaptised child would not grow, and brought bad luck to the family. Christenings were celebrated with a feast, to which friends and neighbours were invited. The godfather (*goisdidh*) had charge of the jar of whisky, while the godmother (*bana-ghoisdidh*) organised the meal.

The child was carried to church in its father's arms, with a chunk of bread and cheese held in the folds of its gown as a luck offering to the first person encountered on the road. Pins were carried to the church, and, on returning to the house after the ceremony, these would be distributed among the young men and women that they might dream of whom they would marry. A dish of highly sweetened gruel, containing a spoon, was passed around the company, and each person was expected to take a spoonful.

There was a belief in Kintyre that if a child died unchristened it gained neither heaven nor hell, but remained earthbound as a *sgrèachan-réilig* — 'graveyard shrieker' — or else lamented quietly in woods and other lonely places.

The story of *Deorsa an Rum* — 'George of the Rum' — was well-known in Kintyre. He was probably the son of Neil Campbell in Innean Gaothach. In the winter of 1753, according to one version, a ship was wrecked on the Moil and her cargo plundered. George's mother, Kate, carried off a cask of rum, with which the christening celebrations were enlivened ... and prolonged. 'Every morning when the guests got up and had breakfast, intending to go home, they would say that they would have a dram before leaving; then they would forget all about home and continue drinking.' In another version, there was no water in the house for the christening, so the baby George was christened with the looted rum. His own children were said to have been better known by the name 'Rum' than by Campbell.

In Kintyre there was a custom of wrapping a new-born child in an old shirt of its father's for good luck. Neil Thomson in Muasdale heard that for several nights after a birth, two or three young men would 'sit up' with the child to guard against fairies stealing it away and leaving in its place one of their own feeble 'changelings'.

Funerals

The waking of corpses was customary in Kintyre until the early nineteenth century — in 1857 MacIntosh recorded the 'superstition' as being 'nearly worn out'. In the eighteenth century wakes were considered open to all. Campbeltown Town Council, in 1727, enacted a bye-law prohibiting attendance at 'late wakes' by other than 'nearest of kin to the deceased and persons of undoubted probity'. The penalty was to be a fine of £5 Scots money or a week's imprisonment with bread and water. The council complained of

> ... the manifold abuses committed ... to the dishonour of God, the scandal of the town, and to the great loss and detriment of the surviving concerned in the dead, by the flocking of a numerous crowd of unconcerned idle persons to such wakes, for no other purpose, for ordinary, than to eat and drink, and often to disgraceful excess; and to use unlawful games and unsuitable diversions, such as cards and hot loof [incomprehensible — author], and other unbecoming fooleries and discourses and, too often, to steal anything that is readiest to hand, all of which has been observed and is well known ...

Wake games — some of them highly elaborate — were common in Ireland until fairly recent times, and are examined in Seán Ó Súilleabháin's *Irish Wake Amusements*, the classic work on the subject.

For the wake, the body was laid on a platform, over which was raised a canopy of linen. Inside that canopy, candles burned night and day. A pan of salt was placed on the corpse's breast, in the belief that it would retard decomposition. A succession of neighbours sat, each in turn, with the corpse from the laying out until removal. These were the *luchd-faire* (watchers). Prayers were said morning and night, oatcake (later bread) and cheese were served at intervals with whisky, and words were spoken in praise of the deceased. It was customary to have the children of the house kiss the corpse, in the belief that they would be spared from dreaming of it. The effect was probably quite the opposite.

The religious service was held in the house and attended by relatives, but if two ministers were present, and the funeral was at a farm, another service would be held in the barn for the rest of the mourners. Before setting off, the company was served with bread, cheese, and whisky. In Southend, in the early nineteenth century, the mourners would be served with three rounds of drink — one of whisky, one of rum, and one of whisky toddy. The coffin was then carried on *spaiks* — spokes, or wooden bearers — to the grave, the men relieving one another in turn; but before the procession was out of sight of the house, the straw from the deathbed would be taken outside and burned.

Coffins were often carried great distances, so that a body could be buried in the parish of birth and among kinsfolk. At the older of the bridges over Allt na Dunaich, near Putechan, two funeral processions were supposed to have met and disputed the right of crossing first. Both parties were drunk and would not yield. A fight broke out and there were casualties on both sides. (There was, incidentally, a pagan belief that bloodshed appeased the spirit of the dead.)

At the funeral, c. 1805, of Torquil MacNeill — 'Little Torquil' or 'The Prophet': see my *Kintyre: The Hidden Past*, p. 6 — ' . . . there were two men fought . . . and the Blacksmith that was there told them just to let the men fight for it was the Devil who could not get the good Christian soul and body (little Torquil who was buried) and therefore had gone into the two men'. That was the recollection of Neil Fleming in Pans, who attended the funeral, at Kilchivan, as a boy.

Frequently, the procession would be headed by a piper or someone on the jew's-harp. After interment, bread, cheese and whisky were again served, and the relatives returned to the house of mourning and were given a big meal which in south Kintyre was called the *Dredgie* (connected with 'dirge', according to the *Scottish National Dictionary*). The Skyeman Martin Martin (p. 168) recorded, about 1695, that the Gigha people were 'accustomed not to bury on Friday'.

When Donald MacIlheanie in Achinsavill, Southend, died in November

1722, his widow Margrett MacMurchy purchased from Malcolm MacNeill twelve boards for the coffin, at £1 4s, and four pounds of cheese and a pound of candles (presumably for the wake) at 13s. Archibald O'Drain, in December 1703, for his daughter's funeral, bought seven pints of 'aquavity' (whisky), four ells of linen (for her winding-sheet, presumably), two pounds of candles, and a half-stone of cheese.

The custom of ordering a coffin while still alive is now quite obsolete in Kintyre. Peter MacIntosh, the author of *History of Kintyre*, carved and raised his own gravestone, which stood for many years in Kilkerran before his death in 1876. The inscription was complete except for the year of his death. Another local historian, Neil Munro Kelly — son of the Rev. Daniel Kelly, minister of Southend — had his name and date of birth cut on the family gravestone in Kilkerran, likewise leaving a blank for the date of his death. He specified that he was to be buried as close to the surface as possible. He was a great eccentric, as his obituary in the *Campbeltown Courier* of 2 June 1906 shows.

Sports

Physique was much admired in men, and most sports were contests of strength. Wrestling, stone-throwing, and weight-lifting with boulders, cartwheels, and 56lb weights were popular amusements when men gathered idly. In newspaper reports of ploughing matches in the latter half of the nineteenth century, spectators are often described as amusing themselves with throwing the stone and leaping. But the main team game was shinty, which has already been discussed in its relation to New Year's Day festivities.

Shinty

Shinty — 'shinney' in Kintyre — was introduced from Ireland, where the game is known as hurling. It has a tradition reaching back to the ancient hero-tales of the Irish: the young Cú Chulainn, with a hurley in his hand, was unstoppable.

The shinty-stick was cut from birch, willow, hazel, oak, or any other tree that would provide serviceable wood. The sticks were usually whittled to make them *cam* — 'curved/bent', from which *caman*, the club, and *camanachd*, the game, derive in Gaelic — but capable hands could put a bend in a straight stick by heating an end in fire and shaping it in a clamp.

Enthusiasts would travel miles for the making of a good *caman*, which would remain in regular use until the head of it was worn thin. Kintyre sticks were always made short, and played with one hand; elsewhere in Argyll, a larger stick was played with both hands. Balls, traditionally, were also carved from wood — preferably a knot — as any person struck by one would painfully realise.

At Machair Uinnein, Machrihanish, in the mid-nineteenth century, a pitch — upwards of a quarter of a mile long — would be marked off. At each end, the goal — or *den* — was formed of stone heaps nine or ten feet apart. 'Lots' were cast for the right to 'put out the ball'. A player in the successful side stood between the den markers and made a 'cogy' by 'beating a little of the earth up with the shinty into a pyramidal shape, about an inch or so above the ground. He placed the ball on this point, and then struck it out with his shinty'. The object of the game, obviously, was to put the ball between the goal markers. No one was allowed to carry or lift and throw the ball (p. 175), but 'crapachs' — no doubt connected with *cnap*, 'to strike', or *cnapag*, a shinty ball — were permissible. That is, a player could catch the ball in flight, throw it from him, and strike it with the stick. At these New Year's Day matches, people — as many as a thousand — would assemble at Machair Uinnein from miles around. Sides were picked from the willing men assembled. Select teams sometimes played under patronage, with wagers at stake.

In 1870, with images of the ball's passing 'swiftly to and fro among the light-hearted and swift-footed Highlanders', the *Argyllshire Herald* correspondent at the Machrihanish match doubted 'whether any other district in the West of Scotland could produce a better set of shinty-players'. In 1874, there was a large turn-out of players and spectators. The match, played at Trodigal, began about 10 a.m. and continued 'until the day was far advanced'. Despite bad weather, many of the players stripped to the waist. Neither side was able to force a win, so, by popular agreement, the teams retreated to Pans Inn to 'refresh themselves' on the strength of a 'handsome sum' dispensed by Captain Hector Macneal, the local laird. Two of his sons played in the junior game, and the *Courier* correspondent speculated that they might 'yet become the leaders of the game'. But in 1882 the complaint from Machrihanish was that 'it is to be regretted that more interest is not manifested in the game'.

According to Andrew McKerral, the New Year's Day shinty match on Strathmore was played between Conieglen and Glen Breackerie sides. (If that is correct, then the arrangement was unusual. Generally, teams were selected by two men choosing in turn: for example, at Glenbarr in 1878, by Major Macallister of Crubesdale and Norman Macallister of Glenbarr

Abbey.) There is no record of when the Strathmore fixture ended, but by about 1880 shinty itself had been forbidden among Southend boys. Rules and restraints were practically non-existent then, and split lips and broken teeth marred many a game. McKerral, when he started school at Southend in 1882, noticed 'a row of confiscated shinty sticks standing up against the chimney place of the schoolroom'.

Soccer, towards the end of the nineteenth century, was gaining popularity, and had that game not been such a counter-attraction it is unlikely that shinty would have died away in Kintyre as quickly as it did. The last vestige of the ancient sport was, in fact, the New Year's Day fixture. But in 1871, at Largie, only boys turned up that day to play the game: 'The people now regard such amusements as too trifling for persons come to maturity.'

From 1880 until 1892, New Year's Day matches were played at Machrihanish, Glenbarr, Saddell, and Largie. Thereafter, the game appears to have declined and disappeared from Kintyre. In 1888, an effort was made, by the newly founded Campbeltown Celtic Club, to revive the sport, but the attempt evidently did not survive beyond that year. At first the club played matches involving only its own members — by February increased to eighty — but challenges were later issued to Glenbarr and Machrihanish shinty-players (these districts, by implication, being the main rural strongholds of the game). One of these matches was played, at Glenbarr, and the Campbeltown side won by six goals to two.

The sport has recently been revived in Kintyre. The Kintyre Camanachd Association was formed, in Campbeltown, in 1985, largely by the efforts of Donald Woodrow (a native of Islay), Niall Brown (of Colonsay) — both of whom had played the game in their youth — and James Robertson of Campbeltown. The sport was introduced at all three primary schools in town, as well as at Drumlemble, Southend and Carradale, and has since become popular. Also in the inaugural year, a senior team was entered in the Fourth Division South of Scotland League. These developments are remarkable considering the long absence of the game, and the eventual emergence of Kintyre as a major force in shinty would be a fine conclusion.

Curling

Curling was evidently of Lowland origin, and evolved from trials of strength with rough boulders. Of its introduction to Kintyre there is no record, but that it started among the Lowland settler stock is a reasonable supposition. The game was certainly being played in Kintyre in the mid-nineteenth century, but was probably much older.

It was naturally a winter sport, and entirely dependent on weather. Without a freeze there could be no curling, and the duration of a freeze determined the success of the season. In some winters, conditions would suit for days only, or not at all; in other winters, weeks of play would be possible.

Curling was mainly played on the lochs around Campbeltown — Durry Loch, the Black Loch and Auchalochy — but in November 1892 a curling-pond was made at Homestone Farm for the Campbeltown Curling Club. A red-brick clubhouse, roofed with corrugated iron, was built there three years later, evidently to replace a wooden house at 'Aros Loch'.

The club was formed in 1881 with a membership of twenty-five, which had doubled by 1885. The subscription fee was 2s 6d, and the membership comprised farmers, professional men, shopkeepers and masons. Lowland names predominated.

Among the records of the club there is a poignant letter, dated 1897, from James S. Peters, schoolmaster at Auchencorvie, close to the Homestone rink. Explaining his resignation, he wrote: 'This is not because I do not love the game, but simply because I have found myself quite unable to get to the ice. When I have no right to be among you, I may be better able to endure the jolly shouts and laughter which reach me unable to leave my post'.

There were also curling clubs at Southend and Knocknaha, and perhaps elsewhere, and inter-club matches were played. Skating was also popular on the frozen lochs, and the two sports often came into conflict. 'It was no uncommon thing', the *Courier* reported in 1882, 'for an incautious skater to extort, from a crusty trundler of the stone, the remark: "Laddie, gin ye cross that rink again, dang me, but A'll break yer legs, A will noo, A'm tellin ye".'

Curling appears to have declined terminally after the turn of the century. In 1909, the *Courier* reported that the game was 'exceedingly rare in the district', owing to a succession of unfavourable winters. A year later, in Southend, there was a 'bold bid to revive the curlers' art'; but the effort failed, and for the same reasons: 'Opportunities for indulging in the pastime are so few here that its devotees seem in danger of becoming extinct in the peninsula'.

Quoits

Quoits — locally pronounced 'kytes' — was very popular in Kintyre in the nineteenth century, but appears to have faded out in the 1920s. Most districts had a quoiting club. The Argyll Club of Campbeltown played at Kildalloig — 'famous for its beautiful and picturesque scenery' — until 1884, when a piece of ground was got at Glenramskill. Knocknaha Club, at that same period, played on a 'capital piece of triangular, but level, ground on the farm of Killeonan'.

The game consisted of throwing, from a measured distance, a heavy iron ring at a peg — or *bab* — in the ground. The ring was sharpened on its outer edge so that it would stick where it fell. The ultimate aim was to 'ring the bab', but the closest throw otherwise succeeded. In a *Courier* report on 16 August 1884, it was remarked that Stewart Morgan — gamekeeper at Limecraigs — 'instead of throwing quoits of 9 lbs weight entered this contest with new quoits weighing about 13 lbs, the result being that his play has greatly improved'. He won that match, against Donald Rae of Kildalloig, by five shots.

A cruder form of quoits was played with horseshoes — or even stones — thrown at an upright stick from a range of about fifteen yards. These games were played in the evenings after work, when men gathered on the farms or at the local smiddy.

John Campbell, as a boy, spectated at the Kyting Green, a piece of ground in a corner of Kinloch Park, Campbeltown, now occupied by houses (2–8 Saddell Street). 'Sometim's ye'd stan' for ten meenits maybe. Other times there ye'd be a whole oor (hour) lookin at them. It'd take yer fancy that way.'

Conclusion

The history I was taught at school was very different from the history I found out for myself. Of the school history I remember some dates, names — of battles, military leaders, kings — and epochal outlines. The 'ordinary people' — my own ancestral stock — somehow did not enter into school history. At the time, I did not wonder at that. Had I thought about it at all I would no doubt have reasoned that they did not belong there anyway — they were not 'important' enough.

But of course they must have been there. Some no doubt fought in battles or were active in other events that I read about or was told about. But mostly they lived their 'ordinary' lives — farming and fishing and doing whatever was necessary to their survival. Not until I had left school did I realise that not only were their lives more relevant to me than the lives of kings and generals, but also more interesting. To be fair, educationalists have also begun to accept that idea, and oral history is now established in the curricula of many schools.

When I think now of my father and his brothers and sisters, and all the old folk in Kintyre that I sat with and listened to, I think of them as individuals who were able to tell me about my own origins and social background. Practically nothing as personal or as immediately relevant ever reached me from books. But historians are increasingly taking that raw material and preserving it, and that is what I have been doing in Kintyre for the past thirteen years.

Whether or not the material is shaped into articles or books is secondary to the urgent task of collecting it. I have been fortunate in having a certain aptitude for writing, but written words are poor substitutes for the words that come out of living mouths. The authentic accent and the whole atmosphere and environment are lost. All that remain are the words, which have become, in truth, the author's words since he trapped them in notebook or on tape and made them work for him.

When I walk that magnificent and peaceful coast between Machrihanish and the Mull, I sometimes remember the late Donald MacCallum telling me that when his father went into High Glenadale as a shepherd about the turn of the century, potatoes were still growing wild around the townships. There is, for me, a marvellous quality to that image, because it increases the sense of human history out there.

The people have gone, but their monuments remain as surely as Nelson's Monument stands in Trafalgar Square: the houses, dykes, cultivations, peat-banks, mountain roads and shielings. There is no true wilderness in Kintyre or anywhere else that people settled.

We need these empty places as the fox and the goat and the eagle need them. Our need is a spiritual one, by any definition. Two centuries ago, sheep were reckoned more profitable in the hills than crops of grain and potatoes. Now, coniferous plantations are reckoned more profitable than sheep, and, in recent years, as the Forestry Commission's interest in Kintyre has declined, private companies have moved in to raise timber crops for wealthy investors. The incentive is tax evasion; the result is landowners who neither know the land nor care about it beyond its profitability.

This, in the history of land use in Scotland, is hardly a new thing. What is new is the total absence of people on these holdings. The land is ploughed and planted, and then effectively deserted until the cutters move in and leave a wasteland behind them.

Land that becomes uneconomic to farm should be bought in the public interest and left to itself and to the creatures that need it, until such time as it may be restored to food production — for who knows when we might again have need of hill ground? Planning permission is necessary to build a garage at the end of a driveway, but the rural landscape can be blotted out by hundreds of acres of uniform trees, and the first the public knows about it is when the forestry ploughs move in.

The farming industry is no longer a big employer in Kintyre. Its effect has been to empty the land of people. Further north, the crofting system was able to hold a population on the land, however tenuously, and the same is true of the Glens of Antrim, where the density of small farms has created a greatly varied landscape, studded with houses and alive with people.

Perhaps the sinister NATO base at Machrihanish points to the future of Kintyre, which is increasingly a centre of military exercises on land, sea and air. But apathy about the NATO presence prevails among the people of Kintyre, and until Scotland has a government which represents, in a real sense, the interests of the Scottish people, Kintyre will remain a geographical appendage of Heatherland, with room enough for armies of trees and men.

Tenants of the Argyll Estate Convicted of Malting or Distilling Illegally, 24 October 1800–2 April 1801 (p. 101)

The following were caught with a still: Thomas Brown, Machrimore; David Reid, Kildavie; Robert Colville, Glenmanuill; Peter MacBride, Largybeg; Colin McEachran, Glenahervie; Donald Campbell, Killeonan; Peter Galbreath, Laggan; James and John Harvie, Skeroblinraid; and Duncan McLean, Kylipoll (Calliburn).

The following had quantities of wash, ranging from 6 to 126 gallons: Donald MacLean, Corrylach; Hugh MacIliver, Remuil; Malcom McMath, Auchinslisaig; John MacPhaill, Darlochan; and James McMillan, Cuilanlongart.

Malting was being carried on by: Donald McConnachy, Baligroggan; Lachlan Bowie, Largymore; John MacNaught, Druimnarianach; Hugh McMillan, Gartvain; Alexander Campbell, Strone; and Archibald Campbell Jr., Dailbhraddan.

Alexander Campbell, Carrine, was caught with five gallons of illicit whisky.

David Reid in Kildavie later satisfied the Duke, on oath, that he had no knowledge of the distilling, which had been 'carried on by his herd, and others not resident upon His Grace's Property'.

Illicit Whisky Distillers who purchased malt from John Colville in Campbeltown during the periods 1814–19 and 1823–26 (p. 105)

Amad	John McNish
Ardnicle	Charles McMillan
Arus	Dugald McTaggart
Auchadaduie	John Taylor
Auchensavill	Mary Blair
Auchyglas	Alexander McDugald
Barr	John McAlister
	Mary McCallum
	William McFater
	Angus McMillan
	Flory McTaggart
Blary	Duncan McCallum
	Archibald McFarland
	John McFarlane
Carnmore	Dugald McClaveren and John Gray
Clachan	James Brodie
	Duncan Gilchrist
	Donald McCoig (also at Lochkearan)
	Charles Mertin
Cloinagart	Archibald McEachen
	Donald McLeod (also at Margmonagach)
Coalhill (Drumlemble)	Nany McArthur
	Mary McKinven
	John (Mc)Murphy
	Bell McSporran
Crubastill	Archibald Blair
Dalbuie	James McGill
Darlochan	Andrew Kelly
Drumlemble	John McInnis
Drumore	Archibald Downie

Drumorebodach	Neill Currie
High Park	Sandy Heman (Hyndman)
Homeston	Thomas McKendrick
Kerrafuar	Robert McGill
	Robert Watson
Killegruir	Neill McDonald (also at Margmonagach)
	John McAlister
Killocraw	John Kendry
	Duncan McLarty
	John McMillan
Kilmaluag	Duncan McCallum
Kilowaraw (Killarow)	William McKellar
Knockhanty	Flory McTaggart
Knockhantybeg	Isbel Smith
Knocknaha	Alexander Campbell
	Mrs Craw
	Malcom Kelly
Knockrioch	Donald Kelly
Lagalgarve	Donald Munro
Licken	John Campbell
Lochend (Campbeltown)	Ket Kenzie
	Ket McNaught
	Donald Tyre
Lochkearan (above Clachan)	John McLean
Lossit	Sandy Cameron
	Gardener
	Gardener's widow
Margmonagach	John McDonald
	John Taylor
Muclach	James Thomson
Paisley (above Lagalgarve)	Mary McKinven
Putichan	John McMillan
Rannachan	John Maloy
Saltpans (Machrihanish)	Donald Cameron
	Dugald McClaverin
	Hector Reid (also at Lossit)
	John Smith
Stockadale (Barr Glen)	Archibald Gilchrist
Tangcoshan (Barr Glen)	Donald McLarty
Torchoillan	Nancy Watson
Tradicle (Trodigal)	William Armour

Index

N.B. Most minor, isolated references to people and places, etc., have not been included in this index.

Achadadunan, 59
Achaloskin, 71, 123
Achansavil (Southend), 27, 146, 185
ale, 98, 100
Algie, John, farmer, 7, 19
Allt Dorie house, 139–140
Allt an Tairbh, 4, 73
Altnaboduy, 74, 138
amalgamation of farms, 8–12, 154
Amod (Glen Breackerie), 37, 103, 115
Anderson, Alexander, exciseman, 106–107
Antrim, County, 53, 82
Ardnacross, 37, 62
Argyll Estate and Dukes of Argyll, 4, 6, 7, 8, 9, 11, 12, 14, 17, 27, 28, 54, 62, 66, 67, 68, 75, 76, 79, 85, 91, 94, 95, 100, 101, 126, 130, 132, 134, 135, 137, 138, 142, 143, 144, 146, 151, 167, 168
Arinarach, 10, 166
Arinascavach, 4, 15, 75, 161, 166
Armour, Edward in Glenramskill, 144, 151
Armour, Mary (McNair), 41
Armour, Robert, coppersmith, 102, 104–105
Arran, 105, 110, 180
Arthur, George, supervisor of Excise, murder of, 99
Auchaleek, 129, 130
Auchencorvie, 20, 60, 189
Auchenhoan, 11, 75, 76, 94, 161
Ayrshire, 47, 48, 57, 59, 74, 80, 81, 82, 96, 97, 105, 157, 180

bagpipes, 119, 124, 182, 185
baile, 2
Balimacconley, 37, 68
Balinatunie, 4, 11, 35, 144 (ill.), 155
Ballochroy (Glen), 67, 113, 114, 169
Ballybrenan, 37, 140
Ballygreggan, 19, 48
Ballygroggan, 22 (ill.), 66, 73, 75
Ballymontgomery, 67, 68, 69, 100, 146
Balmacvicar, 4, 37, 68, 69, 123, 154
Balnabraid, 10 (ill.), 28, 138, 157
Balnabraid Glen, 9–11, 23
Balnamoil, 4, 69, 73, 75
Bannatyne smiths at Barr, 122
Bannatyne, Calum, shepherd, 74, 84, 103, 115, 134–135, 139–140, 169, 170

Barlea, 150, 168
barley, see bear
barns, 37
Barr, 59, 62, 80, 106, 113, 116, 122, 123, 134, 135, 149, 174, 187, 188
Barr Glen, 26, 77, 80, 114, 116
basket-making, 42
Bealach a' Chaochain, 4, 25, 107
beans, 7, 48
bear (and barley), 7, 8, 9, 12, 30, 44–46, 99, 101, 115
Beattie, Alistair, shepherd, 73, 74, 167, 171
Beattie, shepherding family, 73, 84
Bede, Cuthbert, see Bradley, Edward
Bellochantuy, 25, 39, 71, 100, 121, 135, 158, 165, 169
blacksmiths, 5, 85, 99, 118, 120, 185
Blackstock, Peter, shepherd, 72
Blarferne, 11, 123
Bleachfield, 6, 126
Blue, Malcolm, miller at Clachaig, 106, 107
boats, burning of at New Year, 172–173
bogie, hay-, 51; peat-, 86 (ill.)
Borders shepherds, 1, 71
Borgadilbeg and Borgadilmore, 4, 68, 69, 132
Borthwick shepherding family, 73
brà, see quern
Bradley, Edward, 21, 30, 38, 39, 55, 100, 131, 132, 135, 147, 153, 156, 157, 159, 160, 166, 180
braxy, 162, 167
Brolochan, Alexander, cottar at Arinascavach, 161
Brolochan, Duncan, 69
Brolochan, Peter, 66, 68, 69
Brown, Charles in Low Machrimore, 61, 62
Brunerican, 28, 125, 157
butter, 8, 16, 65, 182

cadgers, 92
Cailleach, 33–35, 36
Cailleachan, The, 182
Calliburn, 4, 6
Cameron, Archibald D., farmer, 26, 53, 124
Campbell, Colin and John, 67, 68
Campbell, John, sheep-stealer, 70–71
Campbell, John, tradition-bearer, 46–47, 105, 190

Campbeltown, 5, 9, 21, 23, 39, 41, 45, 46, 47, 51, 52, 53, 54, 55, 62, 63, 69, 72, 79, 80, 81, 82, 91, 92, 93, 94, 97, 98, 100, 103, 105, 113, 115, 116, 119, 120, 121, 122, 123, 126, 129, 130, 133, 134, 143, 148, 150, 152, 168, 170, 172, 178, 180, 188, 189, 190

Campbeltown Town Council, 92, 100, 152, 165, 173, 182, 183, 184

Candlemas, 177, 179, 180

candles, 162, 164, 177, 185, 186

Cantaig, 9, 51

Cara Island, 29, 168

Carradale, 80, 81, 116, 175, 188

Carrine, 63, 103, 122, 138, 150

Carskey, 27, 106, 123

carts, 25–26, 63, 89, 93, 97, 117, 161

cas-chrom, 20–22

Cattadale, 2, 19, 139

cattle, general, 4, 6, 7, 12, 16, 17, 29, 41, 46, 49, 53–59, 69, 70, 81, 85, 121, 126, 142, 143, 153, 154, 170

cattle, Ayrshire, 56

cattle, herding of, 16, 54–55, 59

cattle, native, 53, 57

cattle-stealing, 57–59

Celtic Club, Campbeltown, 188

cheese, 8, 16, 56, 57, 65, 182, 183, 185, 186

children at work, 49, 54–55, 120

chimneys, 156–158

christenings, 183–184

Christlach, 51, 151

Christmas, 167

Clachaig, 35, 58–59, 90, 106, 107, 108, 114, 115

Clachan, 109, 130, 153, 160

clack-mills, see mills, horizontal

Clark, Finlay, shepherd, 26, 75, 77, 80, 95, 169

Clark, Lachlan in Tangy, 6 (ill.), 57, 71

Cleonagart, 114

Clerk, Duncan, writer, 54, 74, 81

Clochkeil, 154, 168

clover, 12, 49

clover, 'stoning', 49

Clydesdales, see horses

coal, 27, 91, 96, 97, 174

Coalwork Company of Campbeltown, 91, 143

Colville, Duncan, local historian, 98, 103

Colville, John, maltster, 48, 105

Cordiners in Machrimore, 11, 62

corn, see oats

Corphin, 11, 119, 121, 123, 155

Corrylach, 75, 78

cottars, 3, 5, 10, 54, 59, 109, 114, 126, 153, 161, 165, 166

Cragaig, 37, 38 (ill.), 66

'crogging' sheep, 77

crop failure, 5, 6, 101

Cross, Campbeltown, 172–173

Crosshill, 18, 23, 98

Crubesdale, 114, 138, 187

cruck-frames, 144–145, 151

cruisie lamps, 74, 162, 164 (ills.)

Culinlongart, 103, 177

curling, 188–189

cutag, see kiln, corn-

Dalabhraddan, 62, 63

Dalaruan, 98, 111

Dalbuie, 51, 75, 77 (ill.)

Dalintober, 110, 173, 174

Dalrioch, 63, 147

Darlochan, 33, 92, 143

Davaar Island, 133

Dearg Allt, 150, 171

Deorsa an Rum, 184

depopulation, 5, 8–12, 67–69

diet, 164–170

distilleries, 92–94

Doig's Grave, 100

Douglas, William, 32, 168

drainage, 12, 13–14, 23, 91; of peat-banks, 84

droving, of cattle, 53–54; of sheep, 79–80

Drumgarve, 37, 121

Drumlemble, 91, 97, 116, 119, 130, 150, 188

Drumlemble, farms, 4, 20, 33, 62, 153

Drumore, 60, 130

Drumore na Bodach, 71, 106

Dumfriesshire, 73

'Dunaverty', see McInnes, John

dung, 29

Dunglas, 11, 19

Durry, 91, 167

dykes, see enclosures

Earadale (Leerside), 9, 51, 61

Earadale (near Cragaig), 141 (ill.)

Elerick, 15

emigration, 5, 71

enclosures, 12, 14–15, 46, 54

English farmers, 1, 17, 27, 48

excisemen, 71, 99, 103, 106–107, 113–116

fairs, 113, 179–182

Falkirk Tryst, 53, 54

fanners, 37

farina, see mills

farms, joint-, 2

farm-labourers/servants, 4, 5, 11, 118–119, 165, 180

feeing, 120, 180

Fenton, Alexander, 23, 123

Feochaig, 9, 51, 76

Ferguson, James of Strathbungo, 20

fertilisers, 24–29, 40

fireplaces, 156, 158

fish, 160, 162, 168–169

fisherman, 104, 149, 168
fishing from rocks, 168–169
flax, see lint
funerals, 179, 184–186
furniture, 159–161

Galbraith, John 'China', 41
Galbreath, John, Tayinloan shinty casualty, 174–175
Gartavaigh, 71, 78 (ill.)
Gartgunnel, 9, 71, 72
Gartloskan, 2, 152
Gartnagerach, 9, 17, 48, 133
Gartvain, 2, 19, 142, 147, 153, 176
Garvachy, 60, 72
Garvalt (Barr Glen), 80, 90, 95
gaugers, see excisemen
Gigha, 18, 24, 30, 40, 43, 50, 96, 105, 114, 135, 136, 161, 168, 181, 185
Gilchrist, Archibald, herd-boy, 55
Glasgow, 41, 44, 48, 51, 55, 57, 58, 126, 130, 132, 180
Glemanuill, 9, 68, 69, 73, 74, 75, 132, 148, 168
Glenacardoch (Point), 150, 169
Glenadale, 60, 75, 103, 126, 139
Glenadale, High, 83, 139, 169, 191
Glenahanty, 37, 115
Glenahervie, 3, 9, 28, 48, 61, 76, 82, 103
Glenamucklach, 37, 139
Glenbarr, see Barr
Glen Breackerie, 39, 103, 115, 176, 187
Glencreggan, 30, 55, 131
Gleneadardacrock, 82, 115, 157
Glenlussa, 127, 171, 179
Glenmurril, 4, 9–10, 11, 60, 157
Glenramskill, 15, 134, 138, 144, 151, 166, 190
Glenrea, 4, 95, 150
gradan, 38
guising, 178

Hall, James M. of Tangy and Killean, 25, 63
Hallowe'en customs, 178–179
harrowing, 30, 40, 48
Harvest Home (see also *Cailleach*), 34–35
hay, 49
Hearth Tax (1694), 37
Helm, Alexander, shepherd, 161, 170
herding, see cattle
Highland Society, 19, 46, 82
holidays, of farm-servants, 181
Homestone, 19, 189
horses, general, 3, 6, 17, 18, 25–30, 37, 41, 51, 53, 60–63, 70, 89, 92, 97, 119, 121, 122, 124, 180, 181; Clydesdales, 61–63
houses, building, 9, 138–142; furnishing, 159–161; roofing, 143–147, 151

improvements, 12–15
Inanbeg (Innean Beag), 69, 72, 133
Inan Beithe (Innean Beithe), 23, 69, 132
Inancalliach (Innean Coig Cailleiche), 68, 69, 132, 169
Inandunan (Innean Dunain), 4, 37, 68, 69
Inangoich (Innean Gaothach), 4, 69, 132, 169, 184
Inanmore (Innean Mòr), 24, 37, 69, 72, 133, 154
Ireland, 27, 28, 29, 43, 44, 53, 68, 93, 94, 142, 150, 177, 186
Irish migrant workers, 32, 94, 150
Irish potato-smacks, 43
Islay, 85, 168, 188

Jackson shepherding family, 73

kail, 4, 49, 72, 171, 178
Keil, 26, 176
Kelly, Rev. Daniel, 53, 68, 186
Kelly, Neil Munro, 186
Kelly, Peter, farmer, 94
Kellys in Darlochan, 143
kelp, 131–136, 165
Keprigan, 2, 95
Keromenach, 53
Kerranbeg and Kerranmore, 74, 75, 81, 171
Kilblaan, 30, 47
Kildalloig Estate, 11, 76, 133
Kildavie, 60, 121
Kildonnel, 23, 48
Kilirvan, 35, 95
Killean Farm, 35, 47, 63
Killean and Kilchenzie Parish, 4, 5, 12, 18, 28, 31, 41, 45, 46, 49, 61, 67, 96, 118, 120, 134, 150, 153, 181
Killellan, 28, 123
Killeonan, 19, 33, 37, 123, 124, 137, 151, 190
Killocraw, 4, 63, 78, 99, 117, 139
Kilmichael (Campbeltown Parish), 19, 48, 121
kilns, corn-, 37; kelp-, 134, 135, 136 (ill.); lime-, 27–28 (ill.)
Kintyre Camanachd Association, 188
Knockhanty, 105, 115, 116
Knocknaha, 115, 124, 125 (ill.), 166, 189, 190
Kylipole (Campbeltown Parish), 6, 123, 158
Kylipole (Lossit Estate), 73, 145 (ill.)

Lagalgarve, 117, 150, 158
Lagan (Ròaig), 8, 104
Laggan (Moss), 13, 81, 90–94
Lammas, 120, 179, 180, 181
lamps, 162–163
Langlands, George, 11, 126
Langlands, Humphrey, 7

Langlands, Matthew, 11
Langlands, Ralph, 126
Langlands, William, 66
Largie, 130, 188
Largie Estate, 70, 79, 81
Largieside, 42, 63, 122, 168
Largybaan, 9, 75, 83, 84
Largybeg, 55, 63, 141
Largymore, 154, 171
lazybeds, 21, 22–23, 24 (ill.), 40
leasing of farms, 7–11, 100, 123, 132, 138, 142, 143, 151
Leerside, 6, 9, 60, 119, 166
Lenagboyach/Lenanboyach, 70, 71, 174
Lephenstrath, 9, 167
lighting, 162–164
lime, as fertiliser, 27–28; as mortar, 141–142, 147
Limecraigs, 52, 190
limpets, 169, 170
lint, 8, 48, 125–127
Lintmill, 126, 127, 129, 130
Littleson, Margaret (Black), 47, 135
Lochorodale, 83, 85, 86
Lossit, High, 73, 82
Loup, 60, 123
lug-marks, 70, 71

Macharioch, 33, 151
Machribeg, 33, 57, 62
Machrihanish, 23, 25, 143, 168, 187, 188
Machrimore, 4, 5, 37, 61, 81, 98, 122, 123, 124, 125, 130, 139, 152, 153
Makepeace, Robert in South Carrine, 17
Malcolm, James, land-agent, 8, 12, 23, 29, 37, 44, 48, 49, 91, 140, 141, 146, 147, 151, 153, 154, 171
malt, 98, 99, 105, 106, 107, 109, 113, 114
maltsters, 45, 101, 105
Margmonagach, 5, 37, 71
marriages, 182–183
Martin Martin, 168, 185
Martinmas, 54, 71, 166, 179, 180, 181
mattresses, 161–162
May Day, 177
meal, see oatmeal
Meal Kist Glen, 166
meat, 71, 79, 166–168
milk and milkers, 41, 49, 54, 119, 164, 171
millers, 99, 100, 106, 107, 113, 114, 118, 124
mills, farina, 129, 130; horizontal, 123; meal, 46, 47, 101, 106, 107, 109, 113, 123–125, 166; waulk or tuck, 109, 128; wool, 129
Mitchell, Samuel in Dalivaddy, 120, 129, 130
Moil Company, 61, 69
Morrison, Agnes, 41
mortar, 140–142
Moss, The, see Laggan

'moss-blocks', 95
Mrs Black's Tree, 104
Muasdale, 26, 37, 39, 54, 80, 103, 106–109, 129, 130, 131, 134, 135, 170
Muasdale, North (Watsons), 43, 46, 90, 97
Mull of Kintyre, 1, 66, 68, 69, 78, 79, 146, 169, 170, 184
multure, 46, 107, 123–124
MacAllisters, illicit distillers, 102
MacAlpine, Dugald, waulk-miller in Clachan, 109–110
MacAulay, James, ploughman in Killeonan, 20
MacCallum, Donald, shepherd, 14, 74, 79, 115, 169, 191
MacCallum, Jenny, herd-girl, 55–56 (ill.)
MacCallum blacksmiths at Machrimore, 122
MacCoag, John, New Year's Day shinty fatality, 176–177
MacDonald, Rev. Donald, 53, 61, 107
MacDonald, Donald in Achinsavill, 27–28
McEachran, Archibald, local historian, 19, 30, 47, 63, 120
MacEachran, Colin, 'grazier', 67, 68
MacEachran, Dr Duncan, 62–63, 122
MacEachrans in Glenahervie, 28, 61
MacGeachy, John in Clachaig, 58–59
MacGougan, William, shepherd, 80, 88, 116, 149, 168, 169
MacIlmichaels in Glenmurril, 9, 60
MacInnes, John, writer, 9, 33
McInnes, Robert, shepherd, 77, 78, 81, 83, 84, 86, 90
MacIntosh, Peter, author, 17, 18, 21, 37, 38, 57, 67, 128, 171, 184, 186
MacIntyre, Dugald, author, 90, 100
MacIntyre, Hugh, sheep-stealer, 71–72
MacIsaacs in Corphin, 9, 11, 119, 121
MacIsaacs in Feochaig, 51
MacKay, John, farmer and peat-cutter, 25, 84, 92–94, 149, 167
MacKay, Peter, agricultural engineer, 51
MacKeith, Duncan, farmer, 36, 39, 42, 78, 81, 116, 149, 171
MacKeith, John, farmer, 36, 149
McKerral, Andrew, author, 2, 124, 125, 158, 177, 187, 188
MacKerrals in Balnabraid, 10, 28
MacKerrals in Brunerican, 19, 20, 127
MacLean, James, tailor and smuggler, 111–112
MacLellan, Neil 'Kipples', 172
MacMillan, Donald, fisherman and smuggler, 110–112
MacMillan, James, blacksmith, 150, 176
MacMurchies in Lenagboyach, 70, 71, 174, 175
McNair, A., blacksmith, 18, 85, 121
Macneals of Ugadale, 124, 187
MacNeill, Malcolm of Carskey, his Estate Journal, 98, 126, 186
MacNeill, Torquil, burial of, 185

MacNeills of Carskey, 69, 81, 146
MacPhail, Adam, farmer, 13, 26, 35, 36, 90, 115, 116, 168, 174

New Orleans, 134
New Year, 34, 115, 172–177, 181

oatcake, 165, 166, 185
oatmeal, 8, 53, 124, 125, 165–166, 167, 170, 182
oats, 6, 28, 30–39, 40, 44, 46, 121, 124

Pans, 185, 187
pantiles, 124, 152
Paris Show of 1856, 82
peas, 48
peats, 13, 16, 37, 46, 83–96, 101, 117, 156, 164, 165
Peninver, Low, 41, 48; Mid, 133; New, 26, 41, 48
Pennant, Thomas, 28, 44, 47, 98, 100, 104, 125, 167
Pennyland, 9, 123
Pennyseorach, 42, 63
pickling, 167, 168, 169
pigs, 167, 169
ploughing matches, 18–20, 120, 186
ploughs and ploughing, 3, 17–18, 40, 121
porridge, 38, 119, 164, 166, 183
pot-chain, 157
potatoes, 4, 7, 25, 40–44, 108, 120, 121, 126, 130, 164–165, 191; markets, 43–44; pits, 42; squads, 41–42
Putechan, 62, 71, 78, 185
Putechantuy, 139, 148, 154

quern, 38–39, 123
quoits, 189–190

rabbits, 41, 168
Raeside, James, weaver, 72
Raeside, James, smallholder, 124
razor-fish, 170
reaping, 30–31
Reid, Gilbert, 'smuggler', 108, 116
rents of farms, 3, 4, 6, 8, 9, 45, 91, 99, 121; produce rents, 1, 8, 53, 98
Revenue cutters (men), 103, 109, 110–112
Rhonadale, 123, 125
Rhunahaorine, 5, 55, 84, 105, 120, 150
rick-lifter, 50–51
Riddell, George in Tangy Mill, 25
rigs, 2, 22–23, 30, 144 (ill.)
Rosehill, 95, 134, 150
rotation of crops, 46, 49

Royal Commission on the Ancient and Historical Monuments of Scotland, 15, 104, 123
Royal Commission on Labour (1892), 26, 134, 154, 166, 181
runrig, 1, 2–3, 15
rushes, common, 35–36, 162; sharp-flowered, 36, 52
rye, 48
rye-grass, 30, 49

Saddell, 122, 123, 179, 188
Saddell and Skipness Parish, 5, 96
'Sailor Jeck', see Morrison, Agnes
sallies, 13, 14
Sanda Island, 66, 106, 134
seagull eggs, 170
seaweed, as fertiliser, 24–26; for kelp-making, 131–136
Second Waters, The, 23, 135
sequestration, 6, 9, 130, 160
sheep, general, 8, 11, 29, 61, 65–82, 167, 182; black-faced, 66, 67; clipping of, 74–79; Leicester, 67; marking of, 70–71; native, 65–67; smearing of, 65, 73–74; stealing of, 70–72
Sheep Island, 66, 168
shellfish, 169–170
shielings, 15–16
shinty, 175, 186–188
shinty matches, New Year's Day, 174–177, 187–188
shinty-sticks, 177, 186–187
shipwrecks, 143, 184
shoemakers, 5, 108, 118, 131
silage, 52
skating, 189
Skernish, 13, 116, 167, 168
Skipness, 8, 33, 71, 72, 104, 105, 111, 123, 125, 126
slates, 124, 151
slipes, 63, 88, 89
Small, James, plough-improver, 18
Smerby, 4, 48, 111, 122, 123, 125, 128
Smith, David in Gigha, 44, 48
Smith, Rev. Dr. John, 3, 8, 11, 12, 13, 14, 17, 18, 22, 27, 29, 37, 40, 41, 44, 46, 47, 48, 49, 53, 54, 65, 66, 67, 68, 74, 85, 96, 99, 126, 137, 141, 145, 147, 164
smiths, see blacksmiths
smuggling, 105, 106, 110–112, 115
Southend, 3, 5, 6, 12, 13, 27, 28, 41, 48, 53, 57, 62, 63, 67, 81, 95, 103, 122, 124, 125, 151, 152, 167, 168, 176–177, 185, 188, 189
sowing seed, 30
spinning, 16, 127–128
sports, 174, 186
sprits, see rush, sharp-flowered
stacks, hay, 51, 52; oats, 35–36; peat, 90, 94

stallions, travelling, 62
steamers, 79, 80, 81, 119
Stewart, John Lorne, Duke of Argyll's
    chamberlain, 6, 56, 82, 130, 182
Stewartfield, 59, 109
Stewarton, 168, 181
stills, illicit — see whisky, illicit
Stramollach, 176, 187, 188
Strathmore, 176, 187, 188
strike, farmworkers' of 1933, 119–120
Strone, 69, 73, 75
sùgan-ordaig, 36
sùist, 36
Sunadale, 39, 42, 116, 149, 170, 171

tailors/tailoring, 5, 118, 128, 129, 180
Talabhtoll, 15, 59
Tangy, 57, 114, 122, 123, 125
tar-barrels, burning of, 172–173
Tarbert, 29, 43, 54, 79, 81, 104, 112, 147, 182
Tarbert Fair, 182
Tayinloan, 58 (ill.), 62, 71, 98, 113, 130, 168,
    174, 181
Tayintruan, 113, 150
Taylor, William in Park Mains, 62
tea, 47, 79, 93, 105, 165, 171
Templetons in Drumgarve, 121, 127
thatching, houses, 138, 147–150, 151; stacks,
    35, 36, 90
Thompson, Christopher in Dalabhraddan, 63
Thompson, Richard in Ballybrenan, 48
Thomson, John, miller at Barr, 113, 114
Thomson, Neil 'P.O.' of Muasdale, 39, 116,
    170, 184

thrashing oats, 36, 119, 181
tileworks, 130
Todd shepherding family, 73, 161
Torrisdale, 4, 175, 179
Trodigal, 69, 187
Tumblin' Tom, 50
Turner, John in Tonrioch, 17, 48
turnips, 46–47; 178; thinning of, 46–47, 120

Ugadale, 62, 125

wakes, 184–185
water, 171
Watson, Donald, farmer, 26, 43, 80, 116
Watson, William, farmer, 46, 54, 97
waulking cloth, 128
weavers/weaving, 5, 118, 126
weddings, 182–183
Weir, John 'Bocan', sheep-stealer, 72
wheat, 47–48
whisky, illicit, 44, 98–117; licit, 45, 98, 99
Whitestone, 26, 36, 43, 81, 127, 179
Whitsun, 179, 180, 181
Wilson, Alexander in Crosshill, 18, 85
winkles, 170
winnowing, 37
wintering of sheep, 80–82
wood, 142–147
wool, 65, 66, 68, 74, 78, 79, 127
'wreck'/wrack, see seaweed
wrights, 5, 63, 118, 130